Conspiracy and Triumph

ALSO BY AARON JOHN GULYAS

*Conspiracy Theories: The Roots, Themes and Propagation
of Paranoid Political and Cultural Narratives* (McFarland, 2016)

*Extraterrestrials and the American Zeitgeist:
Alien Contact Tales Since the 1950s* (McFarland, 2013)

Conspiracy and Triumph

*Theories of a Victorious Future
for the Faithful*

AARON JOHN GULYAS

McFarland & Company, Inc., Publishers
Jefferson, North Carolina

LIBRARY OF CONGRESS CATALOGUING-IN-PUBLICATION DATA

Names: Gulyas, Aaron John, 1975– author.
Title: Conspiracy and triumph : theories of a victorious future for the faithful / Aaron John Gulyas.
Description: Jefferson, North Carolina : McFarland & Company, Inc., Publishers, 2021 | Includes bibliographical references and index.
Identifiers: LCCN 2021044846 | ISBN 9781476680767 (paperback : acid free paper) ∞
ISBN 9781476645506 (ebook)
Subjects: LCSH: Conspiracy theories—United States. | Propaganda—United States. | Communication in politics—United States. | United States—Politics and government. | BISAC: SOCIAL SCIENCE / Conspiracy Theories
Classification: LCC HV6275 .G849 2021 | DDC 001.9—dc23
LC record available at https://lccn.loc.gov/2021044846
LC record available at https://lccn.loc.gov/2021044846

BRITISH LIBRARY CATALOGUING DATA ARE AVAILABLE

**ISBN (print) 978-1-4766-8076-7
ISBN (ebook) 978-1-4766-4550-6**

© 2021 Aaron John Gulyas. All rights reserved

No part of this book may be reproduced or transmitted in any form or by any means, electronic or mechanical, including photocopying or recording, or by any information storage and retrieval system, without permission in writing from the publisher.

Front cover image © 2021 Freeda Michaux/Shutterstock

Printed in the United States of America

*McFarland & Company, Inc., Publishers
Box 611, Jefferson, North Carolina 28640
www.mcfarlandpub.com*

To all those affected by the North Dakota Crash

Acknowledgments

This book materialized between March 2020 and March 2021. I wrote the first word just as news of lockdown restrictions started to circulate. I wrote the last word the day before I received the COVID-19 vaccine. During this time, I was more fortunate than usual to have quality people to rely upon for all manner of support and more fortunate than many to be relatively unscathed by the effects of the year.

I need to thank Cindy Gulyas and Samantha Engel for read-throughs, clarifications, semi-colon suggestions and polite margin notes saying, "you already wrote this two pages back." Any remaining issues are my oversights and—possibly—failure to take their suggestions.

Thank you to Doug Tannas, Paul Kimball, Tim Binnall, Jack Brewer, Adam Gorightly, and the Invisible Frat House for friendly and much-needed conversation and commiseration over 21st-century conspiracy culture, politics, pandemics, and professional wrestling.

Much love to the surprisingly hefty number of listeners to my podcast (*The Saucer Life*) for being an appreciative audience for several topics that were not *quite* right for this volume but were perfect for being an episode of the show when I needed material quickly. Thanks also to my production crew—Simpson, Roberta, Sasha, and Nelson.

And love always to Cindy and Matthew.

Contents

Acknowledgments   vi
Prologue   1

CHAPTER 1. Conspiracy Theory 101   9
CHAPTER 2. NESARA—White Knights, Dark Agendas, and the Appeal to Greed   33
CHAPTER 3. The UFO Disclosure Movement   80
CHAPTER 4. QAnon   128

Epilogue   171
Chapter Notes   175
Bibliography   189
Index   201

Prologue

Most of us expect stories to have endings. When reading novels or short stories we experience the endings their authors craft and we often judge those endings on how satisfying they are based on what we have read. When dealing with stories based in reality—historical narratives, for example—sequences of events seem to blend into whatever comes "after" more or less seamlessly. What we perceive as endings are the product of historians crafting narratives to clearly present complex events and to make an argument about those events. Narratives based upon conspiracy theories often occupy a middle ground—almost a liminal space—between the worlds of fact and fiction. Conspiracists harvest information such as historical events, scientific and medical research, or contemporary cultural events. Often, these are objectively factual. Conspiracists cite legislation, treaties, statements from prominent public figures, and other evidence that is unquestionably "real."

One could describe it as an almost alchemical process: conspiracy-inclined writers, podcasters, YouTubers, and social media influencers take this real information, documentation, or data and transmute it into narratives that often bear only a passing resemblance to reality. Often these narratives possess an intrinsically prophetic nature, foretelling a time when noble, upstanding, right-thinking, and independent-minded Americans (such as themselves) will be stripped of their liberties unless those same right-thinking people (those reading their book or watching their video, for example) take crucial steps. They will be persecuted, prosecuted, rounded up and subjected to imprisonment or death for daring to stand against the malefactors of misery threatening to undermine the sovereignty of the United States and its people. These are "endings" to the stories that are unquestionably grim.

In my previous book on conspiracy culture—*Conspiracy Theories: The Roots, Themes and Propagation of Paranoid Political and Cultural Narratives*—I discussed a number of narratives that fit this description.

Prologue

Fears of the U.S. federal government building death camps in which to imprison conservative Christians or United Nations plots to use environmental crises as a pretext to eliminate private property ownership are only two of the more prominent examples that permeated fringe political discourse—particularly on the right—during the 1980s and 1990s. Obviously, my book was not the first or only one to explore these topics. The more deeply I delved into these worlds, however, I began to notice that there was far more variety in the conspiratorial mindset than I—and many others—may have perceived. It was this observation that led to the research and analysis that culminated in this book, which explores a number of conspiratorial narratives and viewpoints that promise a bright future for either a faithful few or for the American people as a whole. With few exceptions, this study focuses on the United States. This is not the result of a failure to recognize or to ignore the existence and persistence of conspiratorial narratives in other nations and regions but, rather, in the interests of keeping this study to a manageable length.

While most people have a general idea of the shape of a conspiracy theory, the question of what a "positive conspiracy" narrative might look like is complex. Often, at first blush, they may not appear to be very positive at all. They present a world steeped in darkness, controlled by a shadowy elite dedicated to suppressing the masses. In these stories, however, there is a millenarian aspect—a belief that at some point *everything is going to change.* One's economic standing, health, anything one can imagine—they are all going to change for the better. At least, it seems, for those who have kept the faith. It is tempting, but not entirely accurate, to imagine these stories in terms of the Rapture of fundamentalist Christian eschatology.

The example that initially piqued my interest the most was the emergence of the "QAnon" movement. On October 28, 2017, the following message appeared on the website 4chan's "/pol/" board.

> HRC [Hillary Rodham Clinton] extradition already in motion effective yesterday with several countries in case of cross border run. Passport approved to be flagged effective 10/30 @ 12:01a.m. Expect massive riots organized in defiance and others fleeing the US to occur. US M's [U.S. Marshals] will conduct the operation while NG [National Guard] activated. Proof check: Locate a NG member and ask if activated for duty 10/30 across most major cities[1] [bracketed annotations added].

In this somewhat cryptic offering, the reader is promised the arrest of Hillary Clinton. Since the 1990s, both Hillary and Bill Clinton have been at the center of conspiracy theories that included lurid scenarios such as the takeover of the United States by United Nations troops and the imprisonment of conservatives, Christians, and other groups in prison camps. Now, we have a new narrative—one where the villain (Clinton, in this case) faces justice.

Authored by the self-styled "Q-Clearance Patriot" (usually abbreviated simply as "Q") in a discussion board thread with the subject line "Calm Before the Storm," this message launched a narrative known variously as The Storm, The Great Awakening, and—most recognizably—QAnon. This was not the first conspiracy theory to arise during Donald Trump's term as president of the United States. Indeed, the QAnon phenomenon grounded itself in earlier narratives such as "PizzaGate" and the death of Democratic Party worker Seth Rich. QAnon, however, was unusual. Where most conspiracy theories presented visions of the future that their target audiences found oppressive, tyrannical, and otherwise dystopian, QAnon offered something else: hope. Hope and victory for the forces of President Trump and American patriots over Hillary Clinton, George Soros, Barack Obama, John McCain, the Bush dynasty, and the rest of the Deep State, whether they be members of the Republican or Democratic parties.

When will this happen? Soon! How soon? It depends! Regardless of when it will occur, we can all rest assured that the men and women in white hats are riding in to save Americans from disaster.

While this predicted positive outcome is unusual, it is not unique. QAnon is simply the most recent and most visible manifestation of a positive or *triumphalist* conspiracy theory. Spread by social media memes across platforms ranging from free-for-all discussion boards like 4chan and 8chan (and their successors) to your great aunt's Facebook page, stories of the impending arrest of satanic globalist pedophile rings have attracted a great deal of media attention. But triumphalism in conspiracy culture, while rare, is not new. The very stories being promulgated among QAnon followers have their roots in the conspiracy heyday of the 1990s. This book will trace this phenomenon of conspiracies with a happy ending through a number of narrative strands and iterations, each with a colorful cast of characters and connections to the most enduring and significant conspiracy tropes in American history. Closely connected to these narratives is the story of how the evolution of the Internet produced profound changes in conspiracy culture. These changes mirrored the changes in the broader realm of mass media as social media and the potential for constant connectivity to shape and reshape news reporting and commentary. Over the course of this book we will explore and interrogate a number of conspiracy narratives and viewpoints that promise a bright future for either a faithful few, the American people, or humanity as a whole.

The book begins with a primer for those new to the world of American conspiracy theory. It also sets the stage for more fully understanding the sometimes-subtle distinctions between what I term "traditional" and "triumphalist" conspiracy theories, partially through an overview of the scholarship that has emerged over the past few decades and how it has addressed—or failed to address—the notion of triumphalist conspiracy narratives. In particular, it is important to note that despite the "happy endings" of these triumphalist narratives, a healthy dose of negativity often remains. One must, in some eschatologies, pass through the Tribulation before experiencing the Rapture. Part of this background exploration is an examination of some foundational concepts in modern conspiracy narratives that underlie even these newer iterations. The first of these is the so-called "sovereign citizen" movement. This movement has a long, often violent history dating back to the middle of the 20th century. While, to a considerable degree, there is much in here that is akin to traditional right wing conspiracy theories—concerns about the growth of the federal government's power and authority as well as increasing globalization—our focus will be on the legal theories and alternative political structures promoted within sovereign citizen communities. These carry within them a promise of the restoration of a United States more in line, they believe, with how "the founders" conceived of the republic. Many of these theories amount to a system of "magic words." The initiated will know what to say and when to say it and, in doing so, access aspects of the legal system unknown to normal Americans. Despite the fact that these legal incantations are ineffective or, in many cases, lead to further charges, adherents of the sovereign citizen movement foresee a day when the legal system as they perceive it will be repaired and a new government will arise. Or, rather, that the government originally intended by the founders of the United States will be reconstituted. Occasionally, some individuals have used violent action to bring about this restoration, raise awareness of their cause, or resist what they perceive as unjust persecution or prosecution. The second is the broad concept of the "Secret Government." While the more modern phrase "Deep State" has become common, the notion that there exists a cabal of power elites who control politics, finances, science, culture, technology, and the media from behind the scenes is an old one. All of the narratives we will discuss in depth rely to one degree or another on a Secret Government controlling things behind the scenes.

Moving from the earth into orbit, the Unidentified Flying Objects (UFO) Disclosure Movement, which began in the mid–1990s, makes two very basic, very bold assertions. The first—not an unusual one in the world of flying saucers—is that elements of the American government have covered up the "truth" of contact with extraterrestrial civilizations. The other is that the powers that be who are engaging in this cover-up are preventing valuable new technologies from emerging, namely technologies that would solve a variety of problems for humanity. Problems such as hunger, poverty, war, disease, environmental degradation could all be mitigated or even eliminated if only the shadowy cabal would fling wide the doors of disclosure.

This narrative, like other triumphal conspiracy narratives, relies on adherents maintaining a belief in the proclamations of a limited number of leaders in the field despite repeated disappointments and failed predictions. When I discussed the Disclosure Movement in my 2013 book, *Extraterrestrials and the American Zeitgeist: Alien Contact Tales Since the 1950s*, I did so within the broader context of the so-called "Contactee" movement that stretched back to the 1950s. This study requires viewing the Disclosure Movement through a different, more conspiratorial lens. Additionally, the field has continued to develop since 2013. A parallel conspiratorial narrative has developed which posits that a "breakaway civilization"—sometimes entirely human, sometimes involving humans aided by extraterrestrial beings—has been hiding a vast array of technology in order to enrich themselves and enhance their power. Both the Disclosure Movement, in its original, turn of the century form as well as the more recent development of "breakaway civilization" narratives share a belief in the existence of hidden technology and that this technology would, if shared with the public, push humanity into a new age of wisdom and prosperity.

Financial conspiracy theories are one of the most consistent genres of paranoid narratives. In contrast to more arcane conspiracy theories, people find stories of a cabal of the rich and powerful in a system that is perpetually rigged against them to be relatively understandable. Two hopeful conspiracy narratives that emerged in the late 20th and early 21st centuries have built on existing economic conspiracy narratives and present a way out of the supposed nightmare of economic manipulation. The National Economic Security and Recovery Act (NESARA) began as an innocuous thought experiment by an economist and grew into an expansive conspiracy theory about malign forces preventing the implementation of a law (NESARA) that would not only revamp the American economy but instantly reverse the financial misfortunes of individual Americans. This is a classic example of a hopeful conspiracy narrative—an endless treadmill of waiting for the "white knights" to be in a position to make everything better.

These long-standing conspiratorial trends, in many ways, converged at the beginning of Donald Trump's presidency. In 2017, a figure calling themselves "Q" posted on 4chan, an Internet message board. Q claimed to be an insider in the national security establishment who provided cryptic statements to an increasingly rabid fan base. Later moving to the less regulated and more volatile 8chan community, Q would publish over 3000 "drops" between November 2017 and the summer of 2019, when 8chan closed, for a time. Q—or someone accepted as Q—reappeared in November 2019 when 8chan resurfaced as 8kun. This information presented a political world that was, often, at odds with what the "mainstream media," or MSM, conveyed. It was a world where President Donald Trump played an impeccable game of chess against the denizens of the Deep State; where the malefactors of satanic child sexual abuse cults connected to the Democratic Party would finally be stopped. In what became a reassuring rallying cry for the movement, Q would proclaim "patriots are in control." The term "patriots," of course, referring those who support the policies of the Trump administration; those whose lives will become better when the enemies of "American Greatness" are finally laid low.

These narratives of conspiracies with happy endings share two crucial—yet slightly contradictory—features. First, they all display a significant level of mistrust toward authority. From the "deep state" to the very notion of federal power and from entrenched financial and banking systems to the military-industrial complex hoarding UFOs at Area 51, there are always cabals of villains keeping peace and prosperity tantalizingly out of reach. At the same time, devotees of these conspiracy theories—those who hope the hardest for the promised benefits of defeating these villains—place an inordinate amount of trust in their own figures who represent knowledge and authority. Adherents of the sovereign citizen movement follow the advice of "legal experts" who promise to guide them through the arcane procedures involved in separating themselves from the authority of the federal government. Because of what they learn from these experts, they trust that the judges, juries, and government officials will have no choice but to be swayed by their arguments. In a similar way, Americans who cling to the promises of NESARA and other financial conspiracies closely followed the messages of the late Shaini Goodwin, who called herself "Dove of Oneness."[2] She, in turn, passed on messages from unnamed figures who were supposedly in positions of political and economic authority. Goodwin also relied on messages channeled from otherworldly beings. Many of those who believe that the government is withholding knowledge of extraterrestrial civilizations rely on the word of alleged whistle-blowers and those prominent UFOlogists who promote their stories. At least part of the longevity and appeal of the QAnon phenomenon is the belief that the "Q-Clearance Patriot" is a highly-placed figure in the Trump administration or other significant figure in the power structure of the United States.[3]

There is, then, a degree of contradiction inherent in these belief systems. They often rely on the malign power structures to be active participants in their own destruction. This contradiction puts these believers in the somewhat absurd position of exhibiting extreme mistrust of those in authority, *except for the elements of that authority who tell them what they want to hear.* In this sense, they are not too different from those Americans whose views on politics, culture, and society are informed by social media feeds algorithmically tailored to present them with stories with which they are likely to agree. The difference is, as is often the case with extremist beliefs, a matter of degree and of devotion to the cause.

These narratives also, usually, have one of two desired outcomes. The first is a *restoration* of a way of life that had been supplanted by one seen as inimical to liberty and freedom. The sovereign citizen and QAnon narratives are very much in this vein. The second outcome is a *revolutionary* one, in which a new, different, and better paradigm emerges and replaces the old. The extraterrestrial Disclosure Movement is an example of this, as are many of the financial conspiracies discussed. However, as we will see, there is often some overlap—however paradoxical it may seem—between narratives that lead to restoration or revolution.

So, come along on a journey down a yellow brick road to a glorious future where humanity is at peace, freedom is restored, and the enemies of liberty and progress have been remanded to the authorities for trial and—undoubtedly—execution. A bright future awaits us.

CHAPTER 1

Conspiracy Theory 101

Conspiratorial narratives are not new. They are not a 21st-century invention or even a product of the 20th. Many of the key elements of conspiracy theories that became more visible and prominent in the final decades of the 20th century—anti–Semitism, anti–Catholicism, fears about international cabals of Freemasons subverting the legitimate government—had their roots in centuries past. Academic investigations of these narratives, of their origins and impacts, are relatively recent. The scholarly study of conspiracy culture is a multi-disciplinary one. Broadly, when discussing scholarship about conspiracy culture, it is helpful to recognize that there are some commonalities across disciplines. In my 2016 examination of paranoid narratives, *Conspiracy Theories: The Roots, Themes and Propagation of Paranoid Political and Cultural Narratives*, I wrote:

> In general, there is a significant level of skepticism toward many conspiracy claims. Scholars have a tendency to view those who promote such theories and narratives as having motivations and intentions beyond the promulgation of their particular and peculiar version of "truth." Such as class envy, racism or religious prejudice. Scholarly observers and analysts have, generally, viewed the effects of paranoid and conspiratorial viewpoints as irrational and unfortunate.[1]

Since 2016, however, scholars have examined conspiracy theories, paranoid narratives, and their effects on political discourse and the political process with a renewed focus spurred by contemporary events. The election of 2016, the presidency of Donald Trump, and the 2020 presidential election and its aftermath illustrated the increasing power of conspiratorial narratives to motivate political supporters. Conspiracy theory and conspiracy culture shifted from side show to main event, with increasingly visible consequences of the widespread belief in "alternative facts." The triumphalist conspiracy theories of the early 21st century—such as those surrounding QAnon and QAnon adjacent narratives—led their adherents to expect outcomes that were at odds with political and legal reality. In *Conspiracy Theories*, I explored the history of scholarly examination of conspiracy theory. While I do not intend to restate that entire history, before diving into these triumphal conspiracy narratives of the 21st century, it will be useful to orient ourselves to some of the significant turning points in the scholarship that have addressed various aspects of conspiracy culture over the past several decades.

Richard Hofstadter's 1964 essay in *Harper's Magazine*, "The Paranoid Style in American Politics," began the modern era of conspiracy theory analysis and did so firmly within the context of the Cold War conflict between the United States and the Soviet Union. By the mid–1960s, the communist witch-hunts associated with Senator Joseph McCarthy were receding into the past, but anti-communist sentiment was still strong. Indeed, one of the key points Democratic candidates tried to make in the 1960 political campaigns was that the Republican leadership had been too passive in the face of global communist aggression. Caution against communist influence world-wide of course had implications for domestic political culture in the United States. Hofstadter drew parallels between present-day anti–Communist fears with other examples of paranoid and conspiratorial political fears from America's past, such as the anti–Masonic movement of the 1820s and 1830s as well as anti–Catholic and anti–Semitic conspiracy theories that were often linked with concerns over immigration in the 19th century. All of these concerns would persist, in various forms, into the 21st century.

Hofstadter describes the conspiratorial, "paranoid" mindset as one that "sees the fate of conspiracy in apocalyptic terms. The conspiracy theorist 'traffics in the birth and death of whole worlds, whole political orders, whole systems of human values' and 'is always manning the barricades of civilization … constantly liv[ing] at a turning point … he expresses the anxiety of those who are living through the last days and [are] sometimes disposed to set a date for the apocalypse.'"[2] Traditional conspiracy theories have long contained apocalyptic threads. The use of this term usually has a negative connotation of the end of all things, the collapse of systems, and destruction on—literally—a biblical scale. There is, however, another side of the coin: within the traditional Christian conception of the End of Days that Hofstadter evokes in his essay is the ultimate triumph of good over evil, the final destruction of this sinful realm and the final vindication of those whose faith is in Christ. The same is true of the triumphal conspiracy narratives examined here. While there may be destruction—of the global economy, the American government as we know it, of traditional religious structures, of the reputations of scientific experts—the ultimate ending is good for all and is a vindication of believers and justification of their persistence in the face of persecution.

Hofstadter claims that those who believe outlandish and paranoid conspiratorial claims lack "access to political bargaining or the making of decisions" and thus "find their original conception that the world of power is sinister and malicious fully confirmed." They view the "consequences of power ... through distorting lenses—and have no chance to observe its actual machinery ... circumstances often deprive him of exposure to events that might enlighten him—and in any case he resists enlightenment."[3] As true as that might have been in 1964, the explosion of Internet news sources and social media that has taken place even in the last five years has multiplied the number of these "distorting lenses" to a greater number (and to a degree of distortion) than Hofstadter probably could have predicted. These new lenses of both the Internet and social media will play a tremendous role in the spread of these triumphal conspiratorial narratives.

As conspiracy culture grew during the 1980s and 1990s, scholars began to re-evaluate Hofstadter's 1964 analysis. Mark Fenster, in *Conspiracy Theories: Secrecy and Power in American Culture*, connected Hofstadter's view to the prevailing trend of "consensus" history politics of the time. The 1950s and 1960s saw a widespread point of view that there was a "consensus" that American-style representative democracy and free market ideology were accepted as good, proper, and correct across the political spectrum. Racial, economic, gender, and other divides were all able to be addressed within the broad framework of American or Enlightenment liberalism. The social and political upheavals of the late 1960s and early 1970s amply demonstrated that this consensus—if it really existed at all—contained considerable cracks. Out of this consensus view of American politics, Fenster argues, Hofstadter arrived at the conclusion that conspiratorial thought and political paranoia was "a pathology suffered by those existing outside of the pluralistic consensus" which "implied a continuum between proper politics and pathology."[4] Political paranoia was an individual problem rather than the result of broader social and cultural forces. Fenster, to the contrary, argued that "conspiracy must be recognized as a cultural practice that attempts to map, in narrative form, the trajectories and effects power; yet it not only does so in a simplistic, limited way, but also continually threatens to unravel and leave unsettled the resolution to the question of power that it attempts to address."[5] Fenster's description, largely, suits the purposes of our study of triumphalist conspiracy narratives. The degree to which these narratives "unravel" questions of power, however, is a bit different in the narratives we will examine, for they often present attempts to weave something new out of what has been unraveled.

As with more traditional conspiracy narratives, the tales analyzed in this work will illustrate a considerable degree of overlap between the various strands of conspiratorial beliefs that are paranoid but cling to forecasts of specific positive outcomes. Extensive discussions of a coming financial reform (and financial windfall) sit oddly—yet somehow comfortably—alongside predictions of deliverance by benevolent space beings and information passed along to the Internet discussion boards from supposed government "insiders" about the elimination of dangerous political radicals. Michael Barkun, in *A Culture of Conspiracy: Apocalyptic Visions in Contemporary America*, describes similar cross-breeding of conspiratorial narratives when he uses the illustration of the interest Oklahoma City bomber Timothy McVeigh had for UFO conspiracy theories and the rumors of alien technology at Area 51—a conspiratorial trope that had a significant renaissance in the late 2010s. Barkun argues that this supported the notion that there existed an increasing overlap between political paranoia and conspiracy theories that focused on the notion that the government was hiding "the truth" about extraterrestrial visitation to the Earth.[6] If anything, this has increased in the years since Barkun pointed out this overlap. Barkun asserts that there existed three fundamental categories of conspiratorial narratives: "event conspiracies," "systemic conspiracies," and "superconspiracies." These categorizations illustrated Barkun's approach which closely examined conspiracy narratives and their reflection of the changing nature of the cultural and political contexts of conspiracy theory.[7] This book takes a similar approach, while arguing for the existence of an additional category: "triumphalist conspiracies."

Following the election and during the presidency of Donald Trump, the pace of scholars—particularly political scientists—analyzing the role of conspiracy theory in American political culture began to quicken. The most thorough study of the distinctions between more traditional conspiracy theories and narratives and the newer style of conspiracism that has emerged is Russell Muirhead and Nancy L. Rosenblum's *A Lot of People are Saying: The New Conspiracism and the Assault on Democracy*. They define the key differences in this "new conspiracism" primarily by what it lacks:

> There is no punctilious demand for proofs, no exhaustive amassing of evidence, no dots revealed to form a pattern, no close examination of the operators plotting in the shadows. The new conspiracism dispenses with the burden of explanation.[8]

To conceal this lack of explanation, the new conspiracism makes use of "innuendo and verbal gesture":

> "A lot of people are saying...." Or we have bare assertion: "Rigged!"—a one-word exclamation that evokes fantastic schemes, sinister motives, and the awesome capacity to mobilize three million illegal voters to support Hillary Clinton for president. This is conspiracy without the theory.

It tears down rather than builds:

> It is *de* all the way down: destabilizing, degrading, deconstructing, and finally delegitimating, without a countervailing constructive impulse. It is as if whatever rises from the detritus of democracy is less important and less exciting than calling out the catastrophes and humiliations wrought by the malignant agents who claim to represent us. We're witness to the fact that it does not take an alternative political ideology—communism, authoritarianism, theism, fascism, nativism—to delegitimate democracy. Angry, sterile conspiracism does the work.[9]

Muirhead and Rosenblum thoroughly discuss what the new conspiracism does, and does not do, and the mechanisms of its spread, including adherents promoting claims that are "true enough" and relying on "repetition over validation."[10] And, while devotees of the new conspiracism are eager to tear down the old, what comes after is less clear:

> Where classic conspiracism offers hopeful—sometimes utopian accounts of what exposing the conspiracy can accomplish, the new conspiracism is not aspirational. Conspiracists offer no notion of what should replace the reviled parties, processes, and agencies of government once covert schemes are revealed. They are without political prescriptions or an ounce of utopianism. Even when the new conspiracism foresees an apocalyptic climax ... there is no phoenix rising from the ashes.[11]

I would question the assertion that "classic conspiracism" is hopeful in every case. While anti-government conspiracists of the 1990s hoped for a restoration of what they believed to be a "constitutional republic," they were often under few illusions about their odds of making that happen and plans for rebuilding from the rubble of what had been were often vague, boiling down to "we'll just follow the Constitution!" Conspiratorial narratives about gray aliens enslaving humanity or "patriots" being locked away in Federal Emergency Management Agency (FEMA) death camps awaiting execution for the crime of opposing the "New World Order" were singularly hopeless in tone and content.

In the same way, there are aspects of "the new conspiracism" that are aspirational, that do have a "political prescription." These prescriptions, however, are often less well-developed than their forebears. The narratives that *are* aspirational, that have a more—rather than less—well-developed vision for what comes next, are those that have their roots in older conspiratorial traditions, such as the UFO Disclosure Movement. While the new conspiracist is not "aspirational," I argue that it is persistently "hopeful." Adherents of the QAnon complex of beliefs, from their emergence in 2017 through the end of the 2020 presidential election cycle, were hopeful that the defeat, humiliation, and execution of those they saw as enemies was imminent. But as Muirhead and Rosenblum note, QAnon followers did not aspire to anything but the rough justice that awaited anyone who dared oppose the will of GEOTUS (God Emperor of the United States) Donald Trump. Elements of this have seeped into NESARA and UFO Disclosure narratives since 2017. The new conspiracism, as described by Muirhead and Rosenblum, is a valuable phrase and one which I will employ as we discuss more well-established conspiratorial narratives. This is because many of the features of this new conspiracism have become prominent in these older narratives.

Since 2016, there have been several surveys and polls that examine conspiratorial belief in the United States. Two, in particular, are especially relevant to our study. A 2018 poll by the Monmouth University Polling Institute found that while only 37 percent of Americans were "very familiar" or "somewhat familiar" with the term "Deep State," when the term was defined ("a group of unelected government and military officials who secretly manipulate or direct national policy"), 74 percent said it "definitely" or "probably" exists. While the "Deep State" nomenclature exists largely in the rhetoric of right-of-center politicians and conspiracy peddlers, belief in the basic concept the phrase represents cuts across ethnic and party lines:

> Belief in the probable existence of a Deep State comes from more than 7-in-10 Americans in each partisan group.... Republicans (31%) and independents (33%) are somewhat more likely than Democrats (19%) to say that the Deep State definitely exists.
> Americans of black, Latino and Asian backgrounds (35%) are more likely than non–Hispanic whites (23%) to say that the Deep State definitely exists. Non-whites (60%) are also somewhat more likely than whites (50%) to worry about the government monitoring them and similarly more likely to believe there is already widespread government monitoring of U.S. citizens (60% and 49%, respectively). More non-whites (35%) than whites (23%) say that such monitoring is rarely or never justified.[12]

Also germane to the conspiratorial narratives we will be analyzing, Chapman University's 2016 Survey of American Fears (Wave 3) found that significant numbers of Americans believe "the government is concealing what they know" about "alien encounter" (42.6 percent), "plans for a one world government" (32.9 percent), and "[President Barack] Obama's birth certificate" (30.2 percent). Elements of these three conspiracy theories would play prominent (and, in some cases, revitalized) roles in the conspiracy culture that rose during the 2010s. Perhaps more significantly, the survey included in its list of well-known conspiracy theories one that did not actually exist, the "North Dakota Crash." Among the survey respondents, 32.5 percent "Agreed" or "Strongly Agreed" that this was subject to a government cover-up. This number is more than those who agreed that the government was suppressing information about "Obama's Birth Certificate," "the origin of the AIDS virus," "the death of Supreme Court Justice Antonin Scalia," or "the moon landing." Like the statistical disparity between those familiar with the term "Deep State" and those who accepted as plausible the concept behind that label, the fact that nearly a third of Americans accepted the North Dakota Crash cover-up is interesting. Does the acceptance of the fake conspiracy theory indicate a willingness to believe nearly *any* conspiracy theory? Or does it illustrate a broader suspicion of the government: a propensity to assume that the government suppresses information and lies to the public as a matter of course?[13]

Since 2016, narrowly focused, non-mainstream news media has played an increasingly significant role in shaping conspiracy culture. In their 2018 article "Contentions Narratives and Europe: Conspiracy Theories and Strategic Narratives Surrounding RT's Brexit News Coverage," Emma Flaherty and Laura Roselle explore how the Russian state-funded news website RT (originally the much-less ambiguously named "Russia Today") framed the 2016 Brexit debate and the degree to which RT "used conspiracy theories to challenge European actors through its news coverage." Flaherty and Roselle found that "blatant conspiracy theories" were far less frequent in RT stories than "question raising."[14] Question raising, a "method for challenging information by suggesting alternative narratives or questioning existing ones," has become, they argue, "a potential subset" of conspiracy theory that "questions the legitimacy, the actors, or the information involved in ... news coverage" without taking the typical and more traditional form of conspiracy narratives.[15] "Question Raising" allows conspiracy peddlers to promote and spread their theories with the benefit of being able to deflect criticism by insisting that they are "just asking questions." The triumphalist conspiracy narratives we analyze in the coming chapters—particularly the universe of claims orbiting the QAnon phenomenon—often rely heavily on the question asking techniques analyzed by Flaherty and Roselle. Indeed, in some cases, "Q Drops" consisted almost entirely of questions, such as this, from October 18, 2020, regarding Hunter Biden.

> How do you inform your target(s) ["business partners"] what you have?
> Why would H. Biden have such material on his laptop?
> How was the content *originally* received?
> Email?
> Why would H. Biden risk turning over such material to a computer repair shop? [contents unrestricted?]
> On purpose [years of being treated poorly by "Pop"] or simple negligence?
> If such information existed on laptop why wouldn't contents be claimed?
> Several attempts made to contact to claim?
> Messages left?
> Why wouldn't H. Biden want to reclaim *knowing* the contents on the drive could bury *Pops* & family.
> A troubled life?
> A troubled family?
> Looks can be deceiving.
> Q[16]

While belief in the proclamations of Q, in the imminence of a new age of financial freedom due to NESARA, or the coming announcement of full diplomatic relations with an extraterrestrial civilization might lead to stigmatization of believers, the rise to power of politicians like Donald Trump, whose rhetoric reinforced many conspiratorial narratives, lent a greater air of legitimacy to conspiratorial thinking than ever before. In addition to the renewed scholarly focus on conspiracism's influence, studies aimed at a broader audience also highlighted the shifting cultural landscape. Veteran conspiracy researcher Kenn Thomas asserted that, in 2017, when Trump counselor Kellyanne Conway justified demonstrably false statements by Press Secretary Sean Spicer about attendance at President Trump's inauguration as "alternative facts,"[17] it was not "awkward phraseology" but what "amounted to an ideological declaration." In his book *Trumpocalypse Now! The Triumph of the Conspiracy Spectacle*, Thomas examined Trump's history of promoting conspiracy theories such as

> the rumor that Barack Obama was not born in the United States ... that his Christianity made him a target for tax auditing; that vaccines cause autism; that climate change doesn't exist that the 9/11 plane crashes were cheered by thousands in the streets of New Jersey; many claims involving immigrants and immigration; and that one of his political opponents was involved with the JFK assassination.[18]

Trump's history of conspiracy mongering combined with "his career in television spectacle"[19] contributed to cultivating media coverage that moved conspiratorial narratives from the pages of "conspiracy theory books" and posts on Internet forums to the nightly news during the political campaign in 2016 and persisted afterward. This presidential sanction, along with support from other national political leaders, was a significant factor in the way that triumphalist conspiracy narratives thrived. Those adhering to the conspiracy theories were not marginalized outsiders fighting the power structure, they were "digital soldiers,"[20] elite operatives serving their president. This is particularly true of QAnon and Q-adjacent narratives but also affected the worlds of NESARA and UFO Disclosure.

Both scholarly and popular examinations of conspiracy culture since 2015 have noted the increasing prominence of conspiratorial narratives in American political and cultural life. Journalist Anna Merlan's 2019 *Republic of Lies* has a subtitle that emphasizes this prominence: *American Conspiracy Theorists and their Surprising Rise to Power*. Merlan noted that "many of the hard-core conspiracy theorists" she encountered in early 2015 on a conspiracy theory–themed cruise "weren't very engaged in politics" believing that "it's a fake system designed to give us the illusion of control by our real overlords." Over the course of the 2016 presidential campaign and Trump's election, however, "conspiratorial thinking leaked from its traditional confines to spread in new, more visible ways across the country." Merlan emphasizes that conspiracy culture did not begin with the 2016 election cycle, "there [was] something new at work: people who peddle lies and half-truths [had] come to prominence, fame, and power as never before." As a result, during the course of her investigation into the growing conspiracy culture, Merlan witnessed "a disturbing thirst for vengeance, a willingness to punish enemies and vanquish evildoers that is then easily twisted by opportunists."[21] The prospect of vengeance—or justice, depending on one's perspective—is a significant characteristic of the QAnon and NESARA conspiracy complexes. The constant promise that adherents will win their conflict with their enemies includes the tantalizing prospect of righting the wrongs of the past. In some cases, allegations that such punishments have already begun are an integral part of the narrative.

Before delving into the triumphal conspiracy narratives that have dotted the paranoid landscape of the late 20th and early 21st centuries, it is important to examine some core foundational concepts that provide background and context for several of the ideas running through the NESARA program, the UFO Disclosure Movement, and the complex of beliefs that orbited QAnon. The newer triumphalist conspiracy narratives are deeply intertwined and indebted to earlier conspiracy theories and extremist ideologies. The first of these is the so-called sovereign citizen movement. This movement has a long, often violent history dating back to the middle of the 20th century. While, to a considerable degree, there is much in here that is akin to traditional right wing conspiracy theories—concerns about the growth of the federal government's power and authority as well as the increasing globalization—our focus will be on the legal theories and alternative political structures promoted within sovereign citizen communities. These carry within them a promise of the restoration of a United States more in line, they believe, with how "the founders" conceived of the republic. Many of these theories amount to a system of "magic words." The initiated will know what to say and when to say it and, in doing so, access aspects of the legal system unknown to normal Americans. Despite the fact that these legal incantations are ineffective or, in many cases, lead to further charges, adherents of the sovereign citizen movement foresee a day when the legal system as they perceive it will be repaired and a new government will arise. Or, rather, that the government originally intended by the founders of the United States will be reconstituted. Occasionally, some individuals have used violent action to bring about this restoration, raise awareness of their cause, or resist what they perceive as unjust persecution or prosecution.

Key tenets of the sovereign citizen movement developed out of a number of strands during the late 20th century including conspiracy theories about the Federal Reserve System, concerns and paranoia surrounding the U.S. government's decision to take the dollar off of the gold standard, and the tax protest movement of the 1970s and 1980s. J.M. Berger, in a report for the George Washington University Program on Extremism, summarizes the sovereign worldview:

> So-called sovereign citizens believe in an alternate history of the U.S., replacing reality with a vast conspiracy governed by complex, arcane rules. They believe that if someone understands and properly invokes those rules, that person is exempt from many laws, including the obligation to pay taxes, and that he or she can be empowered to seize private property, enforce legal actions against individuals, and claim money from the government. When faced with arrest for illegal actions that they believe are legal, sovereign citizens can become violent.[22]

While Berger's description is accurate, it is difficult to answer the question of "what do sovereign citizens believe." Berger acknowledges that "many variations" coexist within the broad realm of sovereign citizen belief. There is no standard set of "canonical" sovereign citizen writings. There are contradictions in interpretation of legal theories. Some sovereign citizens are closely connected with white nationalist groups, while others display little overt racist ideology. While different sovereigns can emphasize different texts or authorities, Berger asserts that "the most fundamental tenet of the sovereign movement is an alternative version of American history."[23] The notion of a hidden, secret, or alternative history is fundamental to conspiracy theory in general, and it is especially significant to the triumphalist conspiracy theories discussed latter in this study.

There are a number of different parts of sovereign citizen belief. Two of the most important for the purposes of this study, are the secret history of the 14th Amendment and the "redemption" process.

The Secret History of the 14th Amendment

As with most (if not all) sovereign citizen legal theories, the end goal is not merely the gaining of freedom for freedom's sake but, rather, the realization of a freedom from unwanted financial obligations as well as the restoration of a political and economic system allegedly lost to time; the recovery of a hidden history. This is where the optimism and hope lie in such theories and the schemes involved in putting these theories into practice.

In the hidden legal and judicial history of the United States that forms the basis of sovereign citizen belief, the passage, ratification, and implementation of the 14th Amendment during the Reconstruction period plays an enormous role. As with other aspects of this secret, hidden history such as the supposed "Titles of Nobility" Amendment or the "bankruptcy" of the United States in the 1930s, different conspiracists have different interpretations.

The interpretation of the 14th Amendment is contained in the book *The Red Amendment*, which was written by L.B. Bork of the "People's Awareness Coalition" and posits that the 14th Amendment represented the origin of the supposed communist infiltration and takeover of the United States. This book appeared in the early 2010s and provided an overview of many sovereign citizen views of the 14th Amendment. *The Red Amendment* connects familiar sovereign citizen arguments about the 14th Amendment to well-trod conspiratorial narratives and tropes as well as concerns typical of evangelical and conservative moral panics related to the "culture wars" of the 1970s, 80s, and 90s, including an ongoing Cold War fear of communist or socialist subversion. As with most sovereign citizen legal arguments, the book goes into exhaustive (and exhausting) detail for nearly 200 pages. Various versions of *The Red Amendment* have cropped up in different corners of the sovereign citizen Internet over the years. Sometimes it is reprinted word for word but other times, it would be altered or amended. One of the more widely available versions was appropriate/adapted by David E. Robinson, a sovereign citizenship promoter and "tax protester" who styled himself "The

Maine Patriot." The number of different iterations of *The Red Amendment* makes finding a definitive version difficult, if not impossible. I have used the Bork and Robinson versions as the basis for this discussion.

The Red Amendment begins with a touch of hyperbole, declaring the 14th Amendment to be "a conspiracy more evil than any other the [U]nited States of America [sic] have seen in their many years of existence" and asserts that the amendment "is a vehicle for the implementation of Communism in America" as well as being "a vehicle to deliberately bring the United States into perpetual debt." As is typical in 14th Amendment conspiracy narratives, Bork goes back to the beginnings of the United States for the roots of this evil, explaining that despite victory over Britain in the War of Independence and the War of 1812, the "money powers of Europe" or "the World Elite" had taken "covert measures" that resulted in "a veiled takeover (conquest) of our country by way of financial control." Bork goes on to explain that since "America is the New World. The New World Order emits [sic] from America." Guiding this effort are various secret societies and "the Illuminati." It falls back on familiar notions of "occult symbolism" that are common in conspiracy narratives, such as the Washington Monument being "555 feet high with a 20% substructure 111 feet deep, for a total length of 666 feet." He does not, however, maintain this line of argument or explanation about the New World Order and, instead, segues to his main point: the 14th Amendment being a tool for the implementation of communism in the United States.

A key point (and what makes the 14th the "Red" amendment) is that Karl Marx and Friedrich Engels's 1848 *Communist Manifesto* is a "'blueprint' that elites and secret societies use to enslave and control nations with perpetual debt." Their ultimate goal is "to destroy Americans." This, of course, ignores much of the context in which Marx and Engels wrote the *Manifesto*, such as the rising economic and political radicalization in Europe accompanying industrialization, increasing urbanization, and the changes these brought to society. This is just one way in which *The Red Amendment* re-interprets 19th-century Marxism to reflect the concerns and fears of political, economic, and religious conservatives of mid to late 20th century. This is evident in a list of goals claimed to be part of communism's "corrupt dictum." Some of them (such as "Income Tax" or "Elimination of Private Property") are not entirely out of line with the goals that a devotee of Marx would have had in the 19th century. Others, however, are much more familiar to the context of Cold War and post–Cold War concerns. Fears over "corrupt dictum" items like "Destruction of belief in God (Religion)," "Destruction of the Natural Family Unit,"

"Destruction and erosion of Morality," or "Free Love" are much more a piece of the late 20th century than the middle of the 19th. Other items on the communist to-do list are vague to the point of pointlessness, such as "Elimination of Eternal Truths," "Elimination of Freedoms," and "Everyone Working."

As evidence that this "corrupt dictum" is being fulfilled, *The Red Amendment* cites these facts: "government is determined to control the public schools.... Women have been conditioned to be part of the general work force.... The media promotes free love and immorality; you then get the break-up of families." By projecting 20th- and 21st-century concerns back through time, Bork is attempting to establish that these perceived negative aspects of modern life are part of an evil master plan rather than organic social and cultural developments. As to his assertion that "the greatest tool used by the Elite are the people of the labor force.... People should not be burdened to the point where life is all work," Marx would likely agree, to a point.

Having exposed the machinations of the New World Order and the communists, the author turns their attention to the constitutional and legal arguments underpinning his denunciation of the 14th Amendment. This argument is grounded in the definition of "nation" and the question of where an American's citizenship is based. For example, the author asserts that "most Americans are unaware that their true country and nation is not the United States of America." Their true "country and nation" is either the "native state" or their "chosen state." Further clarifying this is the argument that "'one nation [under God]' in the pledge of allegiance [*sic*] to the yellow-fringed flag of war is a misnomer. We are a Union of 50 nation-states." Utilizing a straw man argument, the author warns readers that those who say "'times have changed' or that 'The Constitution is old and no longer applies'" were utilizing "programming by Communist dicta."

Echoing one of the common constitutional arguments of the sovereign citizen movement, the author explains that following the Civil War, the 14th Amendment established a new, different government, "based on Socialism-Communism." This "insurgent democracy" is distinct from the "Republican form of government ... guaranteed to the nation-states ... in Article 4, Section 4, of the Constitution." Highlighting the dangers of democracy over republicanism, *The Red Amendment* presents a bizarre and factually inaccurate historical parallel:

> Rome became a so-called Democracy, what you live in now. The Roman Empire collapsed due to its people over indulging [*sic*] in sporting events, dictatorships, corruption, military aggression, sexual perversions, etc. Does this sound familiar to you?

Returning to the 14th Amendment, the author asserts that its alteration of the nature of citizenship was, in reality, the fundamental goal of the Civil War itself. They argue that Supreme Court cases such as *Dred Scott vs. Sanford* (1857) and the *Slaughter-House Cases* (1873) were orchestrated to—in the case of *Dred Scott*—demonstrate the need for the 14th Amendment and—in the case of *Slaughter-House*—to establish a precedent for the 14th Amendment to be used by courts for purposes beyond guaranteeing the citizenship rights of African Americans. The goal of the Civil War, according to Bork, was the enslavement of the American people:

> The slaves were transferred over to the control of the United States. You may believe that reference is being made to people of African descent owned by Southern plantation owners; as those persons' rights were to be guarded by the United States legislation. On the Contrary! Reference is actually being made to all Americans being tacitly enslaved by the purported government of the Union: the "United States."

The 14th Amendment, according to *The Red Amendment*, "naturalizes all Americans to be citizens and nationals of the United States at birth" and "negates" what he calls the "state nationalities de jure." By law, Americans are citizens of their individual states. The 14th Amendment established the de facto power of an entity called the "United States"— an illegitimate entity distinct from the union of states created at the dawn of independence. In addition to destroying the original "nations or countries of America," the 14th Amendment "puts the land of people in quasi-joint tenancy with the government (feudalism)."[24] *The Red Amendment* explains that "a de facto government is a government of fact exercising power and control, as opposed to the true and lawful government that was established according to the 1787 Constitution." This is, he explains, the "insurgent government" currently ruling the American people. This is not only a political legal issue but is part of a broader plan to implement communism. Like many conspiratorial narratives, it aims to prove its argument by highlighting alleged instances of symbolism or numerical importance.

> The Civil War began in 1861, 13 years after the Communist Manifesto was drafted. The number 13 is representative of "Moral Corruption and Rebellion against God." The 14th Amendment is a Manifesto of the Communist's Declaration of War against the world and God, and the World Elite are behind this "Quiet War."

Beyond the effect of the 14th Amendment itself, *The Red Amendment* examines other aspects of the Civil War and Reconstruction eras to explain what sovereigns see as an ongoing erosion of liberty and freedom. The author cites the Expatriation Act of 1868 [15 Stat. 223]. The passage of the Expatriation Act served as a declaration that the United States denounced the concept of perpetual allegiance to a power and established that naturalized citizens of the United States were no longer subject to the jurisdiction of any previous powers. While that may sound obvious, during the 19th century there were numerous instances of naturalized American citizens being conscripted into the armies of their birth country when they returned to visit.[25] As a nation of immigrants, American legislators and diplomats argued that there needed to be a clear break with the old country when one became a citizen of a new one. *The Red Amendment*, in keeping with its vision of what one's "true" nation is (the individual state rather than the "United States"), argues that the Expatriation Act required citizens to renounce their allegiance to their state in favor of federal citizenship. That the Expatriation Act passed one day before the announcement of the 14th Amendment's ratification is simply one more synchronicity pointing to a vast conspiracy.

In a similar, but much more far-reaching way, *The Red Amendment* also points to the Lieber Code—a set of regulations defining how officers and men of the Union Army were to conduct themselves in fighting, treatment of prisoners, and other exigencies of war—and claims that it is evidence that the United States government is a "military government" and that it "define[s] Americans as enemies of the state and federal governments." Americans, however, have helped to put themselves into this position and have enabled the "insurgent" government to thrive:

> The Expatriation Act desires that you give up your allegiance to your country—your nation-state—but nobody can make you do it. Your allegience [sic] to your native country (the nation-state in which you live) is a natural right held under the Law of Nations.

So how does one renounce your nation-state citizenship? By voting:

> The 14th Amendment induces us (via our voting franchise) to participate in insurrection, hence all voters create a rebellion against their constitutional state government, and such suffrage is deemed treason under international law. By voting we voluntarily give our consent to the de facto government and give away the freedoms protected by the de jure Constitution which is still in force and effect today. This 14th Amendment suffrage creates the Quiet War wherein a voter is actually empowering the communistic totalitarian dictatorship of the world.[26]

While the 14th Amendment does discuss voting rights, *The Red Amendment* seems to be conflating the 14th Amendment with the 15th, which guarantees voting rights regardless of race or "previous condition of servitude." Voting, the author argues, has empowered the United States to move toward socialism, as the people vote themselves public benefits. Immigration has encouraged this, being "the mass importation of common voters who perpetuate the mobocracy that feeds this so-called Democracy."

These notions about the 14th Amendment, while laid out in one particular book, echo broader sovereign citizen beliefs. The "Quick Guide to Sovereign Citizens" produced by the School of Government at the University of North Carolina explains that "sovereigns distinguish between the original state, of which they are citizens, and the false and illegitimate state that occupies the same territory. And, as already mentioned, they view the Fourteenth Amendment as the source of the new separate class of federal citizenship."[27]

Logically, if one voluntarily renounces one's "nation-state" citizenship, one could renounce their "United States" citizenship, exit that system and "repatriate" to the country of their birth (in this case, an individual state). As with other aspects of sovereign citizen conspiratorial narratives, promoters present a constitutional or legal crisis which robs an individual of their rights and liberties by revealing a hidden history that "changes everything." The next step is to provide a solution; to give them the magic words, the right form, or the perfect procedure to restore these rights and liberties. Of course, none of these solutions are free. In the case of exiting the "14th amendment United States" system, David E. Robinson offered a "Declaration of Sovereignty" process. Robinson offered to help people with their "REDEMPTION from the color-of-law world of fiction" by preparing for them "a UCC-1 DECLARATION that will register your newly claimed status as the initial, primary SECURED PARTY, HOLDER-IN-DUE-COURSE of your STRAWMAN" (emphasis in original). People could then file this completed paperwork with their state's Secretary of State.

To achieve this, the soon-to-be sovereign citizen submits their name and address as well as an official copy of their birth certificate and a copy of their Social Security card. To facilitate the entire process, Robinson requires a "donation" of $300 for each filing. This is in addition to whatever filing fee the new sovereign will have to pay their Secretary of State. Expensive, but a small price to pay to be—supposedly—free from most taxes, fees, and government red tape.

Robinson also assured people he would

> Overlay your BIRTH CERTIFICATE, and produce a BILL OF EXCHANGE and CHARGE BACK letter for you to sign and mail to the Secretary of Treasury at the United States Treasury in Washington, D.C., that will activate your UCC CONTRACT TRUST ACCOUNT (UCC-CTA).

This notion of a "trust account" and reference to the UCC—the Uniform Commercial Code—is another foundational concept in the sovereign citizen movement.[28]

Financial Redemption: There's Money with Your Name on It!

The secret history of the 14th Amendment provides a legal and political framework for sovereign citizen beliefs, reframing the parameters of federal and state power in terms of an imagined, idealized past. Paired with this is another significant strand of sovereign citizen theory, a financial component to the "redemption" process one may use to free oneself from the jurisdiction of the federal government. In the sovereign citizen worldview, just as there is the concept of the "de facto" and the "de jure" U.S. government, there is a distinction between types of citizens. One sovereign citizen resource summarizes the distinction between types of citizens in this way:

> A **Sovereign/Citizen** of the United States of America (American Citizen), lives in one of the 50 sovereign states, and has inalienable rights secured by state and national constitutions.
>
> The **artificial person, U.S. citizen,** is a legal fiction that has been created by the federal government, via the social security application, and is a corporate employee of the United States by virtue of being a U.S. citizen. He is subject to the jurisdiction of the federal government and of the state government and subject to the corporate income tax.
>
> The U.S. citizen is created property, created to raise revenue for the government, your employer. You have essentially contracted to be liable for the debts of your master, the federal government.[29]

The distinction between "sovereign citizen" and "artificial person" leads to a financial aspect of redemption based on the notion that the illegal, "corporate" United States government possesses massive amounts of money which citizens can access, if they know the proper procedures to do so. This concept is, perhaps, even more complex and convoluted than the distinction between "de facto" and "de jure" governments and is complicated by the multiple sources and interpretations associated with it.

Despite some variations in the story of this financial aspect, there is a common thread that runs through them all. Like the secret history of the 14th Amendment, this narrative has its origins in the Civil War era, with two parallel strands—the increasing power of the presidency and the emergence of a tax on income. Both of these items loom large not only in conspiracy literature but in right-wing politics more generally. Sovereign citizen history claims that when the southern states seceded in 1861, the exit of southern members of Congress meant that the legislative body did not have a quorum. With Congress unable to "conduct the nation's business," power was left to the executive branch. Abraham Lincoln "declared a state of war and exercised his powers as Commander in Chief, to institute martial law under a state of emergency." Congress, however, still met and passed laws during this period. This was an illusion, to a degree, for "Lincoln ordered Congress to reconvene under his military authority as Commander in Chief (not as President)." Thus, Congress gave the appearance of fulfilling its legislative function under the Constitution, but this was not actually the case. Further, nothing changed at the end of the war. "Congress was NEVER legally reconvened under the Constitution" and "still sits today under military authority, by order of the President." Using this authority, Lincoln established numerous means to fund the war, including war bonds. Sovereign citizen scholars explain that the first income tax, established during the war, was designed to pay the interest on these bonds. The debt from these bonds was, they claim, never paid, forcing the United States into bankruptcy.

That bankruptcy means that the nature of the government changed. Sovereigns argue that it "is a legal maxim that a bankrupt[cy] is 'civilly dead.'" Because of this, "Congress cannot legally make positive law in bankruptcy, because they have no legal standing." Congress still appears to function because "sits at the pleasure of the Commander in Chief, waiting to do his bidding." Presidential power was further expanded, sovereigns argued, through the 1917 Trading with the Enemy Act and the 1933 Emergency Banking Act. The end result was that citizens of the United States (that is, "14th Amendment citizens") were viewed as property of the government—collateral for the fraudulent "Federal Reserve Notes" that have been issued as currency to pay debts that have been accruing since the Civil War. Citizens unwittingly consent and submit to this status almost as soon as they are born:

> Starting in the 1930's [sic], when you were born, you were issued a birth certificate from the state, and this certificate was recorded in the state records. After your birth certificate is recorded, it is sent to the Department of Commerce. Why there? Because the government is creating an artificial person and is just recording the birth of their property, that they will control and use for generating tax revenue. This is done to create an employee of the United States corporation to help pay off the national debt, since it is not legal to use private property to pay public debts.

The birth certificate or, in some interpretations, a Social Security number, is "just a 'Certificate of Title' to the U.S. citizen, just like you get for your car." In a legal sense, sovereigns argue, "you don't own the fictional U.S. citizen, and legally you don't own your car." Rather, the titles are held by the government, which "issues you a Certificate of Title for your car and a Birth Certificate for the U.S. citizen."[30] Once the government issues this title, the Department of the Treasury takes out a "bond" against the value of the new citizen which is held in something usually called a "Treasury Direct Account." The amount held in the account ranges from $650,000 to $20,000,000 per person.[31] Sovereigns usually refer to the entity held as collateral as a "straw man," a legal creation which is distinct from the flesh and blood natural man. Here, Sovereigns cite *Black's Law Dictionary* for their definition. A straw man is "an entity, such as a corporation, created by law and given certain legal rights and duties of a human being."[32]

While we could go into much more depth on the backstory of "redemption," behind all of the arguments and assertions about the nature of U.S. citizenship, currency, and citizens-as-collateral is a fairly simple notion: by carrying out "a series of arcane legal filings," citizens may gain access to the hundreds of thousands, even millions of dollars, held in their Treasury Direct Accounts.[33] There are a number of methods that sovereigns argue will accomplish this and most use the Uniform Commercial Code, as discussed earlier, as the means to redeem their straw man and access the money. It is, however, a complicated process so, just as there are services that claim they will help you file the paperwork to become a sovereign citizen, there are companies that do the same for accessing Treasury Direct Accounts. One of the oldest still on the Internet is The Redemption Service, which has operated since 2005. The Redemption Service explains the solution to the problem of freeing oneself from being human collateral in a somewhat confusing way:

> Thus, the cause was the contract, and the contract was the parent's signature upon the birth record; that birth record (birth certificate) being the tool used that established the cause. The Solution: reversal of the same UCC system (nexus) "backwards" from the effect (enslaved flesh-and-blood) to the cause! (the contract). Simply reverse the positions of the cause with that of the effect, through the nexus, and the result is the remedy! Convert the enslaved flesh-and-blood (effect) into the new CAUSE (signature contract), and at-the-same-time convert the birth certificate contract into the new EFFECT (enslaved property). Now the Live flesh-and-blood is the "contract" (through their signature) and the previous birth certificate "contract" is now the "enslaved property" (secured property title) of the Live flesh-and-blood.

For those who are unsure of exactly how to do this, the Redemption Service will assist in helping them establish a "Secured Private Title

Bond" that will enable them to regain "control of their life and their sovereignty." Once they are "no longer obligated to the fictitious 'bankruptcy' and 'debt'" they will be able to carry out their financial business using gold and silver. Moreover, they will be

> completely "exempt" from any government bankruptcy, debt, tax, interest, or any other type "liability" (especially liabilities that can only be paid in "Federal Reserve Notes"). Sovereign Live flesh-and-blood people can not [sic] be forced or compelled to even "use" valueless unbacked Federal Reserve Notes (FRNs). The Sovereign Live flesh-and-blood Secured Party can not [sic] be forced to "pay" in FRNs for any debt or liability incurred (or supposedly incurred). Thus, they are exempt from any and ALL payment demands made in or subject to FRNs.

Through a "chargeback" to the Treasury Department, the sovereign citizen who has redeemed their straw man creates a new "Treasury Contract Trust Account" which covers all the financial obligations of their strawman.[34]

In order to take advantage of their expertise and skill in negotiating the legal minefield of straw man redemption, one must "be a member in good standing" of their organization. While membership is free, it is subject to their approval and, thus, there is an application process. There are five steps to membership, all of which must be completed, including the requirement that applicants "MUST also read EVERYTHING herein upon these pages." The clumsy pseudo-legal language is typical of sovereign citizen businesses. Once the Redemption Service receives an application, they contact the applicant by phone for an interview and, if membership is approved, grants "a full private 1 on 1 consultation."[35]

The multi-part application process involves a great deal of reading. The first part is dedicated to flattering the potential customer/member and attempting to convince them that The Redemption Service is the only legitimate avenue for redeeming their straw man account. The Redemption Service has high standards for membership, with a "focus" on "assisting and empowering *honorable* people of sound character." These potential members are "strong minded, confident, determined, and SERIOUS about taking powerful control over their lives like you've never known EVER before." They have to be careful about who they admit to membership, for The Redemption Service has many enemies. When they began their work in 2005 (as the "Cracking the Code Webstore") they were targeted by "multiple hostile agents (agencies)" who were "determined to shut us up and shut us down, because we were immediately seen as a serious threat to the establishment." The Cracking the Code Webstore overcame these challenges only to find numerous imitators who "hijacked, stripped away, and convoluted" their work.

While competitors appear to offer similar services, The Redemption Service explains to potential customer/members that these other businesses "are nothing but pretend websites peddling incomplete and ineffective processes" and warns them that if they use these other services they "will never have anything effective with them, nor will you ever complete anything legitimate with them."[36]

After more than a dozen years in the "redemption" game, The Redemption Service explains that there are five different types of people who seek their services. The most desirable are "Quality High-Status People of Honor." These people are "well pulled together, well developed, well established, financially stable." These people the "perfect match" for the knowledge provided by The Redemption Service. There are also "Average or Above Average People," who may be educated but who definitely "have good, solid morals, values, integrity, are usually well pulled together, well developed, well established, financially stable." While they are not the "perfect match" of the first group they are generally "no problem to work with." Less desirable are the "Average to Below Average People." They have lower income, entry-level jobs. Some of them, however, "are resourceful." Unfortunately, "many" of them are "unstable" with regard to their finances or character. They may have even availed themselves of one of The Redemption Service's imitators or competitors, mostly because they were not serious enough to do the proper research. "Most of this crowd," they explain, "are not the perfect match for us. Although, there are some from this camp that do have high integrity and are resourceful." Not a good match are the "Below Average/Low Mentality People." People in this group lack money and desire. They have "no passion, no plan, to ever improve their financial situation or living conditions." Even worse, they possess "no values." They are "complainers, doubters, excuse makers, envious." The fifth and worst group are excitedly described as "Dishonest! Dishonorable!" The people in this group are "immoral and often, typically, is the case, predatory." They possess "serious character defects, personality disorders." Into this category fall all those who "are attempting to imitate" the work of The Redemption Service.[37]

The Secret Government

Another foundational concept not only of "the new conspiracism" but also of older, 20th-century conspiratorial narratives in the notion of the "secret government." Conspiracy theories about a secret government have taken a variety of forms during the 20th and 21st centuries.

These range from the bizarre to the prosaic. On the more prosaic end of the spectrum are conspiracies that theorists extrapolate from the existing political/geopolitical order. Cold War–era conspiracy theories about communist subversion spun out of the real-life chess game between East and West following the Second World War. Fears of a communist takeover of the United States—present during the 1920s and 1930s but taking something of a back seat during the war—gained momentum during the 1950s and persisted throughout the Cold War.

None Dare Call It Treason, John Stormer's 1964 book is emblematic of the anti–Communist paranoia that would inform the post-war era. Stormer claimed that "the hidden tentacles of the communist conspiracy [were] exerting unmeasured influence over the rest of the world."[38] Could the Soviet Union, perhaps, defeat the United States? Could tyranny triumph over freedom? Stormer believed it could for a number of reasons. He cited a slackening of anti-communist sentiment since the McCarthyite heyday of the early 1950s. The U.S. was increasingly involved in the United Nations and fewer Americans than ever were informed about the dangers of international communism. And yet, Stormer was not fully certain that there was a full-blown conspiracy to accomplish this. He asks:

> Is there a conspiratorial plan to destroy the United States into which foreign aid, planned inflation, distortion of treaty-making powers and disarmament all fit? This question divides many knowledgeable and dedicated conservatives. They waste time and effort and split their ranks with senseless debate. It doesn't really matter whether the "parts" have been planned for an "assembly line revolution" as [Indiana] Senator [William E.] Jenner charged, or if they are the work of well-meaning but misguided idealists.[39]

Stormer's position was that the question of conspiracy was almost beside the point, distracting people from the very real dangers of communist subversion.

None Dare Call It Conspiracy was a 1972 book that, while sounding like a sequel to Stormer's, merely aped the title. Author Gary Allen tied together well-worn and anti–Semitic financial conspiracy theories with anti-communism. Allen connected the Rothschild and Warburg banking families, J.P. Morgan, and the Federal Reserve System to the outbreak of the First World War, claiming that these global forces had been planning the war for decades before it took place.[40] We will see echoes of these international banker conspiracy theories in the NESARA narrative, with supporters presenting NESARA as the final judgment on and punishment of those who first established and then benefited from the financial system while keeping the people of the United States in debt and fear. Allen's book also highlights the culpability of "insiders" in politics and international affairs for the state of the world and the looming threat of communism. Allen's particular targets are the Council on Foreign Relations and the Bilderberger organization. Organizations such as these had, in Allen's opinion, an outsized role in influencing foreign policy, working behind the scenes to weaken the nation and effect the victory of communism:

> Yes, the *Insiders* have no aversion to working with the Communists whose ostensible goal is to destroy them. While the *Insiders* are serving champagne and caviar to their guests in their summer mansions at Newport, or entertaining other members of the social elite aboard their yachts, their agents are out enslaving and murdering people. And you are next on their list.... It should not be surprising to learn that there is on the international level an organizational equivalent of the C.F.R. This group calls itself the Bilderbergers. If scarcely one American in a thousand has any familiarity with the C.F.R., it is doubtful that one in five thousand has any knowledge of the Bilderbergers. Again, this is not accidental.[41]

The tension between insiders and outsiders, between members of in-groups that have power and authority and members of out-groups that have none is a common driving force for conspiracy theories. In *None Dare Call It Conspiracy*, Allen explains that since Republicans and Democrats alike are part of organizations like the Council on Foreign Relations and the Bilderbergers, there is no substantive difference between the two parties. The goal of those in government is to stay in government and advance their anti–American, communist, and globalist agendas. They are, essentially, not answerable to the American voter, because no matter who is elected, they are likely to be part of this in-group. This situation is exacerbated by the persistence of the unelected career bureaucrats at all levels of government.

The ideas presented by Allen, echoed by conspiracy theorists decades after, are the foundation of paranoia surrounding the Deep State and calls for a draining of "the swamp" that were prevalent during the 2016 presidential election campaign. While reducing the size and scope of the federal bureaucracy has long been a focus of right-wing politics, adherents of the QAnon conspiracy narrative have been particularly fixated on it. The Deep State was the heart of the evil against which candidate (and later president) Donald Trump fought. There is a direct line from the Deep State conspiracy narrative of the 21st century to the insiders versus outsiders discussion presented by conspiracy theorists like Gary Allen. Though the term "Deep State" is most associated with Donald Trump's campaign rhetoric and those who adopted the term with the QAnon conspiracy community, the concept itself is as old as conspiracy theories themselves, with the NESARA financial conspiracy and the UFO Disclosure Movement both adhering to a version of it.

Communist-focused conspiracy theories, such as those presented by Stormer and Allen, exist at the more prosaic end of the secret government conspiracy theory spectrum. Further along are theories which place the ultimate blame for the spread of communism and the threat of a globalist "New World Order" at a higher level than the pawns working in and for the government. Conspiracy theorists have pointed to secret societies, such as the freemasons and religious forces such as the Roman Catholic Church as supranational movements that are responsible for fomenting threats such as Communist infiltration. These organizations represent the true danger beyond the threats of which the public might be aware. The most outlandish secret government conspiracies place a layer of control at the top that supersedes human-controlled systems. Non-human beings, whether they be gray aliens from Zeta Reticuli or shapeshifting lizard people from the lower fourth dimension, as claimed by David Icke,[42] began playing a role in conspiracy theories near the end of the 20th century. The UFO Disclosure conspiracy narrative, in particular, pushes back against the more traditional "alien invasion" narrative with one that puts extraterrestrials on a moral, ethical, and technological pedestal.

All three of the narratives—NESARA, UFO Disclosure, and QAnon—rely on earlier, and more fundamental conspiratorial tropes that are much more long-standing than these particular iterations. Traditional conspiracy theories speak of an oppressive secret government, of a corrupt American government that ignores the Constitution, of a global cabal that is hiding the truth about our extraterrestrial neighbors. These triumphal narratives do not entirely erase the negative. Rather, they promise that patriots and other true believers will overcome the challenges of corrupt systems and global elites. Those who keep the faith, who keep fighting, will break the back of the traditional systemic conspiracies. The common man and woman are no longer victims of the conspiracy; they are victors over the conspirators.

Chapter 2

NESARA—White Knights, Dark Agendas, and the Appeal to Greed

> There is, RIGHT NOW, a law on the books that when announced IMMEDIATELY Improves YOUR LIFE![1]
> —Message that greeted visitors to Shaini Goodwin's NESARA.us website, 2003–2010

Depending on what results they choose when doing a web search for NESARA, the National Economic Stabilization (or sometimes "Security") and Recovery (or sometimes "Reformation") Act, a curious person could come to the conclusion that it was a thought exercise about needed reforms to America's banking and taxation systems. Another curious person, choosing a different link to click, might come to the conclusion that NESARA was a law that would instantly improve their financial life; that it was passed by Congress and signed into law in 1993; that this fact has been hidden since then by malefactors carrying out a "dark agenda" to keep the bulk of humanity financially and politically oppressed. But wait! There were, fortunately, forces actively fighting this dark agenda, from regular people around the world to extraterrestrial starship commanders and spiritual "Ascended Masters." The conspiracy to prevent the benefits of this law could not, our curious web searcher might read, be hidden forever. Soon the dam would break, and the forces of light would enact NESARA. Our subject's credit card, student loan, mortgage debt, and any other financial obligations would disappear overnight. There were other conspiracies ready to break as well—currency re-valuations that will finally restore gold and other precious metals to their rightful place at the top of the monetary pyramid; new medical and energy technologies that have been kept from the public would revolutionize life on Earth. From what they have read, they also needed to contact their cousin in Europe, for there is a global version of NESARA on the way.

It will be a new dawn for humanity. Soon.

NESARA, and other financial conspiracies that alleged great wealth and prosperity being withheld from the American people by malign forces, provide a challenging and complex glimpse into a world where the hope that is on the ever-receding horizon is often more intensely personal than in other conspiratorial narratives. The NESARA narrative provided a future of tangible financial change. To be sure, it also included more abstract economic, governmental, and geopolitical changes. But, unlike many of the other narratives and theories we discuss in this volume, the focus and appeal were framed primarily in terms of what NESARA would do for the individual citizen, and only secondarily on broader societal and systemic change. During its rise to prominence in the early 2000s, NESARA also illustrated the transition from the "old" conspiracism to the new, with proof of its conspiracy-based claims relying less on rational evidence and complex proofs than it did on repetition and loud assertion.

American conspiracy theories and narratives that focus on financial and economic topics are as old as the nation; older, if we look back to the colonial era. The era of turbulence in the 1760s and 1770s which ended in rebellion, war, and independence was in many ways driven by financial concerns, including the Currency Acts of 1751 and 1764, which restricted the colonies' ability to issue paper money and forbade colonial currency from being used to pay debts. As the colonies crept closer to open rebellion, these issues became part of the vast web of actions colonial activists believed were part of the motherland's effort to inhibit their growth. In the early years of the Republic, fears of financial conspiracy flourished. Many—generally farmers and planters in the southern and western United States—feared that Alexander Hamilton's plan for establishing a centralized banking system and federal assumption of state debts would benefit financial and banking interests at their own expense, as well as lead to a much more powerful and domineering national government than they envisioned at the nation's birth. By the early 1800s much of the furor had died down as the American economy prospered. A new economic catastrophe—the Panic of 1819—resurrected criticism of the centralized banking system. By the 1830s, the Democratic Party and President Andrew Jackson were determined to eliminate the bank in a bid to limit the power of the financial elite many blamed for the unstable economy.

Without the stabilizing force of a central banking system, the American economy throughout the latter half of the 19th century was volatile, experiencing repeating boom-bust cycles and frequent periods of economic recession. Paper money at the time was still backed by precious metals—gold and silver—and the question of how much paper money the government should issue dominated political debate in the latter half of the 19th century. Urban industrial workers and farmers— and the politicians representing those interests—insisted that the silver being mined in the western states should be "coined" and put into circulation. The increased money supply, they argued, would strengthen the buying power of the industrial working class and enable struggling farmers to pay their debts. Banking officials and other members of the financial sector objected that the inflation caused by this policy of bimetallism—basing paper money on silver as well as gold—would be ruinous to the economy. In his seminal article "The Paranoid Style in American Politics," Richard Hofstadter used the pro-silver Populists as an example of the long reach of conspiratorial thinking in political rhetoric. In their 1895 manifesto, the Populists claimed that "every device of treachery, every resource of statecraft, and every artifice known to the secret cabals of the international gold ring are being used to deal a blow to the prosperity of the people and the financial and commercial independence of the country."[2] Although the gold standard would prevail, financial conspiracy theories would persist, particularly in a focus on the role of the Federal Reserve System (echoing some of the concerns about the Bank of the United States in the 1790s and 1830s), and the nation's abandonment of the gold standard.

One of the things that distinguished NESARA from traditional financial and economic conspiracy theories was the prominence of the immediate, personal monetary benefit that waited at the end of the rainbow. Free Silver populists in the 1890s saw the potential for financial benefit if they were to overcome the machinations of "the secret cabals of the international gold ring"—but they would still have debts to pay. NESARA incorporated aspects of these earlier economic narratives but added a personal financial angle to entice believers.

A factor contributing to this personal financial angle is the NESARA story's roots in a financial swindle called "Omega." As a narrative that spun off from a failed get-rich-quick scheme, the "you're gonna be rich!" message makes sense. NESARA, however, was—and continues to be—more than a swindle or get rich quick scheme. It, and related narratives, blend some of the pitches and techniques of classic grifting with a wide variety of conspiratorial tropes and sub-narratives that borrow from many sources.

NESARA began with the work of economist Harvey Barnard. In the early 1990s, Barnard undertook a "search for a root cause and the solutions to America's social problems."[3] By the 1990s, Barnard had developed the ideas that made up the National Economic Stabilization and Recovery Act, which he circulated to members of Congress in the book *Draining the Swamp: The NESARA Story* in 1996. By 2001, Barnard established the NESARA Institute and had begun promoting his NESARA plan on the Internet. Barnard intended NESARA to reform the monetary system of the United States and to provide broader reform of the entire fiscal system. This would be accomplished by placing the monetary system under federal control and out of the hands of the Federal Reserve bank (which would be eliminated and replaced with the "United States Treasury Reserve System"). It also sought to restore the American monetary system to a basis of gold and silver, thus returning the country to "constitutional" currency. In doing so, NESARA would "secure for the American people their unalienable right to Life, Liberty, and Property." Barnard asserted that NESARA has the potential to "eliminate trillions of dollars of public and private debt," which seemed like an extravagant claim. It did not, however, completely change some of the less popular aspects of America's fiscal policy. Barnard's NESARA would only amend "the existing federal income tax system" and it aimed to impose a national sales tax on many consumer items. The despised Internal Revenue Service (IRS) would vanish but be replaced by a new "National Tax Service." Additionally, Barnard emphasized that there would be no immediate elimination of the "entire national debt" and pointed out that it would take time for the NESARA changes to halt inflation.[4]

As Barnard developed his NESARA program, other events transpired in the Pacific Northwest that would forever shape how the public would perceive NESARA. Shaini Goodwin became involved in the NESARA movement in the early 21st century and would be the public face of the ever-evolving NESARA story until her death in 2010. Goodwin went by the online handle "Dove of Oneness" and her contributions to NESARA were based in her involvement in The Omega Trust. The Omega Trust was an investment scheme begun in Mattoon, Illinois, by electrician Clyde D. Hood. In 1994, Hood (along with several co-conspirators) established Omega Trust and Trading, Ltd. Under the aegis of this company, Hood courted various groups, giving lectures in which he claimed to be an "international trader" who had the ability to provide investors with huge (and hugely unlikely) returns on investments. Hood targeted church groups, claiming that he had received a vision from God that he should use his connections in the financial world to help "the little people" and to support humanitarian programs.[5] Exactly how Omega was able to do this was not entirely clear. Hood talked vaguely about being in "the investment business" and said he owned a foreign bank and dealt in "prime bank notes." Investors would give Hood $100, with the promise that they would receive a 50–1 return on this money after 275 days. At that point, they could cash out, or they could let the money ride for another 275 days for another massive—and implausible—50 to 1 payout.[6] Investors from every state in the union as well as China and Australia took part, eventually netting Hood and his co-conspirators over $12,000,000. Hood and his compatriots laundered the money through real estate purchases and interest-free loans.[7] While Hood took no more Omega investors after 1995, he then began a number of other programs and employed existing investors as his ground troops in multi-level marketing plans. Investors did not receive their expected returns as Hood provided numerous excuses and explanations for why the promised money failed to materialize. He provided his investors with pre-recorded "updates" that relayed tales of "unforeseen financial conflicts" of various kinds but always assured them that their money would arrive soon. By 1999, Hood was aware that he was under scrutiny by federal law enforcement, and in 2000, he and several co-conspirators were indicted on charges including filing false tax returns, fraud, and money laundering. Hood pled guilty in 2001 and in 2002 was sentenced to 14 years in federal prison. He died before his sentence was complete, in 2012 at the age of 78.[8]

As Clyde Hood's journey took him inexorably toward federal prison, a new voice arose from Washington State. Shaini Goodwin, using the pen name "Dove of Oneness," began distributing messages reassuring investors that the returns on their Omega investments were just around the corner. She also served as a cheerleader to keep Omega investors' morale up while Clyde Hood underwent his trial:

> Tonight we were told by a very high intelligence agency source that this whole thing in Illinois "has been staged" to try to stop funding! However, this case in Illinois TOTALLY LACKS any ability to stop funding. It's almost a comedy, because the whole case will disappear instantly—VERY SOON.... STAY AWAY FROM THE WEBSITE that has information on this case!!! You will be tracked if you go to that website. And, absolutely avoid filling out any complaints—you could lose your funding if you do that![9]

In this statement, Goodwin used a number of techniques that were familiar in the genre of hopeful or triumphal conspiracy narratives. She had "very high" sources in the intelligence community who—of course—could not be identified. Publicly documented events were "staged." The usual channels of communication and news—even reports of the conduct of the trial—were all untrustworthy. Indeed, they were dangerous, with the threat that even checking the court website for case updates would result in being "tracked." Because of the overt financial aspects of this narrative, Goodwin made sure to provide an incentive for Omega investors to refrain from providing support and information to prosecutors in Hood's court case.

Goodwin often relied on her claims of friends in high places to reassure Omega investors that everything was going to be fine. Her descriptions of these lofty figures were generally even more vague that than her warnings and reassurance about Hood's trial, saying that her "main sources include very important people whose responsibilities require their presence in the most secret and most important activities of this country and all the major countries in the world."[10] Their relationship went beyond simply leaking information to a useful outlet. Goodwin claimed that she had "personal relationships" with these "key people" and that those relationships explained why they chose Goodwin "to be the spokesperson to the [Omega] lenders."[11] In 2001, Goodwin began to shift toward what was, at best, a reinterpretation of Harvey Barnard's NESARA law and at worst a complete misrepresentation of his work.

On the front page of her NESARA.us website Goodwin provided a summary of NESARA's provisions for the people of the United States:

> NESARA initiates PEACE IMMEDIATELY and
>
> 1. Restores Constitutional Law in America as of NESARA's public announcement.
> 2. Removes U.S. administration officials and all members of the U.S. Congress from their positions due to their continuous unconstitutional actions. Bush, Cheney, Cabinet members, and all members of Congress are immediately removed from office by NESARA's public announcement; specific law enforcement personnel shall physically remove Bush government officials from their offices. These removals allow a fresh start at the national level. Using the Constitutional Line of Succession, NESARA installs Constitutionally acceptable NESARA President and Vice President Designates until new federal elections can take place within six months after NESARA's announcement.
> 3. Because NESARA abolishes unconstitutional states of emergency, NESARA's public announcement declares "peace." U.S. military in Iraq and Afghanistan are immediately recalled to the USA.
> 4. As partial remedy for 90 years of government and banking fraud, NESARA requires zeroing out of credit card balances and bank debt relief be given to Americans.
> 5. Initiates the U.S. Treasury Bank System with new U.S. Treasury currency backed by gold. The Federal Reserve is abolished; Federal Reserve facilities and most personnel are absorbed into the U.S. Treasury Bank System.

6. Abolishes Income Taxes in U.S. and creates a national sales tax on new, non-essential items as revenue for government. Essential items such as food and medicine, and used items, are exempt from the sales tax.

While these claims moved far beyond what Harvey Barnard intended with his original NESARA plan, they were in line with his essential focus, which was primarily economic. The end of the Iraq and Afghanistan conflicts were an addition that, of course, addressed events occurring after Barnard created his original plan. Shaini Goodwin continued to broadcast to her Omega contacts, using the benefits of NESARA as a means to fulfill the promise of the Omega scam. Because this iteration of NESARA was significantly different from its original conception, Goodwin had to construct a new creation story or origin myth for the law.

The connection between NESARA and the Omega investment scam rested on Omega's position as one of many "prosperity programs" that promised great wealth to those unfortunate enough to become involved with them. Goodwin explained to her newsletter readers that the benefits from NESARA actually predated the law itself being passed. "Some of the prosperity programs," she explained, "are almost 20 years old and have been kept from being paid out that long by the dark agenda." The "dark agenda" was Goodwin's short-hand nickname for those who strove to prevent the implementation of NESARA and the delivery of NESARA benefits to Americans. Since the early 1990s, both presidents Bush as well as President Bill Clinton had done the bidding of the Dark Agenda overlords. Goodwin then went into the history of these prosperity programs.

She explained that the entire process had begun in 1993, when "the U.S. Supreme Court issued rulings in the Farm Claims lawsuits found that the Federal Reserve banking system and the U.S. government had colluded and committed FRAUD on the people. The U.S. Supreme Court also VALIDATED the Farm Claims evidence that the IRS is illegal." The "farm claims" Goodwin mentioned were a reference to an earlier financial swindle. In the early 1990s, a Fort Collins, Colorado, organization called We The People promoted a scheme to farmers whose property was in danger of foreclosure. Spearheaded by Roy Schwasinger, the organization used many of the same dubious legal techniques as the sovereign citizen movement promoted, including filing fraudulent liens and "common law jury" indictments. *Associated Press* writer Bob Kerr profiled the organization in 1993, and his reporting was picked up across the United States by several newspapers. Kerr summarized the basics of the program:

For $300, evicted landowners are invited to join his campaign against the nation's system of land financing, hoping to share in a court victory and get their land back. Schwasinger's weapon against foreclosure is the court system, where he has challenged bank foreclosures and filed liens against federal judges, attorneys and participants in foreclosures. Legal actions based on Schwasinger's bizarre advice have appeared in several state and federal courts in Texas, New Mexico, Iowa, Colorado, Oklahoma and Minnesota.

In the opening of his story, Kerr highlighted the desperately optimistic tone of Schwasinger's target audience, writing that they "embrace[d] Roy Schwasinger's message with the hope usually reserved for the hereafter."[12] Schwasinger's claims were solidly within the realm of the financial theories underlying many conspiratorial financial narratives, such as the illegality of the American monetary system and the notion that the United States had gone "bankrupt" when it went off the gold standard in the 1930s. Schwasinger also made some rather more outlandish claims, telling audiences that in addition to being a magazine salesman and meat packing plant worker, that he was also involved "in secret operations," that he possessed "a transducer linking him by satellite to Congress," that he had, "been empowered with 'the right to kill,'" and that "the Navy secretly executed 170 judges and lawyers" in February 1993.[13] These claims—particularly about righteous military personnel executing presumably corrupt judges and lawyers—were in line with Goodwin's portrayal of "White Knights" fighting for NESARA against the Dark Agenda. A similar thread would also emerge in both UFO Disclosure and QAnon narratives decades later (see Chapters 3 and 4). This narrative strand also anticipated a more general assumption that there were "good guys" in the government who were secretly on the side of those conspiracy theorists who knew the truth and were actively working to eliminate negative elements within the government, thereby helping to bring about whatever political, financial, or cultural triumph the theorist desires.

Schwasinger's influence within the right-wing patriot community was extensive. One example of this influence is that he shared his teachings of filing fraudulent liens and other legal paperwork with the Montana Freemen militia group and was one of the sources of their broader antigovernment ideology.[14] Schwasinger's influence would come to an end in the mid–90s, however, after a Texas court convicted him of filing fraudulent liens against public officials. In 1995, eleven people associated with We The People, including Roy Schwasinger, were convicted of theft and securities fraud in Colorado, having fraudulently "collected more than $2 million from duped investors nationwide," in the words of prosecutors.[15] Schwasinger's Colorado sentence would not begin until he had served his prison term in Texas. Schwasinger died in 2009, but he and his "farm claims" became tied in with NESARA years before that.

The story Goodwin told—that the Supreme Court had, in 1993, ruled against the government and declared the IRS illegal—is untrue, but emblematic of what we see in conspiracy theories. Such stories are built up from commentators pulling one or two sentences (or even phrases) out of context from various court rulings and other sources. These out-of-context citations have been freely blended with outright fabrications and flights of fancy, such as this non-existent Supreme Court ruling, to craft evidence (or pseudo-evidence) that supports their narrative. For Goodwin, the supposed Supreme Court ruling was evidence that there was an impetus within the federal government for change. Goodwin explained, "In 1993 the U.S. Supreme Court ruled that a VAST REFORMATION of the federal government and banking system was necessary including abolishing the IRS as well as a return to Constitutional Law."[16]

A new villain appeared at this point. President Bill Clinton "fought the U.S. Supreme Court's rulings in World Court and tried to have the U.S. Supreme Court overturned by the World Court." This is not, of course, anything that happened or—constitutionally—could happen. Goodwin, however, reported that the World Court upheld the U.S. Supreme Court's decisions and appointed a group of officials to enforce the ruling. These were the "White Knights"—central characters in Goodwin's ongoing narrative. Throughout the mid to late 1990s, the White Knights negotiated these reforms with the federal government. However, bankers and other members of what Goodwin called "the dark agenda" resisted real change. In March 2000, the White Knights "managed to get the NESARA law secretly passed." Why was this momentous event not part of the Congressional Record?

> ALL White Knights, Congressional, banking and government officials, World Court Judges, U.N. officials and others OFFICIALLY involved in our prosperity programs funding and NESARA are under a STRICT GAG ORDER by the U.S. Supreme Court and also a GAG ORDER by the World Court which PROHIBITS them from "publicly" admitting NESARA is real until AFTER the formal public NESARA Announcement.[17]

Throughout 2001, as Clyde Hood's trial wound through the court system, Goodwin began to increasingly rely on NESARA as the replacement master-narrative for Omega followers. A significant turning point for Goodwin and her NESARA claims came on September 11, 2001. Within hours of the terrorist attacks on New York City and Washington, D.C., Goodwin sent this message to her followers:

"The three targets today were ALL connected to NESARA and the banking changes. I just learned that at 9:00 a.m. in New York this morning, there was an IMPORTANT banking activity set to be activated in the IMF international banking computer center in the World Trade Center!" she wrote. "This was obviously WHY the World Trade Center was attacked TODAY at just before and after 9:00 a.m.! ... The orders for these plane attacks came from U.S. citizens who are trying to stop our deliveries/funding and NESARA."[18]

Over the next several months, Goodwin linked George W. Bush and his administration to the attacks, making her NESARA/9-11 theory one of the first fully formed "9-11 Truth" conspiracy narratives. As her claims spread across the Internet, NESARA pioneer Harvey Barnard denounced her claims as fabrications and a misuse of his original idea. Goodwin, in turn, labeled Barnard part of the "Dark Agenda" working to keep NESARA from being implemented. Further, she renamed the law from the National Economic Stabilization and Recovery Act to the National Economic *Security* and *Reform* Act—making it her own creation, distinct from Barnard's, but keeping the well-known and recognizable NESARA acronym.[19]

Thus NESARA, in Goodwin's presentation, had a history (and a future) that was entirely independent of Harvey Barnard. This history imbued NESARA with a veneer of legitimacy: Goodwin used the trappings of the American legislative and judicial systems and crafted a tale that sounded as though it *could* be true. For an audience that was looking for some kind of hope for their Omega investment returns or new followers who were predisposed to conspiratorial thinking, Goodwin's sequence of events sounded plausible enough, if one didn't do much digging. And even if one did, the fig-leaf of "gag orders" on the subject explained any gaps in the official record.

However, as is often the case with conspiratorial re-writings of history, the NESARA narrative continued to undergo additions and revisions over time. In 2002, as discussed above, Goodwin explained that the World Court upheld the Supreme Court's decisions and appointed the White Knights. Within a few years, the official "History" page on Goodwin's NESARA.us website had been home to a number of slightly different versions of the story. On December 9, 2003, on the page "History behind the National Economic Security And Reformation Act (NESARA)," Goodwin explained that after the Supreme Court found in favor of the Farmers Union, a committee consisting of five USSC Justices (whom Goodwin did not name) was assigned to plan the implementation of the massive changes necessary to reform the American financial system. In order to do this, they sought assistance from "experts in economics, monetary systems, banking, Constitutional government and

2. NESARA—Knights, Agendas and Greed   43

law, and many other related areas" and "built coalitions of support and assistance with thousands of people worldwide." These people who were assisting the justices in implementing these changes were known as the White Knights.[20]

Goodwin explained that this term "is borrowed from The Wall Street Journal and the world of big business hostile takeovers when a vulnerable company is 'rescued from a hostile takeover by a White Knight' corporation or wealthy person." The White Knights—and, as we'll see, the makeup of this group shifts from time to time—were a significant part of the NESARA story. The impact of these financial changes was so significant that nothing could be revealed until the work was done, and the time was right. The Court sought to enforce this secrecy with fairly draconian measures. Goodwin explained, "At every step of the process, anyone directly involved was required to sign an agreement to keep the U.S. Supreme Court's process of negotiating and implementing the required reformations 'secret,' or face charges of Treason, that are punishable by death." This was a remarkably broad group, with the Supreme Court Justices of the implementation committee working to negotiate "accords" with representatives of the Federal Reserve, the International Monetary Fund, and the World Bank as well as the financial officials of numerous other nations. So, what happened? According to Goodwin, "the process of using Accords to implement the reformations was not successful" and, as a result, the Supreme Court "authorized" the passage of NESARA as legislation.[21]

The remainder of the history—with NESARA secretly being passed on March 9, 2000, and everyone involved being subject to a gag order—is essentially the same as she outlined in 2002, with the added revelation that in June 2000, some of the White Knights (specifically "U.S. naval intelligence contacts") released news of NESARA to selected individuals to help spread support for the law. Goodwin does not reveal whether or not these White Knights were convicted of treason and executed for violating the gag order, but it seemed unlikely. Why did people need to be informed? Because ordinary citizens (like those reading the website) can help urge the authorities to formally announce NESARA by sending a postcard to the Supreme Court asking them to do so. It was important, Goodwin explained, to use a postcard rather than a letter because "a 'postcard' bypasses anthrax checking and is delivered more quickly than letters." Goodwin gave a summary of the benefits of NESARA, and then presented "proof" of the law's existence by claiming that "many bank presidents and senior stockbrokers have privately confirmed to close personal friends that they have been briefed about the U.S. Treasury Bank System."[22] Readers would have to take her word for it.

One of the most significant differences between this version and the history Goodwin proclaimed to her followers in 2002 is that there was no mention of the opposition from the Clinton administration with the subsequent intervention of the World Court forcing the implementation of these reforms. In this version, the Supreme Court tried to get it done, could not (Goodwin did not explain why), and delegated the responsibility to the legislative branch. The history underwent another revision in 2005. In this iteration, the Farmers Claims Supreme Court cases had a U.S. Army General as a co-plaintiff. Further, "certain US Generals and Admirals were supportive of" the plaintiffs' arguments about the fraudulent nature of the American financial system. Goodwin also went into more detail on the substance of the Farmers Claim cases. These details and case citations were connected to Roy Schwasinger's scams discussed earlier, with basic facts being misstated and misrepresented.

Goodwin explained that during the 1980s, "some of the farmers investigated why there were so many bank foreclosures on their farms." These farmers—through the claims of people like Roy Schwasinger—came to believe that the foreclosures were illegal and filed lawsuits to overturn the foreclosures and gain restitution. Goodwin cited the case *Baskerville and Foster v. Credit Bank of Wichita, Federal Land Bank, and First Interstate Bank of Fort Collins* as being pursued "through the Federal District Court in Denver and other locations" and ultimately heard by the Supreme Court. The court, of course, issued its favorable ruling in "early 1993."[23] This, of course, was the impetus for the actions that would culminate in the secret passage of NESARA. The problem with this is that it was simply not true. *Baskerville and Foster v. Credit Bank of Wichita, Federal Land Bank, and First Interstate Bank of Fort Collins* was a real court case, but it was ultimately decided by the Tenth Circuit Court of Appeals in June 1994. In the words of Judge John W. Lungstrum, the plaintiffs had "sued several banks, law firms, judges, and individuals, after their farms and personal property were seized to satisfy certain loans." The case was dismissed and, in appealing the case, the plaintiffs "submitted a rambling and almost unreadable brief which raises no issues." The lower court's dismissal of the case was upheld.[24] The fact that it was decided in 1994 made it difficult for the Supreme Court to consider it in 1993, of course, but it did not get taken up by the high court at any time.

Goodwin had provided a defense against anyone who might have done their research and found that her story did not add up. Her assertion that these court cases and the subsequent negotiations, the passage of NESARA, and other official acts were done in secret provided an effective conversation-stopper for anyone who inquired about the documentation of these decisions. The threat of death looming for anyone who discussed the case provided additional "proof" that one would never find mentions of NESARA or the successful Farmer Claim cases in the official records. The mid–2005 iteration of NESARA history also provided additional background information that tied this narrative more tightly to some strands of sovereign citizen thought. Goodwin stated, for example, that "FDR took the US out of Constitutional Law when he declared a national banking emergency and amended the Trading with the Enemy Act in March 1933" and explained further that the 16th Amendment had never been "properly ratified," thus the Supreme Court Justices "had no choice" but to abolish income taxes.

Goodwin's addition to the NESARA story of those "certain US Generals and Admirals" who supported the cases served a vital role in the narrative. She explained that "the presence of the Generals and Admirals is why the majority of the judges felt they had to rule properly and in favor of the farmers." On the surface, this sounds like an outrageous instance of the military exerting dangerous and undue pressure on the judiciary. In Goodwin's world, however, this was part of a process that attempted to make the entire NESARA scenario more detailed and sensible. While the previous iteration of the NESARA history detailed the process of the Court attempting to forge agreements that would initiate the NESARA reforms, but being unable to do so, the 2005 version takes a more derogatory stance, claiming that "the Court made half-hearted efforts to implement the reformations." In response to this failure, "the powerful US military Generals and Admirals" along with "constitutional law experts" wrote the NESARA law and submitted it to Congress in 1999. Its eventual secret passage in 2000 was the result of soldiers from Delta Force and Navy SEALs basically forcing the minimum required number of legislators to vote for the bill. While there is no discussion of it here, other NESARA sources indicate that the same military officials forced President Bill Clinton to sign NESARA into law.[25] The QAnon narrative that arose in 2017 would also cast the American military in a supporting role as savior of the republic.

Here, as in previous versions, the "History of NESARA" presented a summary of NESARA benefits. Then, instead of explaining who has already received confirmation of NESARA as in previous versions, Goodwin revealed that "[t]he NESARA law required that a minimum of one time each year, there must be an effort made to announce NESARA." This "requirement," like many other aspects of Goodwin's NESARA narrative, carried a veneer of plausibility. Through it, she gave the impression that an announcement *must* be forthcoming and at the same time left herself an out: the only requirement was for an "effort" to announce, not an announcement itself. While the White Knights may have been making efforts to reveal the truth of NESARA, others fought to keep this information in the dark. The same Supreme Court given control of "the committee in charge of NESARA's announcement" had been using "their overall authority to secretly sabotage" that announcement. Goodwin claimed that, because of the "gag order" in place, there were few sources of information available for supporters "to learn exactly what has happened to stop NESARA from being announced." This established her as a vital conduit of information and reinforced a sense that her followers depended on her (and her alone) for the truth about their future financial prosperity. While she was a rare and valuable source of information, she did not work entirely alone. By "investigating details with hundreds of people," Goodwin reassured her followers that she knew what needed to be done to ensure that the NESARA announcement happened. The 2005 "History" concluded with the assertion that the United States was facing an unprecedented financial crisis and only by enacting NESARA could Americans "follow the lead of our Founding Fathers and restore America."[26]

This 2005 recounting of NESARA's history would remain unchanged through the closure of the *NESARA.us* site in 2010. Goodwin's revisions between 2003 and 2005 served the broad purposes of giving supporters (and would-be supporters) the story of NESARA's background while also persuading them of reality of the law's existence. The differences between the 2003 and 2005 histories illustrated a shift toward providing more specific details about the origins and passage of NESARA. This specificity, however, was illusory. Goodwin's clever use of the "gag order" narrative meant that any specific details were impossible to verify or corroborate. Moreover, the "gag order" was a signifier that the conspiracy to hide the truth of NESARA from the people of the United States was so wide-reaching that an independent search for truth was likely to lead nowhere. The only choice was to rely on the assurances of those, like Shaini Goodwin, who had connections that normal Americans did not. Goodwin enlarged the 2005 history to include a team of White Knight military officials, special forces troops forcing the passage of the law, and more details on the continuing conspiracy to prevent the implementation of NESARA. These details—viewed objectively—did not do any more to verify Goodwin's claims than the earlier versions of the history but reinforced Goodwin's position as the dispenser of secret truths.

While the NESARA.us website served as a portal for the new and curious, "Dove of Oneness" conducted the bulk of communication with her followers through an email distribution list that ran from early 2002 through 2010, when Goodwin died. It is through these messages that we see how Shaini Goodwin's narrative blurred the boundaries between the fundamentally political and economic nature of NESARA and the world of the occult and New Age thought. The figure of "St. Germain" is what connected those two realms. In her messages to followers, Goodwin differentiated between information she received from supposed terrestrial sources and information she relayed on behalf of St. Germain.

St. Germain and NESARA

"St. Germain" was one of the foundational characters in New Age and spiritualist thought. The Comte de St. Germain was born was born either in the early 1690s or 1712 and died in 1784. He was a documented historical figure who meandered through the upper classes at the dawn of Europe's modern age and appears in several contemporary accounts. One of the most vivid accounts of St. Germain was in *The Memoirs of Jacques Casanova de Seingalt*.

> This extraordinary man, intended by nature to be the king of impostors and quacks, would say in an easy, assured manner that he was three hundred years old, that he knew the secret of the Universal Medicine, that he possessed a mastery over nature, that he could melt diamonds, professing himself capable of forming, out of ten or twelve small diamonds, one large one of the finest water without any loss of weight. All this, he said, was a mere trifle to him. Notwithstanding his boastings, his bare-faced lies, and his manifold eccentricities, I cannot say I thought him offensive. In spite of my knowledge of what he was and in spite of my own feelings, I thought him an astonishing man as he was always astonishing me.[27]

Several aspects of Casanova's colorful description of St. Germain—particularly his claims of extreme old age, or even agelessness—were taken at face value by those involved in various spiritual traditions under the broad umbrella of Theosophy. St. Germain was most identified with the I AM Activity, which was established by Guy Ballard and Edna Ballard in the 1930s.

In 1929, mining engineer Guy Ballard was hiking on Mount Shasta in California. Already at that time, Mount Shasta had connections to occult beliefs. Down to the present day, some adherents claim it is everything from the home of lost Atlanteans to a base for UFOs (both from outer space and the inner Earth). As Ballard drank from a stream, a man appeared and offered him "a vivifying white liquid that the stranger identified as 'omnipotent life.'"[28] This was Count St. Germain—who Ballard would identify as one of the "Ascended Masters" who "has generated enough Love and Power within Himself to snap the chains of all human limitation." For millennia, the Ascended Masters have worked through various humans to prepare the great mass of humanity for an age of enlightenment and translation to a higher plane of existence.[29] Germain explained that he was in the process of "initiating the seventh golden age" on Earth and had spent six hundred years traveling through Europe to find the right person through whom he could release the necessary information. No one in Europe was suitable, so St. Germain expanded his search to the United States. Ballard claimed that St. Germain appointed him, his wife, and their son Donald as "the only accredited messengers of the Ascended Masters." Ballard, writing as Godfré Ray King, published a two-volume account of his meeting with St. Germain in 1934 and established the St. Germain Foundation and St. Germain Press to spread the word about the work of the ageless count and his fellow Ascended Masters.[30]

Goodwin rarely, if ever, provided her followers with any sources for material she "hear[d]." When she did cite a basis for her claims it was usually in the form of messages either received from St. Germain or about things St. Germain might be doing. Channeled information from Ascended Masters or, as seen in Chapter 3, extraterrestrial beings has a dubious benefit. As with any supernatural or divine revelation, its followers must take such information on faith. It existed in a different category than Goodwin's more prosaic claims about Supreme Court decisions, gag orders, and cabals of White Knight military officers. Goodwin had a lengthy history of involvement in New Age and occult organizations, such as the Ramtha School of Enlightenment[31] and was adept at weaving together diverse spiritual, political, and economic strands. Goodwin's NESARA narrative and the multi-faceted way she constructed and presented it appealed to a wide audience. Goodwin presented information as being from St. Germain in her "Dove Update" email newsletters as far back as 2002. Often, she indicated when St. Germain was sharing a message in the subject line of the emails with the preface "The Dove Speaks for St. Germain" followed by a specific topic. In the April 27, 2002, edition, Goodwin revealed:

> Saint Germain has been working for hundreds of years to get Americans to the point that we can carry out our TRUE missions on Earth. If necessary, Saint Germain will get NESARA announced THROUGH EXTRAORDINARY MEANS, because NESARA is the ONLY vehicle for giving Americans the LIBERTY and EMPOWERMENT we NEED to do our true missions of improving and assisting the world.[32]

The "Dove Speaks for St. Germain" emails were particularly heavy during April 2002 and in an email newsletter sent to followers on

2. NESARA—Knights, Agendas and Greed   49

April 28, Goodwin provided authorization for her habit of speaking on behalf of St. Germain:

> I, Saint Germain, Ascended Master and Chief Representative of the High Council of the Great Light Brotherhood of Earth's Ascended Masters, hereby RELEASE ALL Earth Humans and Members of the Extraterrestrial Forces from their vows of secrecy and silence regarding interactions and communications with the Ascended Masters who are involved with Earth. I, Saint Germain, encourage all of you to SPEAK FREELY regarding the Ascended Masters overseeing the Divine Plan activities on Earth. So say I, Saint Germain, Ascended Master and Chief Representative of the High Council of the Great Light Brotherhood of Earth's Ascended Masters, through My Chosen Messenger, Dove of Oneness.[33]

From this point, Goodwin scaled back on explicitly signposting certain pronouncements as being from St. Germain. The "authorization" Goodwin proclaimed on behalf of St. Germain had the effect of granting all her missives a sheen of otherworldly prestige. This extended to others who spoke on behalf of various Ascended Masters as well. Also of note in this April 28 message was the news that St. Germain extended this clearance to share communications with the Ascended Masters not only to humans but to "Members of the Extraterrestrial Forces" as well. There was significant overlap between the world of Ascended Masters and that of spiritualist-oriented extraterrestrial contact narratives, with some figures pulling double duty as both spiritual teachers and alien benefactors.

As Goodwin and others developed the role of St. Germain in the NESARA narrative, he became a figure whose primary purpose throughout his supernaturally long life had been to enact NESARA. Goodwin's presentation of St. Germain was slightly at odds with the stated intentions of St. Germain as expressed through the teachings of Guy Ballard and the I AM Activity. She used Ballard's writings, however, as evidence of NESARA's truth. One example was this passage from the Godfré Ray King book, *Unveiled Mysteries*, which Ballard published in 1939. The bracketed additions and capitalizations are Goodwin's:

> Many changes were shown to take place in the next seventy years [1930s–2002]. These affected Europe, Asia, India, North and South America, and revealed to us, that regardless of all appearances at the present time, the SINISTER FORCE attempting to create chaos and destruction throughout the world, WILL BE COMPLETELY DESTROYED.

Obviously, dating from the 1930s, this prophecy did not specifically refer to NESARA but the general thrust of a defeat of the sinister force equated to the fall of the "Dark Agenda" that worked to prevent the NESARA announcement. The selection continued:

When that is accomplished the mass of humanity will turn to the "Great God Presence" within each heart and also governing the Universe. "Peace shall reign on earth—and man send out good will to man." This revelation was stupendous. The closing scenes followed next and these concerned principally the United States in the next century. [2000+] The progress and advancement she will make is almost unbelievable.

This sounded enough like what NESARA promised without sharing any actual, specific connections. More specific to the political aspects of NESARA was this message from St. Germain in Ballard's *I AM Discourses* that Goodwin included in the same newsletter.

See that all authority is in the hands of Thy trained and trusted Messengers; that they may govern fully all governmental offices in America, and be ever divinely sustained; that America be healed, blessed, and forever prosper; that all sinister influence be consumed and forever repelled from within the borders of America.[34]

Like the excerpt from *Unveiled Mysteries*, this prediction of St. Germain did not specifically connect to NESARA. The themes of evil forces being defeated and new, righteous government taking control were, however, compatible.

The email newsletters and alerts that Dove of Oneness regularly distributed to her followers tended to follow a fairly set pattern or cycle. First came confident predictions of NESARA's imminent announcement and enactment, often with clearly specified timelines. When those timelines were not met, Shaini Goodwin explained what had happened. Goodwin often positioned herself as the key figure pushing for NESARA when even the "White Knights" were not doing their duty to proclaim NESARA to the masses. The email newsletters Goodwin published in April of 2002 illustrated the cycle that repeated itself multiple times over the years.

In her April 2, 2002, newsletter ("NESARA Before Mid-April; Debt Forgiveness; Keep $ Onshore"), Goodwin claimed she was told "the NESARA announcement is the trigger for the banks to begin processing the official bank debt forgiveness required by NESARA." Here, she emphasized the immediate, individual, personal financial benefits of NESARA rather than the broad structural changes to the American economy. While, in terms of the NESARA mythology, it may seem elementary to discuss the need for the NESARA announcement for benefits to occur, Goodwin was cognizant of the fact that any given newsletter might be someone's introduction to NESARA. Thus, there was often a great deal of repetition of basic NESARA points to bring new followers up to speed. In this April 2 missive, Goodwin expanded a bit on the process by which Americans' credit card debt will disappear and explained that once the government announced NESARA, "the banks are required to run computer programs to ZERO OUT the credit card balances of everyone in the U.S." She discussed neither the source of the "computer programs" nor the means by which banks who lent the money would be made whole (if, indeed, they would be). Lest anyone fear that they might miss the NESARA announcement, Dove of Oneness explained the announcement process:

> I understand that the media will get very extensive press kits giving them the full text of the TRUE NESARA law and also a great deal of background information from which they can fill in the thousands of details.... For once, TRUTH will be given by our federal government.

In response to follower questions, in this email Goodwin also advised those awaiting their NESARA riches not to establish offshore bank accounts for their incoming wealth:

> Based on all my research, I advise that we keep MOST of our prosperity funds in the Treasury Banks of the country in which we receive our funding. Our funds are huge GIFTS made possible by monetary and financial geniuses and visionaries who are FAR WISER than any of us about the BIG PICTURE ... this is to KEEP the WORLD economy in BALANCE and STABILITY.[35]

In her April 4 newsletter ("Current Activities Bringing NESARA"), Goodwin reported that NESARA would be announced that evening, if "all the required processes were completed properly prior to today." This was a common caveat Goodwin provided to allow an out when NESARA failed to materialize. The references to "required processes" were vague but certainly sounded sensible given the complexities of overhauling the entire financial system. Goodwin went over the announcement process once again, revealing that there may be a brief announcement by "our Great Lady of White Knight World Court Justice"—a figure who often appears as a representative of the White Knights—explained that "a U.S. Supreme Court ruling requires that banking and government changes take place immediately." Then, "the full announcement and full details" would emerge the next day.[36] By this point, on April 4, 2002, Goodwin had shifted from a "mid–April" date for the NESARA announcement to April 4, but only if those mysterious "required processes" had been completed. The April 5 newsletter ("America is Way Shower, Heralding Golden Age") saw the Dove of Oneness explain that NESARA was imminent; there were just a few more details that the White Hats needed to arrange:

> I'm told that the funding process is being done in such a way that all the prerequisites for NESARA are being DONE DONE DONE and VERY SOON.

This includes completing specific activities which are irrefutable proof and CAUSE the U.S. Treasury Bank system to BE 100% LEGALLY EXISTING at the completion of these activities. Therefore, after these specific activities are completed, most of the banks will be legally required to open up as U.S. Treasury Banks the next time they open. This means that once the target objectives are attained, we must have NESARA announced regardless.

Victory was, as always, just around the corner. Here, the delay was the result of more vague "specific activities" (which may have been related to the "required processes" she mentioned the night before). The wheels were still in motion. To provide reassurance to her followers, Goodwin also relayed the following information about how deeply support for NESARA ran within the military:

> I asked the Forces' Intelligence Agents today about the percentage of our U.S. Military who ARE White Knights. TODAY, I'm told that 92% of the U.S. Military CONSIDER themselves to be WHITE KNIGHTS! NINETY-TWO percent! This means that the vast majority of our U.S. Military are STANDING TALL for NESARA and PEACE because NESARA brings PEACE to our country and the world. This means that 92% our U.S. Military men and women have realized there is ONLY ONE CHOICE and that is to get NESARA announced and bring these wonderful improvements to our country and people! These people have decided, just like you and I, that we MUST have NESARA.[37]

As in Goodwin's summary of NESARA's history, the American military played an important role in support for and implementation of NESARA. The Farm Claim negotiations were dead in the water before the high-level generals and admirals got involved. NESARA would never have been passed or signed if special forces troops had not asserted themselves. With this, Goodwin brought the rank and file of the nation's military—not just a cadre of flag officers—into the NESARA fold. Doing so created two impressions. First, it led readers to believe that the nearly the entire might of the military would be brought to bear in initiating the NESARA reforms. Second, Goodwin's "92%" claim reinforced the idea that the NESARA reforms are a broadly democratic, popular initiative.

In the April 6, 2002, email ("NESARA on Target BEFORE Mid-April"), Dove of Oneness fell back on a more general timeline, but still asserted that "certain groups of the White Knights and Forces are very busy participating in key activities that lead to NESARA's announcement SOON." She concluded the email newsletter with this instruction to her readers as an example of the increasingly spiritual dimensions that NESARA would take on as the years progressed:

> Let's continue our prayers, meditations, and energy work focuses daily at 4 p.m. in our time zone. We can help by calling upon the Divine Assistance

of Heaven to STRENGTHEN AND PROTECT all our White Knights as they carry forth the activities of improving governments and banking systems around the world and bringing liberty and prosperity options for all. We can also call forth WORLD PEACE for truly our support of World Peace will assist us and the White Knights in bringing NESARA and the wonderful uplifting changes worldwide into all our lives. NESARA Now! Prosperity Now![38]

This call for prayer prefigured a recurring theme in Goodwin's appeals to her readers and followers—that they could, in some way and to some degree, bring about NESARA's announcement through their prayers, intentions, or some other force of will. Of particular interest was the assertion that calling forth "world peace" would "assist" in bringing about NESARA, since Goodwin had usually argued that NESARA would, through its implementation, bring about that peace. This placed the onus for action on the NESARA believers, not just on the White Knights. Goodwin played her part by urging everyone to implement NESARA—both the believers who read her newsletter and the White Knights themselves. By establishing for herself the role of St. Germain's spokesperson, Goodwin placed herself above both run-of-the-mill NESARA followers and the governmental and military officials who supported NESARA implementation.

Dove of Oneness reinforced this responsibility shift from the White Knights to the NESARA supporters themselves, with a new addition to the NESARA mythos in her April 23, 2002, newsletter:

> I'm told there is a provision in the secretly-passed [sic] NESARA LAW which enables WE The People to ANNOUNCE NESARA and REQUIRE NESARA's implementation if, two years after the passage of NESARA in March 2000, the NESARA law is still unannounced. This provision is a SAFEGUARD in case the "authorities" are unable to get NESARA announced.

A skeptical reader might have asked any number of questions about this. Who "told" her? Since the requisite two years had been up for a month, why was she not informed earlier? Later in this newsletter, she attempted to forestall these questions by placing some additional restrictions or requirements on an announcement of NESARA by the people:

> In addition, I'm told that IF the White Knights NESARA Team fail to get NESARA announced and it becomes NECESSARY for WE The People to get NESARA announced, some of the White Knights will be RELEASED from their "gag order" restrictions by the MOST HIGH AUTHORITY so that they can help get NESARA announced by We The People.

So, while the March 2002 deadline had passed that would allow the people to announce NESARA, Goodwin explained that the White

Knights had to complete (and fail at) their current effort before this could happen. While explaining this bad news, she sweetened it by hinting that the "gag order" might be relaxed. Throughout this newsletter Goodwin issued a barrage of bad news, such as the continued delays and potential failure of the White Knights' efforts blended with good news. The biggest piece of good news—like the instant debt relief discussed in the April 2 newsletter—appealed directly to readers' greed and desperation:

> In addition, last night and today I have learned that the HIGHEST AUTHORITY over the first 31 prosperity programs is ABSOLUTELY DETERMINED that we receive our prosperity deliveries for these first 31 programs, including the big program, by April 30, 2002. This HIGHEST AUTHORITY will also make certain that we have access to the full amounts of our funding as set forth in the funding schedules, including for us in the big program to have a VERY LARGE amount of PROGRAM funds which we may use as we wish. Our PROGRAM funds are IN ADDITION to the GIVE-AWAY funds.[39]

Since, by the 23rd of the month, Goodwin's mid–April prediction for the NESARA announcement had passed, she again leavened the disappointing news that the White Knights had not yet secured victory with another date-sensitive prediction. The "Prosperity Programs," to which Goodwin referred in her message, concerned not only to the Omega Trust program with which she was personally affiliated, but also other financial scams of a similar nature. The NESARA narrative provided a hook to keep those who had been victimized by such frauds emotionally and—through donations to Shaini Goodwin—financially connected to these systems. Over time, the mythology of these prosperity programs integrated the Count Saint Germain narrative as well and drew an array of financial scams into the realm of spiritualism and conspiracy.

In August 2002, Goodwin provided an updated summary of the "prosperity programs" that she often mentioned in her email updates. These prosperity programs made appearances in her announcements as a prompt or incentive to encourage people to keep the NESARA faith. Discussion of the prosperity programs also served the purpose of providing continued hope to those who had taken part in financial "investment" schemes. Goodwin related that in late 1999 she "began tracking the progress of certain prosperity programs." She discovered that "there were more than 50 prosperity programs, some of them over 15 years old, which were supposed to be funding to program members at about the same time as the big prOgram I was tracking." The capital "O" used in "prOgram" was a reference to the Omega Trust scheme. These trusts

2. NESARA—Knights, Agendas and Greed

were set up by "certain Wealthy Visionaries" as a means of developing sufficient funding to "make crucial world improvements." Who were these visionaries?

> I learned that a number of these Wealthy Visionaries came from some of the most powerful families of the world, such as the top thirteen banking families who controlled the major banking systems of the world. I learned that these Wealthy Visionaries from the powerful families disagreed with their families' future plans to obtain increased control of the world's resources and people. The Wealthy Visionaries could see their families' plans would result in disastrous consequences for the world and the world's people.

The Wealthy Visionaries were, in a sense, another category of White Knights. People from within corrupt systems that saw the error of their (or their organizations') ways and were trying to make a positive change in the world. The Wealthy Visionaries worked with the International Monetary Fund to manage the seed money they had put up to begin the prosperity programs. There were, of course, "dark agenda" forces that sought to prevent the "prosperity deliveries and funding." Goodwin explained the failure of Omega (or the "big prosperity prOgram") as being the work of the Bush and Rockefeller families. "George W. Bush, Senior [sic] and David Rockefeller" were on the board of trustees and used their position to prevent funds from being paid out. Later, elements of the Central Intelligence Agency (CIA) and financiers (who used "slick banker tricks") joined in fighting the release of money from Omega and other programs.[40]

While the mid–April deadline came and went, and while the White Knights seem to be unable to get the job done, Goodwin urged her followers to take heart in the incoming flood of money as well as the knowledge that they could take control if the White Knights are stymied.

Four days later, on April 27, with NESARA not yet announced, Dove of Oneness rallied the troops with an email titled "NESARA is KEY; Avoid Anti-NESARA Info."[41] Her tone in this email was scolding, as she informed readers that "anyone who fails to understand NESARA's importance, after seeing 9/11 and ensuing activities against our people, is showing extreme ignorance." She implied that by reading her email updates and keeping the NESARA faith, her followers were more fully informed than their peers. She continued this encouragement to stay on board with both NESARA and her email guidance with—once again—an appeal to greed:

> It is NOT NECESSARY for you to be a member of the Dove egroup list in order to receive your BIG FUNDS. However, to one High Authority over the World Trust funds coming to us, IF YOU are someone who has EMAIL on the Internet, being on the Dove egroup list is a GOOD indication you are the

"right person" to receive the BIG funds. However, it is NOT NECESSARY to be on the Dove egroup list to receive your BIG funds.

The "right" people would receive the large financial benefit from NESARA—the right sort of person is the person who is part of Goodwin's email list. But she hedged this by emphasizing that the "BIG FUNDS" were not dependent on being part of the email list. If the influx of personal wealth was the result of being on the Dove of Oneness' email list, it would undermine the narrative that NESARA was legislation that would benefit all Americans. She still placed herself in a key position to mediate the benefits of NESARA, with her followers benefiting the most.

Goodwin continued the email with some excoriation of those involved in various financial programs who continued to doubt her NESARA information or who otherwise denounced NESARA and declared that "speaking out against NESARA is the stupidest thing anyone in the prosperity programs can do." She claimed that she stated nothing but facts about NESARA, and her facts were backed up by "numerous people" in her email group who had done their own research. These people "have proven for themselves that NESARA and the new U.S. Treasury Bank system are real." Her sources included an array of figures as impressive as they were anonymous, such as "bank presidents and many stockbrokers have confirmed this as well as White Knights in the Navy Seals, Delta Force and other key White Knight units in the U.S. Military."

Time, however, was running out for Shaini Goodwin's April 2002 NESARA prediction. On the 29th, she reported that the wheels were (again) in motion for NESARA to be announced, in an email titled "Media Prepares for NESARA Announcement."[42] Goodwin reported that "Saint Germain and key White Knights had a meeting with media executives this morning in New York regarding their cooperation in doing the NESARA Announcement." Of course, the media promised to "cooperate fully in bringing us the NESARA Announcement and very extensive follow-up coverage over the next week or two." The meeting had been made possible by former president Bill Clinton, who "made the initial contacts with the media executives to provide an introduction for Saint Germain." One might assume that if a heavy hitter like St. Germain had contacted major media outlets, that Goodwin's prediction of an April announcement might come to pass. On April 30, however, she reported a snag in an email entitled "About the NESARA Announcement & Deliveries:"[43]

> I'm told the [sic] Ashcroft, Rumsfeld, the FBI Director, CIA Director, and others were demanding "concessions" about WHAT was included in the

2. NESARA—Knights, Agendas and Greed   57

NESARA Announcement. The Bush gang demanded a last minute meeting yesterday evening to put forth their demands to have facts detrimental to them removed from the Announcement. This meeting went until after 11 p.m. EDT last night, I'm told, and therefore caused the NESARA Announcement to be delayed.

I've heard for some time now that the White Knights intend to include information in the NESARA Announcement about the Bush administration's involvement in causing the 9/11 attacks. This was one of the things the Bush gang wanted removed. Furthermore, the Bush gang "threatened" to denounce the new NESARA government unless their demands were met.

This was her out: negotiations broke down at the last minute and the White Knights, apparently, could not move forward with the NESARA announcement. Given, however, the strong support within both the American military and the media for NESARA, it is difficult to determine exactly how the Bush threat to "denounce" the plan would have affected the implementation of NESARA. As with previous disappointments, Goodwin provided some relief with additional promises related to the "prosperity programs":

> I'm also told our remaining mass U.S. prosperity deliveries should be happening quickly. I'm told the "rules" changed when Saint Germain personally took over control of the funding of the World Trust in the last few weeks. Therefore, the deliveries and funding window can be extended if necessary. This means we can still receive our remaining mass deliveries after April 30th and in the NEAR future.

Again, there had been a change. April 30 was no longer feasible, but the change was for a good reason: St. Germain himself was taking control! Thus, what could have been considered bad news was not. Even though the Bush administration blocked NESARA, those who placed their trust in the distribution of funds from the prosperity programs would see relief. Goodwin ended the email—and the month of April—with some advice for those responsible for bringing about NESARA:

> IF I WAS RUNNING THIS OPERATION, I would say to the White Knights:
> 1. CANCEL any more meetings with the dark agenda;
> 2. TELL the Bush gang to pack their bags;
> 3. Do the initial short NESARA Announcement IMMEDIATELY TODAY during regular business hours just as any professional organization does important press releases;
> 4. Set the TIME for the BIG ANNOUNCEMENT for later today and STICK TO YOUR DECISION—JUST DO IT—DO the NESARA Announcement and Implementation Immediately!

I challenge YOU in authority to DO THE ABOVE and DO NESARA's Announcement immediately!

Goodwin's tough talk to the White Knights accentuated the image she built for herself as being at once both intimately connected to the powerful figures behind NESARA and just an ordinary American trying to spread the truth about NESARA to her fellow citizens. She benefited from the status of being a conduit for information from White Knights, St. Germain, and other elite figures but avoided any personal blame for the failure to announce NESARA. At the end of this roller coaster of a month, with its shifting announcement deadlines and tales of prosperity programs coming to fruition, the Dove of Oneness made a show of speaking truth to power, cementing her position as the advocate for all who would benefit from NESARA.

As a coda to April's unmet expectations, Goodwin's May 1 email ("To WKs: END Meetings; DO NESARA NOW!") was even more forceful. In it, she accused the White Knights of causing "the delays in the realities and paradigms shifts embodied in NESARA that are REQUIRED BY the Divine Plan." She warned them that they will be "OVERRIDDEN" within 48 hours "by Divine Right Authority and Power" if they "continue to WASTE TIME and fail to make NESARA's Announcement!"[44] In her June 12 email ("Let's Take ACTION & Get NESARA Announced!"), she softened her criticism of the White Knights and explained that "the dark agenda are able to attack the White Knights and others helping with NESARA in ways that you and I would find totally despicable and unacceptable" and that "the dark agenda has twisted elements of our world to serve them and use as weapons against the White Knights and us."[45] This effectively brought her readers and followers back to the top of the cycle that repeated over and over in the coming years. The cycle began with a declaration that NESARA's announcement was imminent, followed by a reiteration of NESARA's benefits and a discussion of steps being taken to ensure the announcement. When the announcement failed to materialize, there were explanations as to what went wrong, which nearly always blamed the "dark agenda."

Until her 2010 death, Shaini Goodwin was the closest thing available to an authoritative source for the NESARA narrative. Her website and email newsletter list not only provided regular updates on what was happening with the announcement of NESARA but also served as platforms for trumpeting the efforts of NESARA supporters who were doing their part to get the word out. The "Supporters" page on the NESARA. us website[46] proudly displayed pictures of—usually small—groups at demonstrations and marches carrying signs bearing slogans such as "NESARA NOW!" as well as of NESARA supporters handing out flyers about the law in cities across the world.

After 2010, the world of NESARA had no real "center." The foundational narrative developed by Goodwin survived but as new voices emerged, the conversation splintered. In order to discuss NESARA developments after Goodwin's death, I have chosen number of sources which are representative of the NESARA "field." It is thorough, but not exhaustive.[47]

The NESARA Work of David E. Robinson

In the early 2000s, David E. Robinson wrote and distributed the *Maine Republic Email Alert*, which routinely circulated information related to NESARA, currency revaluation, sovereign citizen legal theories, and related topics. In April 2015, David Robinson was convicted in U.S. District Court of "conspiracy to defraud the United States and corruptly endeavoring to impede the lawful administration of the Internal Revenue Code." In the Justice Department press release on the conviction, it was noted that "Robinson claimed to be the 'Interim Attorney General' of the 'Maine Republic Free State' and advocated that people not pay federal and state taxes."[48] In 2011, David E. Robinson self-published *NESARA I: National Economic Security and Reformation Act* and a sequel, *NESARA II*, which had the same subtitle. These books combine transcripts of YouTube videos, with additional uncredited material from NESARA promoters such as Nancy Detweiler and Elizabeth Trutwin. These books drew from a wide variety of sources and provided a useful example of how NESARA, by the start of the 2010s, had begun incorporating a broader array of triumphalist conspiracy strands than ever before. Once again, this was a situation in which someone (in this case, Robinson) compiled numerous texts from a variety of authors and blended it with his own work. Just as, during the 1990s and early 21st century, the burgeoning World Wide Web provided a platform for people to present and discuss conspiracy narratives, the advent of affordable print-on-demand services led to an explosion of independently published print and electronic books. Because of the very low overhead and cost compared to older "vanity publishing" models, there was relatively little effort and expense involved in producing books. This new technology and the commercial models that went along with it, however, made no provision for ensuring the quality or originality of the many, many works produced. David Robinson's NESARA I and NESARA II books illustrated the democratization of conspiracy publishing and, at the same time, demonstrated how the content of conspiratorial works became—in some cases—increasingly diluted and derivative.

Although, as discussed earlier, Robinson cribbed his summary and explanation of NESARA from a number of varied sources around the Internet including, of course, the original work of Shaini Goodwin as well as NESARA advocate Nancy Detweiler's timeline of NESARA events,[49] which he also reprinted in full in a 2012 edition of his newsletter, the *Maine Republic Email Alert*.[50] Using those sources, Robinson compiled an expanded NESARA narrative that provided a coherent history and overview for those unwilling to trawl through dozens of defunct webpages, message board posts, and email newsletters. This examination of the Detweiler/Robinson version of NESARA's history was lengthy but provided valuable insight into the ways in which the NESARA narrative expanded. As the online NESARA community became increasingly splintered after 2010, this expanded history filled in some of the gaps left in Goodwin's history and incorporated details she scattered throughout hundreds of email updates. It also tied the NESARA narrative to an expanded universe of conspiratorial thought.

The first example of this expanded, integrated NESARA universe involved the story of Roy Schwasinger—as discussed earlier in this chapter—which would undergo a number of alterations as it was tied into the broader narrative of NESARA. It began with Roy Schwasinger, Jr., "a retired military general," who inherited land in Colorado from his father. Schwasinger Senior had used a loan from the Federal Land Bank (FLB). After Schwasinger Junior inherited the land, the FLB notified him that they were foreclosing on the property. Schwasinger unsuccessfully attempted to file a class-action suit against the FLB, which was "dismissed for filing incorrectly." This setback launched Schwasinger on an "investigation into the inner workings of the banking system." In Robinson's recounting of this tale, within a few years, in 1982, Schwasinger "was given a contract by the US Senate and alter the Supreme Court, to investigate banking fraud." Do not bother looking for any official documentation of this contract, because—as was common in these cases—Schwasinger was subject to a "strict non-disclosure order." By the late 1980s he had begun teaching what he had learned to various groups including "high-ranking military personnel" who were involved with a class-action lawsuit against the federal government. Here, Robinson provided a citation, "CV920C-1781." This docket number has been floating around right wing patriot movement circles since the mid–1990s and referred to a federal court case in which two families, the Baskervilles and the Fosters, both of Colorado, sued to prevent foreclosure on their land. Despite the case being dismissed, a "press release" began circulating. In this press release two men—Scott Hildebrand and Darrell Sturgess claimed the court had ruled that

2. NESARA—Knights, Agendas and Greed 61

> the entire Farm Credit System, Federal Land Bank, Production Credit Association, Farmers Home Administration, National Banking Associations, the City of Fort Collins, Colorado, and the County of Larimer Colorado are hereby placed into receivership by order of the U.S. District Court of Denver, Colorado. Darrell Sturgess and I, Scott Hildebrand, are activating the National Guard to ensure National Security. These entities are hereby placed on notice that the assets of those placed in receivership are to be turned over to the receivers Darrell Sturgess and Scott Hildebrand immediately to be recorded with the Court and be disbursed against the Affidavits of Damages submitted to the receivers.[51]

In other words, the assets of those entities were now to be distributed among those who had been wronged by the federal farm credit system. As the Robinson account of NESARA explained, by using this decision, farmers have been to file numerous class-action lawsuits against the federal government, which dodged the suits by "hitting them with either outrageous IRS fees or by imprisoning the legal team under frivolous non-related charges." Roy Schwasinger and other "military generals" then began observing the hearings to ensure "that the bribed judges would vote according to constitutional law."[52] In the early 1990s, Schwasinger argued before the U.S. Supreme Court in a sealed case and "almost unanimously the US Supreme Court Justices ruled that the Farmers Union Claims were indeed valid." This invalidated all of the foreclosures that had taken place under the Federal Land Bank or Farm Credit systems.[53]

This was the point at which Robinson's Schwasinger narrative moved beyond mere restitution for foreclosed farms and into territory that tied directly into the extravagant claims of the NESARA. It was not just the farmers who had been taken advantage of but, in fact, "the Federal Government and banks had defrauded the farmers *all United States Citizens* out of vast sums of money and property." Further, the court revealed the Internal Revenue Service to be "a Puerto Rican trust," that the Federal Reserve System was against the law, and that the 16th Amendment, which allowed collection of federal income tax, had not been properly ratified. Robinson's narrative reveals that a secret from of "benevolent visionaries consisting of politicians, military general, and business people, who had been secretly working to restore the Constitution since the 1950's [sic]."[54] One of these people, "a four-star Army General" was given "title over the United States" by the Supreme Court.

The history then diverged into sovereign citizen territory, discussing the impact of such laws as the Organic Act of 1871 and the Trading with the Enemy Act of 1933 to explain the supposed "corporate Federal Government which has been masquerading to the public as the

Constitutional Government" [capitalization as in original].⁵⁵ "General" Schwasinger, in 1991, presented evidence of all the government's "criminal activity" and the corporate government's connection to the "New World Order" and its plans for "a Fascist One World Government ruled by the international bankers." It was at this point that the task force of military officials described by Goodwin comes into existence, with members including CIA director William Colby, Admiral Jeremy Boorda, and Air Force General David McCloud. Significantly, all three of the men named had died before the publication of this history and those deaths were well-known within the conspiracy community for their supposedly suspicious natures. Colby had died in a canoeing accident in 1996, Boorda committed suicide the same year, and McCloud died in a plane crash in Alaska.

Following an audit of the Federal Reserve, officials found that the central bank "trillions" of dollars sitting in accounts when it "should have been applied to the national debt." The auditors also discovered that the nation's foreign debt was a lie and that, in truth, "most nations owed money to the United States." The trillions of dollars were placed into "European bank accounts" to pay off the Farm Claims and would "become the basis of the Prosperity Programs."⁵⁶ These "Prosperity Programs" included schemes like Omega; NESARA advocates could use this narrative to appeal to victims of any number of financial swindles—their money was coming, they had not been fooled. They simply had to persevere until government officials finally implemented NESARA.

Dark forces, however, were still in control. In 1992, the military task force confronted President George H.W. Bush and demanded that he never use the term New World Order again and sign "an agreement that he would return the United States to Constitutional Law" [capitalization as in original]. He agreed, but this was a ruse. After losing his re-election bid, Bush "secretly planned to sign" an executive order on Christmas ordering the closure of all banks. This would give him "an excuse to declare martial law" and the opportunity to implement a "new Constitution" that would permit all elected officials to remain in office for a further 25 years. The military intervened, however, and the plan was thwarted.⁵⁷

With Bush Senior's plan thwarted, the history moved into Bill Clinton's presidency and began with an explanation for why Roy Schwasinger and his Farm Claim compatriots ended up in trouble with the law and, eventually, in prison. The author explained that in 1993, members of the administration, Supreme Court Justices, select members of Congress, and the military task force created the "Farmer Claim Process." This would allow Americans to receive restitution for a variety of reasons:

2. NESARA—Knights, Agendas and Greed 63

A claim of harm could be made on any loan issued by a financial institution for all interest paid; foreclosures; attorney and court fees; IRS taxes or liens; real estate and property taxes; mental and emotional stress caused by the loss of property; stress related illness such as suicide and divorce; and even warrants, incarceration, and probation could also be claimed.

This process was sabotaged, however, by the imposition of a $300 filing fee. The history made a vague assertion that connected this fee to the arrest of Schwasinger, et al. It never explained how, only claiming that it was "used in 1994 as a basis to arrest the leaders of the legal team, including Roy Schwasinger."[58]

While the evil Clintons were busy locking away patriots like Schwasinger, Attorney General Janet Reno was committed to helping "restore Constitutional law." She "ordered the Delta Force and Navy Seals to Switzerland, England, and Israel to recapture trillions of dollars of gold stolen by the Federal Reserve System from the strategic gold reserves." For her actions, Reno was quietly assassinated and—along with also-assassinated Treasury Secretary Robert Rubin—replaced by a clone. This clone was "responsible for covering-up the various claim scandals."[59] This portion of the account in Robinson's book varies from the original timeline complied by Nancy Detweiler. Detweiler wrote that the Reno-clone was "responsible for covering-up the various Clinton scandals" rather than merely the "claim scandals." Curiously, Robinson would publish Detweiler's original version in an issue of his own *Maine Republic Email Alert* newsletter a year after he published his book.[60]

The narrative about clones of figures such as Reno and Clinton was reminiscent of theories put forward in the late 1970s and early 1980s by conspiracist Dr. Peter Beter. Beter claimed that the Soviet government had developed the technology to create near-perfect duplicates of humans that he called "organic robotoids." Beter explained, "A robotoid is alive in the biological sense but it is an artificial life form. Robotoids respond to conventional routine medical tests…. Robotoids can also think, but they think only in the sense that a computer does." However, the robotoids were limited by their brief life expectancy—their usefulness was outlived fairly quickly. Further, their utility was inhibited for other reasons. Organic robotoids "are extremely expensive, troublesome creatures to produce and utilize; and robotoid capabilities do not exceed those of human beings. All they can really do is simulate human beings." However, as Beter explained, "for intelligence purposes that's all they have to do!" Beter asserted that the Soviets had worked with perennial conspiracy theory villains the Rockefeller family to use organic robotoids as replacements for powerful and prominent public figures around the world.[61]

The remainder of the Detweiler/Robinson history of NESARA in the 1990s expanded slightly on Goodwin's summary. The White Knights, including the group of military leaders, were dissatisfied with the progress of the reforms that the Supreme Court had ordered, and engineered the passage of NESARA and forced President Clinton (or his clone—the text is unclear) to sign the bill.

The clearest illustration of how the NESARA narrative had metastasized is Robinson's enumerated list of reforms NESARA would put into place. The list Robinson presented had 19 items, more than tripling the outcomes provided for in Shaini Goodwin's telling.

1. Zeros out all credit card, mortgage, and other bank debt due to illegal banking and government activities. This is the Federal Reserve's worst nightmare, a Jubilee for Forgiveness of debt.
2. Abolishes the income tax.
3. Abolishes the IRS. Employees of the IRS will be transferred into the U.S. Treasury national sales tax area.
4. Creates a 14% flat rate on non-essential "new items only" sales tax revenue for the government. In other words, food and medicine will not be taxed; nor will used items such as old homes.
5. Increases benefits for senior citizens.
6. Returns Constitutional Law to all courts and legal matters.
7. Reinstates the original Title of Nobility Amendment. Hundreds of thousand [sic] Americans under the control of foreign powers will lose their citizenship, be deported to other countries, and barred from reentry for the remainder of their life. And millions of people will discover that their college degrees are now worthless paper.
8. Establishes new Presidential and Congressional elections, within 120 days after NESARA's announcement. The interim government will cancel all National Emergencies and return us back to constitutional law.
9. Monitors elections and prevents illegal election activities of special interest groups.
10. Creates a new U.S. Treasury rainbow currency backed by gold, silver, and platinum precious metals, ending the bankruptcy of the United States initiated by Franklin Roosevelt in 1933.
11. Forbids the sale of American Birth Certificate Records as chattel property bonds, by the U.S. Department of Transportation.
12. Initiates new U.S. Treasury Bank System in alignment with Constitutional Law.
13. Eliminates the Federal Reserve System. During the transition period the Federal Reserve will be allowed to operate side by side of the U.S. Treasury for one year in order to remove all Federal Reserve Notes from the money supply.
14. Restores financial privacy.
15. Retrains all judges and attorneys in Constitutional Law.

16. Ceases all aggressive, U.S. government military actions worldwide.
17. Establishes peace throughout the world.
18. Releases enormous sums of money for humanitarian purposes.
19. Enables the release of over 6,000 patents of suppressed technologies that are being withheld from the public, under the guise of national security, including free energy devices, antigravity, and sonic healing machines.[62]

There was the same emphasis on a restoration of "constitutional" law and courts and disdain for the present system of taxation in the United States, but this iteration of NESARA also incorporated several concepts central to many sovereign citizen conspiracy narratives such as the "sale" of birth records as collateral, and the claim that the United States entered into bankruptcy in 1933. Item 19 incorporates the world of hidden technology conspiracies, a hallmark of other triumphalist narratives such as those promoted by the UFO Disclosure Movement (see Chapter 3). To be sure, Goodwin used many of the same concepts in her writings, but she did not go so far as to incorporate them within the foundational (and, to a degree, canonical) enumeration of NESARA's benefits.

Robinson explained the "gag order" and the threat of execution for government officials who dare speak about NESARA. He included an alleged quotation from Minnesota Senator Paul Wellstone: "We're here in the nation's capital to tell the story that we've got an economic convulsion in agriculture; we've got a lot of broken dreams, a lot of broken families, a lot of broken lives, and we're not going to take it an [sic] longer."[63] This quotation is similar in spirit to portions of a speech that Wellstone gave to the Senate in September 1999.[64] The themes presented here painted Wellstone as being someone amenable to the aims of NESARA. Indeed, the NESARA narrative claimed that he was about to "break the gag order" and the 2002 plane crash that killed Wellstone and his family was engineered to prevent this. Who engineered it? The Detweiler/Robinson timeline did not say, but it did accuse the CIA of bribing Senators to prevent violating the gag order and claimed that "every Senator has been bribed with a minimum of $200 million dollars deposited into a Bank of America account in Canada."[65] Humanity would never hear "the major media networks report about NESARA," for these networks were being bribed as well (CNN receives billions of dollars per year, laundered through "the Mormon Church in Utah"). Any government of military figures with the authority to announce NESARA refused to do so. The rewards were too high and the punishment too severe for them to take action.

The Detweiler/Robinson narrative expanded on the sequence of events of the planned 2001 announcement of NESARA. The Supreme

Court ordered Congress to approve it ("18 months after NESARA became law," inexplicably) on September 9, 2001. The next day, former president George H.W. Bush moved back into the White House "to steer his son on how to block the announcement." On September 11, the Detweiler/Robinson narrative claimed that Federal Reserve Chair Alan Greenspan was set to initiate NESARA reforms by announcing "the new US Treasury Bank system, debt forgiveness for all U.S. citizens, and abolishment of the IRS." Thus, in their view, President Bush targeted the World Trade Center for destruction, to prevent "the international banking computers" in the North Tower from launching the new Treasury Bank System. The attack on the Pentagon (carried out with a remote-controlled aircraft full of explosives) was intended to destroy the White Knights who were coordinating the implementation of NESARA.[66] At this point, Detweiler's NESARA timeline ended, and Robinson continued on, explaining that because of the wars in Afghanistan and Iraq, it was impossible to implement NESARA. He claimed that in 2007, a new "US Treasury of the Republic went on line [sic] with a new gold backed banking system." This was, he explained, unable to be used, because the banks were trying to sell off their worthless "derivative" investments. He then transitioned to a confusing and convoluted explanation of the interconnection between the 2008 derivatives-driven economic crisis, the international Basel Accord banking agreements (Basel I, Basel II, and Basel III), and the U.S. government's economic stimulus programs (particularly the Troubled Asset Relief Program, or TARP) as reasons for the continued delay in implementing the NESARA reforms.[67]

This expanded NESARA timeline took up a third of Robinson's book *NESARA I*. The remainder consists of transcripts of other NESARA promoters' YouTube videos and more detailed explanations of what each aspect of NESARA would mean for the American people. He sourced these from a number of websites, including a now-defunct (but archived) Canadian NESARA site, "NESARA—The Reformation Act."[68] This site explained how NESARA's rejigging of the monetary system would have rapid effects on people's lives:

> Within about a month of the announcement, there will be a reduction of 90% across the board in the prices of ALL goods and services, to counter inflation and bring us back to the pricing of the 'fifties [sic]. All countries involved have already made arrangements to implement that change industry-wide. Prices will then be tied to the price of gold.... Cash (in hand or at the bank) is NOT devalued. That means that if you have $50,000 right now and wish to buy a new home costing $250,000 the new price of the home would be just $25,000? ..so instead of making a down-payment you

2. NESARA—Knights, Agendas and Greed

could purchase it outright and still have $25,000 left over—as the value of money held right now is NOT devalued.

On its face, this plan sounded unworkable, but the author attempted to make sense of it and explained that any shortfalls on the part of the retailers who would—seemingly—be losing massive amounts of money under this system would be reimbursed from government funds. NESARA would have a major impact on nearly every aspect of the world, even beyond finances.

In general, "technology" would be greatly enhanced as a result of new innovations and sources of energy. "Science will take on a new meaning as new technologies are released" and "the way we do things" would be "radically different." "Oil and gas" use, for example, would be greatly diminished, if they were used at all. As a natural consequence, "oil tankers will become redundant" and "gas-lines will no longer be required." This new independence from traditional fossil fuels "will be one of the greatest contributions to environmental wellbeing on this planet." The authors explained that "other, renewable energies will be used instead"[69] but they did not provide any specific examples of what these sources of energy might be. Several NESARA promoters tied the benefits of NESARA to the release of supposedly suppressed technology, such as the rumored inventions of Nikola Tesla.[70] Beyond the very broad category of "technology" and energy production, the implementation of NESARA would bring about myriad other changes.

Medical science and health would be transformed by the new monetary system ("There is enough wealth in the world to provide FREE health-care") but the impact of NESARA on health care—like its impact on most things—goes beyond economic factors:

> The monopoly of the pharmaceutical companies will be broken, and their products will have to be proven effective and without side-effects before they can be distributed to doctors, hospitals and the general public. According to medical journals, less than 30% of pharmaceutical products receive any real testing at all before they are launched on an unsuspecting public. Natural products will take their place, resulting soon in a reduction of the requirement for hospital beds, or allowing full use of current facilities. With the emphasis on preventive medicine, illness will drop drastically.[71]

Suspicion of the modern medical systems and the pharmaceutical industry is common within conspiratorial narratives. These range from anti-vaccination crusades to the belief that the pharmaceutical industry (aided and abetted by their unholy allies in medical schools and governments) has systematically suppressed miracle cures and treatments for cancer and other diseases. This account followed some of the general rules of conspiratorial reporting, such as providing very specific data ("less than 30% of pharmaceutical products receive any real testing") with the support presented for such a claim being quite vague ("according to medical journals"). Doctors, in a post–NESARA world, would "return to being the physicians of old, rather than doctors of medicine, or true 'Doctors of Health.'" They did not explain precisely what they meant by "physicians of old"—the lack of specificity served the broad purpose of suggesting that there was, at one point, a golden age of health that those working for the "Dark Agenda" have taken from people. There was an emphasis on "natural products" which is also typical of medical conspiracy theory narratives, as was the author's assertion that a shift to natural treatments would drastically reduce the incidence of illness and disease. There was an element of status anxiety in these predictions about post–NESARA healthcare as well:

> The role of nurses in hospitals will be fully recognized and they will play a major role in returning patients to full health. Many of those displaced over the years will return to their profession. Practitioners of alternative or complementary medicine will receive recognition for their expertise and ability to treat imbalances in the physical body. Prevention rather than cure will be the new byword in health care.[72]

Like many of the financial aspects of NESARA, this author framed medical reforms not as a set of innovations but as a restoration of a bygone era. NESARA would bring about the return of the way things used to be before the world went so wrong for so many. Like the gold standard and an economy free from control by a central bank like the Federal Reserve System, "natural" treatments will set things right. This also served as an example of the way that NESARA narratives inverted or otherwise altered long-standing conspiratorial storylines. There is no shortage of narratives in which governments and their cohorts in the medical fields and pharmaceutical industries are hatching schemes to outlaw nutritional supplements or mandate vaccination.[73] In these narratives, there is a status quo; often a favorable one in which you can take whatever supplements you wish and are under no legal obligation to vaccinate your children. If the dark, conspiratorial predictions come to pass, these freedoms will vanish. The NESARA narrative moved the needle in the opposite direction. The status quo was the broken world and this legislation that lies at the edge of an ever-receding horizon is what will bring it back. Both types of narrative appeal to the dissatisfied, fearful, and angry, but they approach their chosen topics from different angles.

NESARA's economic reforms would also bring about improvements in education. There was a call for more funding, with schooling being "completely free up to at least tertiary level." NESARA would also initiate more fundamental changes. The coming technological changes would lead to opportunities for "the authoring of new textbooks" that teach "the Truth rather than man-manufactured tales, or misleading so-called 'scientifically-proven' statements." Unsurprisingly, for example, "Nikola Tesla's work will receive full recognition." Not only would teachers now be "competent to teach in the subjects allocated to them," the materials they use would contain the "truth" rather than textbooks "dictated by New World Order psychologists and spin-doctors." Of course, teachers would need to be re-educated. In particular, they need to be familiarized with "the proper handling of Indigo ... children—children of this 'New Age.'"[74] Indigo and Crystal children are a concept popularized in some New Age circles beginning in the 1970s. Nancy Tappe, who originated the term, claims that Indigo Children are an "anomaly in human evolution" that comprise "over 95% of children born in the last 20 years,"[75] which does not seem particularly anomalous. Doreen Virtue, quoted in a *New York Times* article about the Indigo Children explained that "They're vigilant about cleaning the earth of social ills and corruption, and increasing integrity.... Other generations tried, but then they became apathetic. This generation won't, unless we drug them into submission with Ritalin."[76] While a full examination of the Indigo Children is outside the scope of this study, Virtue's concern about over-medication of children matches the concerns that NESARA's medical effects will supposedly address. Some UFO Disclosure advocates will appropriate the Indigo Child notion, weaving it into their narrative tapestry of extraterrestrial contact—another example of the connections between aspects of the NESARA narrative and the UFO/Extraterrestrial Disclosure narrative discussed in Chapter 3.

The NESARA narrative, as originated by Harvey Barnard and especially as expanded upon by Shaini Goodwin/Dove of Oneness, was largely an Internet-driven phenomenon. As such, it is difficult—if not impossible—to coherently and concisely trace all the different permutations and interpretations through which it has gone. The most efficient way to understand some of the ways in which these stories have developed and how various actors have shaped them to fit various ideological paradigms is to trace their use by conspiratorial thinkers outside of the NESARA "universe." Two very different views have been promulgated by Sherry Shriner and Stan Johnson of "The Prophecy Club."

Sherry Shriner: An Anti-NESARA Narrative

The late Sherry Shriner's online writings and Internet broadcasts focused mainly on her interpretations of "Bible Codes," demonic interference in the political realm and the dangers of various "New Age" beliefs. Shriner would come to believe that the UFO Disclosure Movement was part and parcel of a Satanic takeover of the human race (see Chapter 3). She would also argue that NESARA was not the bountiful boon for downtrodden Americans its promoters claimed. Shriner reinterpreted and reshaped these conspiratorial concepts to fit her own paranoid worldview.

A native of Cleveland, Ohio, Shriner claimed to have been engaged in a life-long struggle against Lucifer. This conflict was due to the fact that "Lucifer knew I had a prophetic calling on my life, and that as an adult, I would grow up to become one of his arch enemies. I would learn as an adult how to expose, attack, and tear down his strongholds that he would create to control and destroy mankind. To prevent this from happening, he had assigned one of his top-ranking generals to kill me." Shriner claims that this was the reason she was tormented by demonic beings throughout her childhood and adolescence. Shriner studied broadcast journalism at Liberty Baptist University and Kent State University but, unable to find work in the field, returned to the Cleveland area and raised a family.

At this point, the demonic torment returned, and Shriner "embarked on an intense research over the next 5 years into spiritual warfare, hell, demons, Satan, and continued into my favorite areas of end time events and last days prophecies." In addition to these religious topics, Shriner also taught herself all about "UFOs, government black operations, the New World Order, and much, much more." In the early years of the 21st century, Shriner established an online presence with numerous websites examining various conspiracy theories. She claimed to have been individually called by God (whom she always referred to as "Yahweh") as a "prophet to the nations" and she maintained a consistent presence on her Internet radio show and over twenty different websites until her death in early 2018.[77] Like other extreme conspiracy theorists—notably the UK's David Icke—Shriner believed that some humans were reptilian entities in disguise. Those who followed her teachings through her website, YouTube channel and Internet radio program took this notion very seriously. In one instance, the paranoia fed by Shriner's teachings ended in murder.[78]

As difficult and confusing as it is to present a coherent summary of Shriner's worldview, it is important for understanding her fringe position on conspiratorial topics like NESARA and extraterrestrial Disclosure and how she perceived them as part of a wider catastrophe for humanity. Like many conspiracists who weave together narratives of political paranoia and alien invasion, Shriner proclaimed that there was an alliance between "the Black Military, or Black projects, or Black technology" and the stereotypical "gray" aliens. Shriner recycled narratives that had been extant since the late 1980s, claiming that the secret government of the United States had a secret treaty with an alien nation, allowing the aliens to abduct Americans in exchange for advanced technology. The end result of this would be a "New World Order." Shriner added elements of Christian mythology to this, claiming that "Satan wants a New World Order, and our government has been creating and promoting it for him." In addition to Satan being the mastermind behind the New World Order, the alien presence on Earth has its roots in the ancient past. "There's nothing new about the New World Order," Shriner asserted. Shriner equated modern "aliens" with the Nephilim discussed the sixth chapter of Genesis in the Hebrew Bible. "It's the same world our Biblical patriarchs lived in," she claimed, "a world of hybrid giants and the crossbreeding of man and aliens." Shriner defined these beings as "fallen angels," and claimed that they are the source of mythological characters such as Hercules. Shriner not only used her many websites, streaming audio program, and YouTube platform to inform people about this threat, she combatted it personally.

Shriner fought hard against these beings and the Ascended Masters who controlled them. Her key weapon was a concept called "orgone." Orgone was the name given by psychoanalyst Wilhelm Reich to a supposed universal life force. His student, Charles R. Kelley, who would continue to promote these ideas after Reich's death, defined orgone energy as "the substratum from which all nature is created…. Orgone energy is the creative force in nature [emphasis in original]."[79] Reich's ideas about this universal life force or energy led to numerous other developments such as the "cloudbuster" device which Reich asserted could influence weather patterns. The use of a substance—orgonite—to channel the orgone energy was the root of Sherry Shriner's efforts to repel the Satanic invaders. Shriner constructed what she called "orgone blasters." She claimed that orgone blasters could "keep chemtrails from sticking over your home and area … destroys aliens and demons won't come near them, and they will kill zombies and evil beings!!"[80]

These malefactors planned, Shriner claimed, to "come back with a new story of who they allegedly are. In this century they are propagating the lie that they are extra terrestrial [sic] life forms from other galaxies." They are "the same cast [sic] of fallen angels from the past, only now they refer to themselves as Ascended Masters in the New Age Movement."[81]

Shriner died from what public health officials described as "natural causes" in 2018[82] but several years later, her many websites, her YouTube channel, and Twitter feed have remained online, and her Facebook page still received multiple posts from supporters every day, in which they shared news stories and their interpretations of those stories in light of Shriner's teachings. Shriner was not the originator of the building blocks of her conspiratorial worldview. She did not invent shapeshifting lizard people, orgone, or the concept of demons masquerading as space aliens. The way in which she configured these elements, however, was singular and was consistently concerned with providing counter-conspiracies to the narratives like NESARA.

NESARA advocates have roundly condemned Shriner for spreading "dis-information" about NESARA and claiming that she has received her "messages from psychopathic spooks."[83] One particular aspect of this—the presence of "ascended masters"—connects NESARA to Shriner's conspiratorial cosmology. On one of her nearly two dozen websites—the simply but evocatively named www.nesarasucks.com—Shriner reported that the "Bible Code" software she used produced the following in response to her entering the name of Count St. Germain: "Satan—Tyrant—Dictator—Deceitful—Phony—Fake—Swindler—Fraudulent—Abomination—Disgusting—Repugnant—Desecrator—Fraud—Deceit—Hoax."[84] Shriner wrote that NESARA is also known as the "New Global Financial System." It was "an excuse to plunder and pillage America under the false pretense of peace and prosperity and an imaginary return to constitutional law." For Shriner, NESARA was a ruse; a plan that would lead to ruination rather than redemption. The "Nesara [sic] Sucks" home page also highlighted Shriner's predilection for juvenile name-calling, remarking that NESARA was "better described as a National Evil Snake, Annunaki (and) Reptilian Association or simply, Neo-logical Excrement Spread Artfully Round America." She warned readers not to allow Ascended Masters like Maitreya and "Sananda Esu Immanuel" to deceive them, claiming that Maitreya was involved in "the H1N1 Vaccine and RFID Bracelets…. Mass Chip Implantation and Murder" [capitalization as in original]. As an aside, Shriner also claimed that she destroyed Maitreya with her Orgone Blasters and that Sananda (who Shriner claims is one of the two leaders of NESARA, along with Count St. Germain) had taken control.[85]

The powers that be, Shriner explained, would present NESARA in a way that largely mirrored what promoters like Dove of Oneness claimed: "a Restoration of our Constitutional freedoms, cures for illnesses and new energy sources, financial and banking improvements, removal of corrupt government officials, and the beginning of more peace on Earth and more." But this would merely be a ruse; the plan would never be implemented and its failure, Shriner claimed, will be blamed on Christians (or "true believers of the Most High") who will then be exterminated to make way for the new order to emerge. This new order, a "first contact" experience, will implement NESARA as part of a treaty system between the United States and "Space Aliens." They will present, she claimed, as Ascended Masters, "Space Ship Commanders," extraterrestrials, "those who have reached godhood," as well as Al Gore and Barack Obama.[86] She goes on to identify the economic aspects of NESARA to the thirteenth chapter of the Revelation of St. John: "And he causeth all, both small and great, rich and poor, free and bond, to receive a mark in their right hand, or in their foreheads: and that no man might buy or sell, save he that had the mark, or the name of the beast, or the number of his name."[87] Once the evil ones are able to fully implement NESARA and "these Reptiles and Lizards are in control they will ratify parts 2 & 3 of NESARA that nullify part 1 and begin their own agenda of cannibalism and murdering the inhabitants of America."[88]

The Prophecy Club

The Prophecy Club blurs the lines between church, broadcaster, and event promotion company and it has often veered away from the standard themes and messages of Christian evangelistic organizations and has weighed in on a surprisingly wide array of conspiratorial narratives. Each time it does, leader Stan Johnson—and the rotating cast of guest speakers he presents—reframe the narrative to fit within their pre-existing prophetic paradigm.

The Prophecy Club began in 1993 as a radio program in Topeka, Kansas. Stan Johnson, who had spent his career in sales, focused the program on playing presentation by prominent Bible prophecy promoters and evangelists. By the late 1990s, the Prophecy Club was promoting live events with a number of different speakers and had expanded their radio footprint to over 80 stations.[89] Like many on the political and religious fringes, the Prophecy Club promoted fears of societal and economic breakdown as a result of the so-called Y2K computer bug, asserting it was part of the "tribulation" period that would usher in the end times. Like many others, Stan Johnson and the Prophecy Club also found ways to profit from the potential disaster. Besides selling dehydrated food supplies, the Prophecy Club promoted dubious investments, such as "Blaze Diamonds":

> Hedge Your Y2K Assets with Blaze Diamonds
>
> All money managers recommend diversification. Convert a portion of your assets into this proven, appreciating, and safe investment. CERTIFIED Diamonds are real, portable, tangible, easily hidden, and therefore protected; kept and controlled by no one but you. Unlike stocks and bonds, diamonds are easily insured against loss. They are internationally recognized and convertable [sic] into any currency. Jews sewed them into the lining of their clothes and use them to buy their freedom.[90]

When the predicted Y2K related disasters failed to materialize, the Prophecy Club admitted they had miscalculated while at the same time offering an explanation that shoehorned the Y2K non-event into their prophetic worldview. In a newsletter to supporters, Johnson argued that the Y2K bug had not been solved by human computer scientists and engineers. He asked, "how do you explain the fact that third-world countries which had massive Y2k bugs had no problems?" There was, he explained, "only one answer. God gave the world some more time!"[91]

Stan Johnson, along with his wife Leslie Johnson, have continued to lead the Prophecy Club despite the decline in reach and popularity. As of this writing, their radio program is on only one terrestrial station and has transitioned to a podcast format. While they no longer conduct their regular live events with an array of speakers, the Johnsons operate the Spirit of Prophecy Church in suburban Dallas, which serves as an additional platform for their teachings. In the decades since the Y2K debacle, these teachings have remained fairly consistent and combine elements of positive- and negative-outcome conspiracy theories. On the program Johnson, and occasional guests, discuss current events and seek "to be an information source on current events in Bible prophecy."[92] Many episodes of the Prophecy Club consist of Stan Johnson explicating current news events in light of his own interpretation of Bible prophecy and the messages from later figures who Johnson believes are carrying messages from God. Chief among these is Dumitru Duduman (1932–1997), a Romanian who claimed to have had a number of visions, many concerning the future of the United States and Israel. The vision that Johnson cites most often, occurred in September 1984:

> The Russian spies have discovered where the nuclear warehouses are in America. When the Americans will think that it is peace and safety—from the middle of the country, some of the people will start fighting against the government. The government will be busy with internal problems. Then from the ocean, from Cuba, Nicaragua, Mexico…. (He told me two other countries, but I didn't remember what they were.) …they will bomb the nuclear warehouses. When they explode, America will burn!

2. NESARA—Knights, Agendas and Greed

Central to Johnson's interpretations of current events is Duduman's prediction of people "fighting against the government" while the government (presumably the federal government) is "busy with internal problems." Nearly every time protests or demonstrations of some kind occurred (particularly where the protests were focused on politically progressive issues), Johnson would link them to this prophecy. From 2014 in Ferguson, Missouri, to later concerns about "Antifa," the United States has, in Johnson's interpretation, nearly continuously been on the verge of some manner of "internal revolution." Duduman's September 1984 prediction also encompassed international affairs beyond a joint Caribbean–Central American attack on the United States:

> I have blessed this country because of the Jewish people who are in this country. I have seven million Jews in this country, but they do not want to recognize the Lord. They didn't want to thank God for the blessing they received in this country. Israel doesn't want to recognize Jesus Christ. They put their faith in the Jewish people in America. But, when America burns, the Lord will raise China, Japan, and other nations to go against the Russians. They will beat the Russians and push them all the way to the gates of Paris.
>
> Over there they will make a treaty, and appoint the Russians as their leaders. They will then unite against Israel. When Israel realizes she does not have the strength of America behind her, she will be frightened. That's when she will turn to the Messiah for deliverance. That's when the Messiah will come. Then, the church will meet Jesus in the air, and he will bring them back with Him to the Mount of Olives. At that time, the battle of Armageddon will be fought.[93]

Stan Johnson frames nearly every analysis of current political, geopolitical, social, or cultural events within the context of this "prophecy." Even when Johnson utilizes the work of other prophets—from the Hebrew Bible, the New Testament, or "present-day prophets"—he comes back to this 1984 message from Dumitru Duduman. That they have been able to fit so many new political and religious conspiratorial narratives into this very Cold War–era prophecy is remarkable.

In June 2016, the Prophecy Club devoted six of their daily Internet radio broadcasts to NESARA. An examination of these broadcasts illustrates the ways in which a conspiratorial narrative may be reinterpreted for a variety of needs. It also provides an example of Muirhead and Rosenblum's arguments about the "new conspiracism" relying on repetition rather than rational proofs and of the standard for conspiratorial acceptability being "true enough."

Johnson began the June 23, 2016, broadcast by reminding listeners that "it's been [his] heart as a watchman to try to warn the people when

[he] see[s] a sword coming."[94] Just as he did with the prophecy of Dumitru Duduman, he has a warning for listeners. He then made clear that none of what he "is about to read" is his own writing, and that the message he is going to convey was "downloaded from the internet"—specifically an article entitled "'HISTORY BEING MADE RIGHT NOW'—New Republic via GCR—'220 Points of Fact' as of May 2016" from the "nesaranews" blog site.[95] "None of this is me actually saying this," stammered Johnson, making an effort to convey the news as important while, at the same time, distancing himself from it. "Some of this, and I really can't say.... I want to make a lot of comments, but I dare not make very many comments because some of it I know to be true. Much of it I know to be true but I really have to limit my comments on this [chuckles] because it is so true. Maybe that's the way I should say it. I have to be careful, but I'm about to bring you some very important information." Johnson masked the fact that he was simply reading bits of a blog post by intimating that he had deeper information that the blog post "confirms." This was consistent with one of Stan Johnson's standard arguments. He often cites the first verse of 2 Corinthians, Chapter 13 (KJV): "in the mouth of two or three witnesses shall every word be established." Taken with the surrounding context, most readers of the New Testament realize that this verse referred to settling disputes between members of the church. Johnson takes that sentence, removes the context, and uses it as biblical proof that if "two or three" sources make a conspiratorial claim, that claim is true. This is a particularly pernicious example of the use of "repetition" in verifying conspiratorial claims as discussed by Muirhead and Rosenblum. It is the basic "new conspiracist" habit of saying that the same article posted on five different websites means there are five *different* sources corroborating a claim. To this, Johnson has added the sanction of scripture.

Before beginning his discussion of the article, Johnson issued yet another disclaimer: "I cannot verify a word of this, although much of it I have heard from various sources and have heard it is accurate." Johnson read the beginning of the article, which claimed that 450 years ago the "Vatican Historical Asset Trust Accounts" were created and that the nations of the world once had currencies that were backed by the "ancient Chinese Royal Dragon Families" and that "Certain sovereign families of Asia and Europe had pooled their assets into a series of very complex and secretive off-ledger private banking trust accounts" that were intended for "humanitarian projects to help the world for the better." Johnson commented that the article was an overview of the last four hundred years of the banking system and "about how we're going into, in my opinion, a world government, a totally new financial system, a new

2. NESARA—Knights, Agendas and Greed 77

religious system, everything is going to be different in the New World Order." Like Sherry Shriner, Johnson saw the coming financial changes through a lens of eschatological horror. For Johnson, these changes signaled the coming of the Tribulation—the seven-year period of intense persecution for the Christian church. Johnson continued his recitation of the article, which cited the Rothschild family as the controlling factor of England's central bank and, thus, secret rulers of the British Empire. It also repeated the sovereign citizen-derived claim that "the cabal" created a "Corporation of the US" in 1871 and that this corporation was under the control of "the world monetary organizations: International Monetary Fund, World Trade Organization, Bank of International Settlements, North American Union, Council on Foreign Relations, Committee of 300 and the Trilateral Commission." This claim ignored the fact that most of those organizations did not yet exist in 1871. The tool to manage all of this would be the U.S. Federal Reserve (which also did not exist in 1871). Johnson goes on to relate that the "global elites" attend "child exploitation get-togethers" and work for the "Khazarian" mafia. It was interesting that Johnson did not comment on the obviously anti-Semitic coded language of "Khazarian mafia"—the Prophecy Club is remarkably devoted to the preservation of the State of Israel and is on the end of the conspiratorial spectrum that is much more likely to demonize Roman Catholics than Jewish persons and Israeli or Zionist positions and policies. The simplest explanation is that Johnson did not actually know what "Khazarian" refers to or how it is often used as a substitute for "Jewish" in conspiratorial discourse.[96]

Next, Johnson related details of internationally organized pedophile rings involving sexual abuse and "the Satanic Ninth Circle Child Sacrifice Cult." Johnson summarizes it by saying "these ruling elite global bankers have a little fetish, they have a little problem. They have to sexually abuse and sometimes use as child sacrifice and apparently this is how they get their power." Johnson correlated this both to Old Testament accounts of people sacrificing their children to the god Moloch as well as legal access to abortion in the present day. As with his contextless use of the verse from 2 Corinthians, Johnson here reinforced biblical verification of these conspiratorial stories and connected the villains of the Old Testament to the villains and concerns of his present-day listeners. He reiterated that "America is about to become a new republic … the corporation called 'The United States of America' is going, going, and some say gone." In the audio, it was apparent that Johnson saw this passing away of what he calls the "capital letter" U.S. corporation as a negative, despite it being part of the ultimate NESARA goal. Like the use of the term "Khazarian," Johnson did not seem to fully grasp some of the core concepts he was repeating but was still happy to work them into his own worldview.

Johnson continued reading the document, and related accusations that Barack Obama and television host Bill Maher were responsible for covering up pedophile rings. Johnson quickly broke off from reading and emphasized that he was not accusing anyone of anything, but his motivation was that listeners "can better understand Bible prophecy." The article discussed the Federal Reserve's role in establishing the dollar as the world's reserve currency, despite being "fiat currency" that was "backed by nothing." The article (and Johnson) finally got into NESARA at this point and supposed return to gold-backed currency on a global scale (part of the "global currency reset" often referenced in NESARA writings after Shaini Goodwin's death). When Johnson read that following China's 2016 return to the gold standard, "privately owned US Federal Reserve Dollar was no longer being accepted for world trade" he again broke off and presented this information as confirming what other Prophecy Club guests had predicted about the fall of the dollar; again, Johnson presented this as a disaster rather than the dawn of a new, better system. Johnson ended by telling his listeners that this information was "real serious" and asked them to pray for his safety as he read this information.[97] The remaining segments of the NESARA series followed in much the same vein, with Johnson linking various parts of the NESARA narrative to his, and his ministry's pre-existing narrative. The NESARA effects on which Johnson focused were largely concerned with currency valuation, and he shoehorned this into the overarching "Fall of America" story as promoted by Dumitru Duduman. Where Sherry Shriner saw NESARA as a deception being foisted upon the ignorant by a cabal of fallen angels and reptilian aliens, Stan Johnson ignored the vast majority of the NESARA narrative, picking and choosing what fit the Prophecy Club message.

Conclusion

The rambling, sprawling story of NESARA is emblematic of the blend between the old and new conspiracisms and the transition from one to the other since 2001. Though still grounded in a mythology that echoes conspiratorial narratives that first emerged in the sovereign citizen and "tax protest" movements, NESARA became conceptually unraveled, especially since the death of its primary voice and promoter, Shaini Goodwin, although hints were there during her lifetime that NESARA was morphing and expanding in its scope and implications.

2. NESARA—Knights, Agendas and Greed

Within two decades, NESARA had expanded from a piece of suppressed legislation that would reform the American financial system to a global system of salvation encompassing centuries of history from Asia to Europe and from the United States to outer space and the astral plane. As it did so, the "proofs" of NESARA's imminent announcement—which were never strong—diminished in rationality to the point where—in the pattern described by Muirhead and Rosenblum—repetition began to take the place of even the weak evidence provided by Shaini Goodwin at the height of her powers as the arbiter of NESARA truth. The advent of widely available media platforms on the Internet—particularly YouTube and social media outlets—engendered an endless game of "telephone" where half-heard and partially-remembered folk legends of "farm cases" and a hidden law are blended with new and revitalized conspiracy narratives such as child trafficking and satanic sacrifice. Through all of this is a persistent insistence that the benefits of NESARA are right around the corner. That people only need to keep the faith for a *little* while longer and everything will be all right; maybe even better than all right.

The pattern of narrative sprawl and transition from the old to the new conspiracism that NESARA illustrates will also apply to the development of the UFO Disclosure Movement and, to a degree, will become intertwined with it.

Chapter 3

The UFO Disclosure Movement

What has become known, broadly, as the "Disclosure Movement" is the premier optimistic or triumphalist conspiracy narrative within the American UFO culture. In its broadest and most inclusive sense, the Disclosure narrative has posited that political, military, and intelligence officials are aware of the existence of intelligent extraterrestrial life and will reveal this information to the public. When they do so, there will be a number of tangible material benefits, intangible spiritual benefits, or some combination of both. While there are numerous variations on this theme, that basic structure has remained fairly constant. The modern age of Unidentified Flying Saucer sightings, theories about their origins or meaning, and conspiratorial narratives surrounding them have contained elements of optimism and hopefulness since 1947. This hopefulness and optimism, however, has not always been a consistent aspect of conspiracy theories surrounding mysterious objects in the skies. UFO culture in the United States since 1947 has followed a number of tracks that largely have run parallel but, occasionally, intersect. While a discrete and identifiable "Disclosure Movement" emerged in the 1990s and developed rapidly in the early 21st century, its basic assumptions were the result of theories, suspicions, and stories that spanned the nearly eighty-year history of the UFO phenomenon. They also existed in opposition and tension with darker and more pessimistic theories and Disclosure advocates often have to counter the more prevalent pessimistic claims about the nature of Earth's alleged extraterrestrial visitors when making their own case. While an extensive history of that culture is outside the scope of this chapter, the optimistic conspiracy strands surrounding UFO belief exist within a well-established context extending back decades. This context has largely been comprised of several forces that, in general, have been at odds with each other.

The first of these consists of official government efforts to investigate, explain, or otherwise come to terms with UFO sightings. From Air Force programs like Sign and Project Blue Book to the CIA's "Robertson Panel" and Congressional investigatory hearings and government-sponsored scientific research into the phenomenon, there is a long history of official interest in whatever the nature of the many and varied Unidentified Flying Objects and their implications for science and defense. Consistently, however, these programs have arrived at the conclusion that the vast majority of UFO sightings may be explained as having fairly prosaic causes. Shadowing these official government efforts were the efforts of individual UFO activists and organized UFO groups that have persistently and publicly pressured government entities to investigate further. This is often followed with skepticism, dismay, and claims of conspiracy from these groups when government-sanctioned investigations do not validate the claims of UFO believers that there is an extraterrestrial element to some of the cases. Alongside these investigations and, especially, after the American military moved away from investigations into UFO sightings at the dawn of the 1970s, civilian UFO investigation groups such as the National Investigations Committee on Aerial Phenomenon (NICAP), the Aerial Phenomenon Research Organization (APRO), and the Mutual UFO Network (MUFON) took the lead in investigating UFO sightings while urging the government to reveal what they knew. A second strand, which emerged in the early 1950s and continues to this day, are those known, collectively, as "Contactees." The Contactees' claims extended beyond UFO sightings to personal, often on-going, relationships with the occupants of these interplanetary and interstellar craft. While the contact movement's prominence in the wider UFO Disclosure Movement faded after the 1950s, it would persist on a smaller scale. A third strand, emerging in the 1980s, was a conspiratorial narrative that insisted the United States government had long been in contact with extraterrestrial civilizations, brokering deals that traded human lives for alien weapons technology.

A Brief History of UFO Belief and Activism

On June 24, 1947, Idaho businessman Kenneth Arnold was flying from Chehalis to Yakima, Washington. As he flew toward Mount Rainier he saw "a chain of nine peculiar looking aircraft flying from north to south at approximately 9,500 feet elevation and going, seemingly, in a definite direction of about 170 degrees." Arnold reported his sighting to the *East Oregonian* newspaper and the Associated Press picked up the story. For several days, readers around the world learned of the strange objects that "flew like a saucer would if you skipped it across the water."[1] June 24, 1947 thus marked the beginning of the modern "UFO Phenomenon" narrative.

Throughout the summer of 1947, there were additional "flying disk" claims from varied witnesses including law enforcement personnel. The Army Air Force (AAF) issued a statement denying that any of their current projects were responsible for sightings and that the sightings that had been reported did not warrant investigation. But in July of 1947—in addition to the so-called "Roswell Incident," which will appear in several of our conspiracy narratives—several military pilots allegedly encountered these disk-shaped aircraft but were unable to match their speed or maneuverability.

By the end of the summer of 1947, the newly independent U.S. Air Force initiated project Sign. Sign's assignment was to "collect, collate, evaluate, and distribute to interested government agencies and contractors all information concerning sightings and phenomena in the atmosphere which can be construed to be of concern to the national security."[2] Project Sign was the first instance of the Air Force taking a serious, organized investigative approach to the mystery of the flying discs. Sign investigated a number of sightings and encounters that would become well-known in the UFO community, including the case of Captain Thomas Mantell, a pilot in the Kentucky Air National Guard.

On January 7, 1948, Mantell was flying an F-51D fighter from Marietta, Georgia, to Standiford Air Force Base in Kentucky. As Mantell and his three wingmen approached the Kentucky base, they reported seeing a large metallic object. They did not recognize it as any aircraft with which they were familiar, and all four pilots pursued it. As they approached 25,000 feet, three broke off pursuit, but Captain Mantell continued until he ran out of oxygen. His fighter went into a steep descent and crashed near Franklin, Kentucky. Although Air Force officials claimed there was no evidence that the crash was anything more than an accident, the *Louisville Courier* dramatized the story with the headline "F-51 and Capt. Mantell Destroyed Chasing Flying Saucer."[3] At this point in the story of the flying saucer phenomenon there was no shortage of theories as to what the objects might be. Observers with a bent toward traditional occult esotericism and spiritualism, such as the members of the Borderland Sciences Research Association, speculated in 1948 that the objects seen "might be craft constructed by the Ancients and preserved in underground caverns, and now brought out for the training of crews against the time of coming war."[4] Others proposed that some of the objects could be experimental American or Soviet aircraft. Some even proclaimed the sightings were of spacecraft from other planets. The "Mantell Incident" (as it would come to be called) solidified the notion that whatever these objects might be, they possessed hostile intent.

Project Sign considered a wide variety of explanations for the aerial phenomena Americans reported, including extraterrestrial ones. Appendix C of the final report, "Some Considerations Affecting the Interpretation of Reports of Unidentified Flying Objects," examined "possible causes" for the reports, addressing three broad categories: "natural terrestrial phenomena," "man-made terrestrial phenomena," and "extraterrestrial objects."[5] That third classification included three possibilities. These included meteors (with the report authors noting that "the reported objects lose little of their interest, however, if they are of meteoritic origin"), extraterrestrial animals ("there are few reliable reports on extra-terrestrial animals"), and spaceships.[6]

The passage on the possibility of some UFO sightings being manufactured craft from another planet is highly speculative, with the authors assuming that any civilization that could "make such objects" would be "far in advance" of any human civilization. As to the purpose of these craft and their operators visiting earth, the report argued that

> such a civilization might observe that on Earth we now have atomic bombs and are fast developing rockets. In view of the past history of mankind, they should be alarmed. We should, therefore, expect at this time above all to behold such visitations.[7]

The notion that aliens beings had begun observing Earth due to the development of nuclear weapons would be a key assumption going forward and would often be part of the narrative put forth by Contactees—those who claimed to have direct interpersonal communication with otherworldly beings. Project Sign's musings on the possibility of and reasons for alien visitation were, however, speculative, with the report authors acknowledging that "all information so far presented on the possible existence of spaceships from another planet ... have been largely conjecture."[8]

Sign was phased out—with the official explanation being that the project cryptonym was compromised—but was quickly replaced by Project Grudge, which was operational from February to December of 1949. This nominal explanation might not, however, have been the whole story. Captain Edward J. Ruppelt was an Air Force officer that had been involved in these early Air Force UFO investigation efforts and would go on to head Project Blue Book. In his 1956 book, *The Report on*

Unidentified Flying Objects, Ruppelt asserted that in the last months of Project Sign, there was an increasing antipathy toward the speculation on an extraterrestrial origin for UFOs—mostly born out of a desire to provide quick, conclusive explanations for sightings. Ruppelt explained it this way:

> The people on the UFO project began to think maybe the brass didn't consider them too sharp so they tried a new hypothesis: UFO's [sic] don't exist. In no time they found that this was easier to prove and it got recognition. Before if an especially interesting UFO report came in and the Pentagon wanted an answer, all they'd get was an "It could be real but we can't prove it." Now such a request got a quick, snappy, "It was a balloon." Everybody felt fine.⁹

Grudge sought to eliminate the ambiguity which affected the Sign project. Although the program would run through the end of 1949, the report on Project Grudge emerged in August of that year. Its conclusions allowed for little of the ambiguity of Project Sign:

> Evaluation of reports of unidentified flying objects to date demonstrate that these flying objects constitute no direct threat to the national security of the United States.
> Reports of unidentified flying objects are the result of:
> Misinterpretation of various conventional objects.
> A mild form of mass hysteria or "war nerves."
> Individuals who fabricate such reports to perpetrate a hoax or to seek publicity.
> Psychopathological persons.

The Grudge Report also asserted that the "planned release" of UFOs alongside the "release of related psychological propaganda" could result in "mass hysteria." On the bright side, "employment of these methods by or against an enemy would yield similar results."¹⁰ Given the conclusion that the phenomena—whatever it might be—were not a direct threat, the Grudge Report recommended that the Air Force study of UFOs be "reduced in scope" and a press release issued explaining the Air Force's conclusions to the public.¹¹

Grudge phased down and its personnel were transferred. While the Air Force would continue to field UFO reports, it would do so as part of its routine intelligence gathering and analysis efforts rather than through a dedicated program.¹² Soon, however, the Air Force would be back in the flying saucer business in a very public way. In March 1952, the project formerly known as Grudge became the Aerial Phenomenon Group and a new codename assigned: Project Blue Book. Blue Book chief Edward Ruppelt explains that the codename "was derived from the title given to college tests. Both the tests and the project had an abundance of equally confusing questions."[13] Within a few months, Ruppelt had revised and updated reporting procedures for the Air Force, leading to an increased number of detailed UFO sighting reports.[14]

Increased UFO sightings, especially in 1952, led government agencies besides the Air Force to scrutinize the mystery. The summer of 1952 saw the Air Force's investigation efforts overwhelmed with sightings from all over the country, including a so-called "Saucer-fly-over" of Washington, D.C. which radar operators were powerless to explain. As mysterious lights flashed in the night over the Pentagon, White House, and Capitol Hill, the Air Force scrambled fighters to intercept. By the time the planes were airborne, the lights had disappeared from the skies and the radar screens.[15] This incident convinced many in the government that whatever was going on, it was vital to determine whether or not these sightings represented a new threat to national security. By early 1953, one of the governmental institutions most emblematic of the Cold War would try its hand at understanding the situation. Over four days in January 1953, the Central Intelligence Agency (CIA) convened the "Scientific Panel on Unidentified Flying Objects," chaired by physicist Howard P. Robertson of the California Institute of Technology. The report of the Robertson Panel, as it would become known, would be one of the foundational pieces of evidence for the assertion that the military and intelligence agencies were manipulating public perception of the UFO phenomenon. One of the areas the panel investigated was the Air Force's procedure for taking and investigating UFO reports through Project Blue Book. They noted that the Air Force's concern over for the issue "was probably caused by public pressure" and that Project Blue Book was the recipient of "reports of nearly anything anyone sees in the sky and fails to understand." This led, the group argued, to a huge number of "low-grade reports which tend to overload channels of communication with material quite irrelevant to hostile objects that might someday appear." Such reports had little scientific value and the entire reporting structure had the potential to suggest that UFOs "might be potential direct threats to national security." There was a need, the report asserted, for authorities and the media to de-emphasize UFOs.[16] Members of the committee were not averse or resistant to the possibility of life on other planets or the possibility that such beings might visit Earth, but "they did not find any evidence that related the objects sighted to space travelers."[17] The panel reported that while there might be no apparent direct danger from these objects, there were "related dangers" that might well exist. These included "misidentification of actual enemy artifacts by defense personnel," the possibility of a flood of "false information" overwhelming reporting channels, and the possibility of "mass hysteria" among the American public and increased susceptibility to "enemy psychological warfare."[18] To counter this, the Robertson Panel proposed an "education program." This program would have "two major aims: training and 'debunking.'" The training portion would involve educating military personnel and civilians in a variety of capacities (such as "radar operators; pilots; control tower operators")[19] in identifying various terrestrial craft and atmospheric phenomena in order to reduce the number of reports coming in that simply misidentified ordinary things as extraordinary. The "debunking" portion of the program aimed to reduce the public's overall interest in the UFO phenomenon.

> This education could be accomplished by mass media such as television, motion pictures, and popular articles. Basis of such Education would be actual case histories which had been puzzling at first but later explained. As in the ease of conjuring tricks, there is much less stimulation if the "secret" is known. Such a program should tend to reduce the current gullibility of the public and consequently their susceptibility to clever hostile propaganda.[20]

The panel went on to suggest that productions from companies such as educational filmmaker Jam Handy, Inc., and Disney would be possible outlets for such educational efforts.[21] The panel also took notice of national flying saucer organizations such as APRO, the Aerial Phenomenon Research Organization. The panel "believed that such organizations should be watched because of their potentially great influence on mass thinking if widespread sightings should occur," opined that such organizations were irresponsible in the way they handled reports and suggested that "the possible use of such groups for subversive purposes should be kept in mind."[22]

As the Air Force and the CIA struggled to deal with both the mystery of the UFOs and persistent public interest in the subject, American citizens took matters into their own hands, forming local clubs and national organizations. The national UFO investigation organizations strove to address the subject in a manner that was, if not totally objective, at least nodding in the direction of a scientific approach. Arising in the late 1950s and 1960s, these organizations boasted thousands of members, published regular newsletters and magazines, and their leaders were the go-to figures for media outlets wanting a memorable line or two about the flying saucers. Clara L. John and T. Townsend Brown founded the National Investigation Committee on Aerial Phenomenon (NICAP) in August of 1956 with the goal of directing "a united scientific investigation of aerial phenomena."[23] NICAP presented itself as a serious, scientific organization that was dedicated to finding answers about the UFOs. The organization's board of directors included scientists and retired military officers. Also on the board in those early days was Donald E. Keyhoe. Keyhoe was born in 1897, served as a pilot in the Marine Corps, retiring due to injury in 1923. During the 1930s and 40s, after a stint working for the U.S. Commerce Department, Keyhoe became a freelance aviation writer. Keyhoe's penned his first UFO story for the January 1950 issue of *True* magazine. This article formed the basis for his 1953 book, *Flying Saucers from Outer Space*. In this early work, Keyhoe focused on sightings and speculation on the origins and purpose of the UFOs. Later, he would shift to developing theories to explain the seeming cover-up of UFO truth by various government entities. The book cemented Keyhoe's position as an authority on UFOs[24] and led to numerous television and radio appearances to discuss the topic. Unlike many of the UFO authorities at the time, Keyhoe had a great deal of experience working within the cultures of the military and the federal government. Styling himself as "Major Donald E. Keyhoe, USMC, Ret." on his books and articles, Keyhoe was somewhat ahead of his time in terms of establishing a brand for presentation to the media and the public. His experience and connection—and the constant reminders that he was a former military man—gave him a veneer of credibility that other saucer commentators lacked.

Keyhoe was the unquestioned leader of NICAP by 1956 and worked to broaden the organization's focus from investigating and cataloging individual UFO stories to an approach that included pressuring members of the U.S. Congress to hold open, televised hearings on the saucer problem. This, he believed, would force the Air Force to release evidence on the UFOs that he was convinced they were keeping from the public. Taking control of the organization was the culmination of plans he had been making for several years. Historian David Jacobs explained Keyhoe's belief that the way to "solve" the UFO mystery was to

> either force or to wait for a "big breakthrough," which could take several forms: a flying saucer could land on the White House lawn, thereby putting an immediate end to the UFO controversy; a series of spectacular sightings could occur, which would create enough public pressure to force the Air Force to reveal all its findings; or rational argument could swing the public to Keyhoe's position, giving him the leverage to compel the Air Force to disclose its "hidden" findings publicly.[25]

There was, of course, no way to predict or control a landing on the president's lawn or a massive sighting event. Thus, Keyhoe's attention was on persuading the public that the Air Force was sitting on the solution to the mysterious craft in the sky. NICAP positioned itself as the rational, serious UFO organization, eschewing the wild tales of the Contactees and channelers. Rather, while investigating plausible sightings, the organization also pursued the angle of pressuring Congress to hold open hearings, putting pressure on the Air Force. Through the 1950s, these efforts gained a toehold, with the combination of NICAP's work and Edward J. Ruppelt's 1958 book *The Report on Unidentified Flying Objects* casting a bright light on the Air Force's efforts. The Air Force, throughout the late 1950s and early 1960s, dodged several attempts by members of Congress to hold hearings. The usual Air Force tactic was to privately brief concerned Representatives and Senators on their findings, casting UFO organizations like NICAP as meddlesome troublemakers who were set on embarrassing the Air Force and having little understanding of what the military was doing to address the issue.[26]

For his part, NICAP leader Keyhoe became convinced that there was a high-level effort to hide the truth about the UFO phenomenon from the American public and humanity in general. As early as 1955, Keyhoe believed there was an organized cover-up. It was not, however, necessarily the mainline policy of the U.S. Air Force:

> In revealing this censorship, I am not attacking the Air Force as a whole. Most of the officers and officials I have encountered are simply obeying orders. Nor do I attribute unpatriotic motives to the "silence group" members who originate these orders. Undoubtedly they are actuated by a high motive—the need, as they see it, to protect the public from possible hysteria.... If the public is not informed of the facts, fear of the unknown may prevail.

Denial of UFO truth, he wrote, "only heightens the possibility of hysteria."[27] Here, Keyhoe mentions "the silence group." This was his label—picked up by many UFO writers in the 1950s and 1960s—for a cabal within the national security structure that managed the flow of UFO related information to the public. In the 1960s, Keyhoe began to focus on the intelligence agencies rather than the military as the source of the Silence group, writing that he was "convinced it's the CIA that sets the policy ... they think people should be kept from worrying, until it's certain there's nothing to worry about."[28]

As NICAP and other organizations were dueling with the Air Force and the Central Intelligence Agency in the battle of UFO public opinion, another strand of flying saucer belief emerged that was less focused on scientifically proving the existence of extraterrestrial visitation than they were on their alleged personal encounters with UFO crew members. The first of these was George Adamski (1891–1965), who claimed that he met a man from Venus in 1952. That November, near Desert Center, California, Adamski encountered a flying saucer on the ground. He met the pilot who, while looking "like any other man," had unfashionably long hair and was clad in a futuristic-looking jumpsuit. Upon meeting him, Adamski quickly learned that speech communication was impossible, but there were other ways to communicate, for "people who desire to convey messages to one another can do so, even though they neither speak nor understand the other's language. This can be done through feelings, signs, and above all, by means of telepathy."[29] Using telepathy and hand gestures, Adamski learned that the visitor came from Venus. The Venusians, Adamski reported, believed that humanity's development of nuclear weapons presented a danged not only to Earth but to other planets as well. The extraterrestrial was not angry, however. Adamski related that "on his face there was not trace of resentment or judgment. His expression was one of understanding and great compassion; as one would have toward a much loved child who had erred through ignorance and lack of understanding."[30] These caring, compassionate beings were here to help humanity through a difficult phase in its development. Not through overt manipulation but by providing a positive example.

Adamski wrote several books about his encounters with the "Space Brothers," in which he expanded on their cosmic philosophy, described their ships, and explained how the residents of the various planets in the solar system had already passed through the stage of development with which Earth now struggled. In 1955's *Inside the Spaceships*, for example, Adamski spent time describing the customs and habits of the other denizens of our solar system, their food, and the way they decorated their flying saucers. He also met "the Great Master"—he was "a greatly evolved being" and a thousand years old (at least "in his present body"). The conversations between Adamski and the Master centered on the basic theme that the Earth was at the lowest stage of development of all the planets in the solar system. Because of humanity's lack of maturity, the Space Brothers did not believe that Earth people were ready for travel to the stars. The Space Brothers would, the Great Master explained, "gladly give you this knowledge which has served us so well, except that you have not yet learned to live with one another in peace and brotherhood." Humanity, they feared, might set out on a plan of conquest throughout the solar system, just as they had done throughout the Earth.[31] There was, however, a way for humanity to move forward. The Great Master told Adamski that "understanding of the universal [cosmic] laws both uplifts and restricts. As it is now with us, so it could be on your Earth. Lifted up by your knowledge, this same understanding would make it impossible for you to move against your brothers."[32] Humanity was not lost—the people of Earth could advance, could move beyond their petty squabbles and eventually take their place among the other advanced societies of the solar system.

The philosophical and ethical ideas that suffused Adamski's extraterrestrial visitation stories emerged before the flying saucer phenomenon. During the 1930s and 1940s Adamski had run various esoteric and theosophy-inspired study groups, most notably the Royal Order of Tibet. During this time, he authored pamphlets that expressed many of the same ideas discussed in his tales of extraterrestrial contact. In 1937's "The Kingdom of Heaven on Earth" Adamski explained that "heaven" was not an afterlife but could—if humanity embraced brotherhood, peace, and love—exist on Earth in the present. "Such is the heavenly state," Adamski wrote, "'peace and brotherhood of man, which is something that must be evolved gradually out of chaos.' If there is to be peace among nations, there must first be peace in the hearts of the individuals making up those nations.' All humans must emulate Jesus, since 'he did not discriminate between races, colors, creeds, or theories.... His law was not hate, but love.'"[33]

In 1949, Adamski more closely anticipated his flying saucer writings in the utopian science fiction novel *Pioneers of Space: A Trip to the Moon, Mars, and Venus*. In this travelogue-style journey though the planets of the solar system, he wrote, "man upon earth is progressive ... [and] could be taken as a good measuring stick of the vast university within which he lives. Even though he makes many mistakes which are against himself, we still see nothing but steady progress."[34] The human astronauts who travelled throughout the solar system were from an Earth that was still disunited, fractured, backward. On their journeys, however, they had the opportunity to learn from beings who had overcome those issues and had moved to a higher level of consciousness. The encounters with people on Venus, Saturn, and the Moon were very similar to what Adamski would claim to have experienced himself less than a decade later. His purpose was not only to tell a story: he encouraged readers to form discussion groups to talk about *Pioneers of Space* and its ideas. *Pioneers of Space* was, in some ways, a study guide for bringing about the "Kingdom of Heaven on Earth."[35] Adamski, in addition to seeking a measure of fame as a UFO author and lecturer, sought to express concerns about terrestrial issues as well, particularly ethical and philosophical. Of course, given the context of the Cold War, the destructive potential of nuclear weapons often cast a mushroom cloud–shaped shadow over the philosophical utterances of Adamski and other Contactees.

And there were other Contactees. Within months of Adamski's initial contact tale reaching the public in 1953, others came forward to share their own tales of contact with space beings, often back-dating them to stake a claim at being the first human contacted by extraterrestrials. George Van Tassel was a post–Adamski Contactee whose ideas would resonate down the decades and remain part of UFO culture. Like Adamski, Van Tassel claimed to have had contact with space brothers. Many of his contacts were psychic in nature, and he channeled messages via automatic writing and other means. Van Tassel also had an interest in meditation and led transcendental meditation sessions in the cavern beneath a boulder known as Giant Rock in Landers, California. In August 1953, Van Tassel declared that he had a taken a trip in a flying saucer from Venus. He would go on to write several books about his encounters and the channeled communications from beings on a fleet of spaceships orbiting the Earth, commanded by a being named Ashtar. Van Tassel also built a device called the Integretron. This device—a 16-sided dome built of wood and concrete, held together by glue—reportedly would rejuvenate the user, eliminating disease and allowing for a very long life. The radiological effects of nuclear war would be negligible, as long as one reached the safety of the Integretron in time. Van Tassel claimed that he received the concept and designs for the device from extraterrestrials. While George Adamski focused on how humanity could (and must) change to avoid disaster, Van Tassel's ideas—including the Integretron—offered an escape from the seemingly inevitable calamity. Both writers were influenced by and responding to the looming threats of the Cold War but differed in their confidence in humanity to avert calamity.

The Contactees promoted a vision of extraterrestrials that was overwhelmingly positive in nature. The extraterrestrials were like us—human—but more advanced. Through their enlightened philosophies and technological know-how they had transcended the petty rivalries and concerns of 20th-century Earth. Humanity, too, could become like them if they would only abandon the path of materialism, greed, division, and violence. Unlike organizations like NICAP, Contactees were much less concerned with whether or not the Air Force revealed the truth about the extraterrestrial presence. Why would it matter? For the Contactees, their own alleged personal experiences were more than enough evidence. If the Contactees had no real need for NICAP and its work, for its part NICAP was disdainful of Contactees and dismayed at the way their outlandish claims threatened to discredit the organization's serious, scientific efforts to expose the truth. There were, however, some commonalities. By the early 1960s, Adamski had adopted Keyhoe's concept of "The Silence Group" to describe nefarious efforts to keep hidden the truths that the Space Brothers shared. While Keyhoe focused his attention on the efforts of the CIA or the U.S. Air Force, Adamski chose a different target:

> What happened to the money-changers Christ drove out of the temple? It seems as though they have gathered over the centuries in Zurich.... The invisible reins of financial influence extend from Zurich to puppet organizations in every nation.[36]

Thus did Adamski connect the flying saucer conspiracy to more traditional anti–Semitic financial conspiracy theories. He would not be the last to do so.

By the mid–1960s, the Contactee movement had fallen out of favor in the face of exposes which demonstrated the falseness of many Contactee claims and photographs, including Adamski's. NICAP's scientific/political approach was winning out. Contacteeism, however, would remain part of the broad spectrum of UFO belief and the Disclosure Movement that emerged in the 1990s would integrate its influence, particularly the need for spiritual and social renewal and development.

Beginning in 1965, media coverage of a series of high-profile UFO cases led to increased public scrutiny of Project Blue Book's handling of sightings. The turning point was a wave of sightings that culminated in the spring 1966 UFO events over southeast Michigan. Dozens of witnesses reported sightings and, by the time Blue Book scientific advisor and astronomer J. Allen Hynek arrived on the scene in Dexter and Hillsdale, Michigan, the national media had descended. Rushed into a press conference, Hynek offered the possible explanation of "swamp lights"—lamination caused by the ignition of swamp gas—for some of the sightings. Despite Hynek asserting that he could not conclusively prove that this was "the full explanation of the sightings," the public's opinion would be set by the reporters who were relaying Hynek's words. As Hynek's biographer Mark O'Connell explained, the reporters "were all announcing to the world what the U.S. Air Force's number one UFO expert had just declared: that more than one hundred people in Michigan—policemen, college students, and civil defense authorities among them—had been duped by swamp gas."[37] The media subjected Hynek and his swamp gas explanation to outright mockery and Congress took more decisive action than it had in the past. Writing to the House Armed Services Committee, Representatives Weston E. Vivian (D–MI) and Gerald R. Ford (R–MI and House Minority Leader) criticized the Air Force's handling of the Michigan sightings and called for formal hearings.[38]

As a result of these Congressional demands, the U.S. Air Force established the University of Colorado UFO Project, which ran from 1966 to 1968. Often referred to as the "Condon Committee" after its director, physicist Edward U. Condon, the project examined hundreds of sighting reports from Project Blue Book, and sightings reported to private civilian organizations like NICAP and APRO. The study's goal was to determine whether or not there was scientific value in continuing to put resources into the UFO mystery. After two years, the report, which received wide exposure with a paperback edition published, concluded that "nothing has come from the study of UFOs in the past 21 years that has added to scientific knowledge. Careful consideration of the record as it is available to us leads us to conclude that further extensive study of UFOs probably cannot be justified in the expectation that science will be advanced thereby."[39] For the scientific community, the Air Force, and the mass media, the question was largely settled. During the remainder of the 1960s and into the 1970s, the Condon Committee report became the go-to source when UFO cases penetrated the public consciousness. The Air Force, relying on the report for its justification, closed Project Blue Book in 1970. As James W. Moseley, publisher of numerous UFO newsletters—notably *Saucer Smear*—from the 1950s until the 21st century, explained in his memoirs, "public interest in UFOs evaporated almost overnight.... NICAP ... had defined itself in terms of government cover-up and demands for disclosure and objective investigation.... People reasoned that it had gotten what it wanted, the answers were in, and that was that."[40]

During the 1970s, 1980s, and 1990s, a number of new trends emerged. The story of a crashed UFO near Roswell, New Mexico, in 1947 was the subject of a number of detailed studies which took advantage of new witnesses. Despite researchers routinely dismissing it during the previous decades, Roswell became firmly cemented in the public mind as the beginning of the modern flying saucer age and Kenneth Arnold's sightings of the same summer faded into the background. Ever more elaborate conspiracy narratives emerged, with tales of secret government collaboration with evil aliens which involved mass abduction of and experimentation on human test subjects. At the root of many of the UFO conspiracy theories that emerged in the 1980s was a secret government group of experts tasked with managing the cover-up of extraterrestrial contact, exploiting technology gained from crashed UFOs, and defending humanity (or at least the United States) against the extraterrestrial menace. The so-called MJ-12 papers were anonymously given to UFO researchers William L. Moore, Stanton Friedman, and Jamie Shandera in 1984. The document seemed to indicate that this group (Majestic 12) was established following the Roswell Incident. The MJ-12 papers have been the subject of much scrutiny, including an FBI investigation into the documents in 1988, finding that they were "fake."[41] Despite this, some UFO researchers have maintained that a Majestic 12 group existed, although it might not have been connected to a UFO cover-up.

Stories circulated about underground bases where aliens and humans worked side by side. These dark conspiracies became the public face of UFOlogy, with television programs like *The X-Files* and films like *Independence Day* illustrating this vision of elaborate government cover-up. In the late 1990s, a new narrative emerged that emphasized not only government secrecy but a decades long parallel governmental structure—again echoing the perennial "secret government" trope—that had been managing the UFO cover-up, concealing technology developed from crashed alien craft, and arranging for the abduction of humans in exchange for these boons.

The Disclosure Movement and Interplanetary Diplomacy

The UFO "Disclosure" Movement blended elements from a broad swath of UFO history. It combined the suspicions of a government cover-up that emerged via NICAP in the 1950s and 1960s with the optimism and socio-political consciousness of the Contactee movement. These two strands intersected with the more elaborate conspiracy theories of the 1980s and 1990s and, by the turn of the 21st century, converged in ways their forebears could never have imagined. Contactee-style stories overlapped with claims of terrestrial conspiracy and cover-up. New stories about benevolent star nations seeking to help humanity counterbalanced the dark stories about evil human cabals cooperating with sinister gray aliens; the new stories absorb the older ones, and hybrid narratives emerged. The Disclosure milieu is vast and in order to explore the scope of the field, this study will focus on two Disclosure advocates who come at the subject from divergent directions. Dr. Steven Greer popularized the term "Disclosure" as a shorthand for the ending of the UFO cover-up while Dr. Richard Boylan began his UFO journey as a therapist working with alleged UFO abductees and, gradually, came to elucidate an elaborate cosmo-political narrative placing himself in a key diplomatic role among the peoples of the universe—overall a much more radical and fanciful interpretation and presentation than Greer.

Steven Greer

Since the 1990s, Steven M. Greer, MD, has been one of the UFO Disclosure Movement's prominent figures. Calling himself "the father of the Disclosure movement," since the early 1990s, Greer has created and overseen a number of initiatives to spread his vision of extraterrestrial contact and to speed the inevitable disclosure of the alien presence. These initiatives have included the Center for the Study of Extraterrestrial Intelligence (CSETI), the Disclosure Project, the Orion Project and Sirius Technology Advanced Research. Through these initiatives, Greer promoted Disclosure but also used the issue of alien visitation to highlight issues of war and peace, government accountability, and environmental responsibility. Greer's work utilized a number of well-worn tropes from the history of UFO belief in the United States. Like the work of the Contactees during the Cold War, however, Greer's efforts combined alien stories with political and social concerns. He urged citizen engagement to effect change in politics and society, criticizing aspects of the *status quo*. Greer attributed the negative state of affairs in the world to the U.S. government's persistent cover-up of alien contact. In particular, Greer (and the Disclosure Movement more broadly) focused on the benefits that advanced technology allegedly sourced from extraterrestrial craft could bring to humanity if made public. While there are deep flaws in American society, Greer's work promoted the idea that improvement will happen and that humanity's future depends on the people of the world working for Disclosure, fighting against the efforts of those who would keep the truth of the aliens hidden away. Greer has targeted his various initiatives to different audiences and utilized a variety of approaches to appeal to groups ranging from those who might consider themselves part of the "New Age" sector to others who would identify as being more skeptical and materialistic.

One of Greer's earlier writings on the UFO situation was 1991's "One Universe, One People." In this brief article, Greer asserted that "the firmest, most enduring and transcendent foundation on which human unity is based then, is consciousness itself, for we are all sentient beings, conscious, self-aware, and intelligent," and that these principles "must be directed not only towards our fellow humans, but towards extraterrestrial people as well, for the same fundamental basis for unity which exists among humans also exists for the relationship between humans and extraterrestrials."[42] This broadly positive view of those from other worlds persisted throughout Greer's work and was very similar to the outlook of the earlier era of Contactees, who painted a vivid picture of a universe populated with beings like humanity, but more advanced, more wise, and more benevolent. In 1990, Greer established the Center for the Study of Extraterrestrial Intelligence (CSETI), which he described as "an international nonprofit scientific research and education organization dedicated to the furtherance of our understanding of extraterrestrial intelligence." This was a means to operationalize the ideas Greer laid out in "One Universe, One People."

CSETI had two key goals. The first was to establish "real-time diplomatic" relationships with extraterrestrials and "develop bilateral and human-initiated contact" with them. To accomplish this, CSETI launched the CE-5 Initiative. The other goal, to "educate all sectors of human society about this subject in a credible and non-harmful manner," was the responsibility of the "Project Starlight Coalition."[43] The CE-5 Initiative was named after the concept of the close encounter of the fifth kind, which Greer described as "conscious, voluntary and proactive human-initiated or cooperative contacts with ETI [Extraterrestrial Intelligence]." Greer discussed several aspects of the initiative and describes the ETI as "peaceful" and "benign." As to the perennial question of why these peaceful visitors from other worlds have not engaged in wide-scale, open contact with humanity, Greer explained that this is in humanity's best interest:

> ETI's enigmatic and elusive behavior may be understood as human-protective when viewed from their perspective: a war-torn, aggressive, nuclear armed and disunified Earth civilization must not receive further potentially harmful technologies until a lasting world peace and unity is achieved, and international human goals become peaceful, cooperative and unified in nature. Such a transformation will then indicate a readiness for a fuller contact and exchange between humans and ETI. We must respect and accept ETI's control and wisdom in this regard ... we may expect a certain limited nature to ETI contact so that the disruptive potential of such contact will be minimized. Certainly, a massive influx of ETI culture, technology, etc. would prove harmful to long-term human evolution if said influx was sudden or ill-timed. Though the exact limits of such contact are not known, we are probably destined to experience an expansion of these limits as human civilization evolves and grows in peace and unity, or at times of significant worldwide crisis.[44]

The CE-5 contacts between humans and ETI would be a step in a positive direction for expanded connections between their respective civilizations. The need for such a program is the consequence of the ongoing UFO cover-up. Looking back on the creation of CSETI and the CE-5 program in his 2017 book, *Unacknowledged: An Expose of the World's Greatest Secret*, Greer cites the mythical 1954 meeting between President Dwight Eisenhower and aliens as being the last time the U.S. government was engaged in an effort to "establish peaceful contact" with extraterrestrial beings. If there were later communications from aliens, Greer says, they "were most likely hijacked by the military industrial complex who did not want to disclose anything about UFOs and ETs to the public." This cabal had worked to keep this information way

3. The UFO Disclosure Movement

from elected officials, including the president, preventing them from knowing about "technologies that should have led to major advances across the globe." History took a wrong turn, and it was up to the people to repair the damage and set humanity onto a new path.

> What the military industrial complex could not do is stop civilians from initiating their own contact with the extraterrestrials. The ultimate disclosure is millions of people making OPEN, peaceful contact and documenting it on social media! ....
> Civilians establishing contact.
> Not the U.N.
> Not the State Department of the United States or the foreign ministries of European or any other nations on Earth.
> And most definitely not the secret government ... a cabal dominated by the military industrial complex that have been profiting off the secrecy since 1947.[45]

The key was to remove governments from the equation. Greer developed "protocols" for members of the CE-5 initiative to use when attempting to achieve contact with the extraterrestrials. Reasoning that there is a shared consciousness underlying all living beings, one protocol involved "group access to non-local consciousness followed by remotely viewing (through consciousness) ET craft or persons which may be passing by at a great distance or which may be nearby and phase-shifted beyond the visible spectrum of human sight." Using these techniques resulted in "an ET object literally 'popping in' overhead."[46]

Along with the CE-5, the Starlight Coalition's began in 1993 with a mission to facilitate UFO disclosure to humanity. Greer laid out a four-phase plan. First, the organization would collect evidence and testimony from "senior government, military and intelligence witnesses on the UFO/ETI subject" and also begin the process of "early pre-briefing of senior world leaders." As is typical of Disclosure narratives, the Starlight Project positioned people of high, official status as being a gold standard of testimony. Their goal is not only to prove the existence of extraterrestrial visitors to the Earth—although that question, in their minds, had been settled—but also to prove the existence of a government cover-up and to end that cover-up. The goal of briefing world leaders illustrates another aspect of Disclosure conspiracy narratives—the trope of a secret government controlling things behind the scenes and keeping elected officials in the dark. Once Project Starlight collected sufficient amount of evidence and testimony, they would begin the second phase, "the formal briefing process," which would target "the world's senior government, scientific, cultural and religious leaders and organizations" rather than the general public. Only when the world's leaders are fully informed about the ET presence will the public learn about it. This was phase three: "an event covered by the world's media where the best evidence and witnesses will be presented publicly, making an undeniable case for the reality of UFOs and ETI." Following this public revelation, Greer explained, humanity would enter the "Post Announcement Era," which would provide a "continued educational program"

> to ensure a calm, orderly and ultimately constructive assimilation of the knowledge that we are not alone in the universe, and to empower the world community to assume open responsibility for management of the subject, thus ending current exclusive covert control.[47]

Throughout the 1990s, Greer related accounts of his efforts to brief high level officials and publicly released copies of "briefings" he prepared for various figures, including presidents Bill Clinton and Barack Obama. Greer claimed that members of the anti–Disclosure cabal threatened him in 1992 at a UFO convention in Atlanta. When confronted by two cabal agents, Greer explained the goals of the CE-5 project, telling them that he had to develop ways to contact alien civilizations "outside governmental channels because the government was broken." The cabal members were not pleased with Greer's explanation. Greer recounted that "they informed me that it was none of my business and not to do it. My response was, 'Try stopping me.' We kind of had a 'mano a mano' in a hotel room until three in the morning."[48]

Clearly, Greer was onto something. Soon, he was in contact with "a trusted emissary" of "a senior CIA official" who told Greer to stay the course because, as Greer had suspected, the government could not accomplish the type of contact that Greer and his CE-5 project could, and his contact's alleged flattery positioned Greer as a necessary crusader and savior:

> Dr. Greer, do what you were planning on doing and don't give up. Someone's got to do this because it's completely out of control; moreover, someone's going to have to spearhead a contact protocol—right now, the system is completely dysfunctional.[49]

In 1993, after Bill Clinton assumed the presidency, friends of Justice Department official Webb Hubbell informed Greer that Clinton was hoping to figure out the truth of the UFO phenomenon while in office. Greer was also approached by "military people who were in favor of disclosure." Greer and these new contacts began to develop ideas for how to brief senior officials on the extraterrestrial presence. If this sounded like an unlikely plan, that is because Greer was, as yet, unaware of how the government actually worked:

3. The UFO Disclosure Movement

> This was back in 1992–93, when I actually thought we had a functional constitutional government. Since then I've learned it's all window dressing, that there's a parallel governmental process that operates completely independent of the people we elect.[50]

This highlighted Greer's growing acceptance of the standard "secret government" conspiracy theory that drove the Disclosure Movement. The visible, public government was not the real—or, at least, the only—government. The only way that this secret government could be defeated was for those within the government with direct knowledge of this extraterrestrial cover-up to openly testify to the truth. Since the government was not functional enough to allow this to happen, civilian groups—like CSETI and its Project Starlight—would have to facilitate the revelation of the truth.[51]

Within a short time, Greer had met with a number of influential people, including Laurence Rockefeller (of the politically prominent Rockefeller family) and John Petersen, who was a friend of then–CIA Director James Woolsey. Greer met with Woolsey on December 13, 1993, but not at CIA headquarters. Rather, the "briefing" could come during a dinner party at John Petersen's home with Greer, Woolsey, and their wives. Despite fearing that he was being set up, Greer and his wife went to dinner. At the end of the evening, Greer handed Woolsey a "white paper" he had prepared.

> Woolsey looked at me and he said, "How can we disclose something which we have no access to?" That was a very chilling question. If we were to push on this, it would unveil the biggest constitutional crisis in the history of the United States.

Greer often cited this December 1993 dinner party (or "briefing") with Woolsey as one of the key pieces of evidence not only that the extraterrestrial cover-up was real but that even the Director of Central Intelligence was unable to get to the truth. This narrative came under scrutiny in 1999 when Woolsey and Petersen sent Greer a letter expressing concern that he had published his account of the 1993 dinner party without giving the others present "the opportunity to comment":

> You portray this dinner party conversation during which the four of use listened to your views and politely asked questions as a "briefing" with a "cover story." You further assert that Mr. And Mrs. Woolsey reported a UFO sighting to you and agreed with your views. You include specific alleged quotations from them.
>
> None of this is accurate. You have portrayed politeness as acquiescence and questions as affirmations. Your conduct in this matter contravenes both accuracy and simple manners.[52]

When this letter became widely known in the UFO research community, Greer was forced to address the issue in an effort to reassert control of the narrative that he was the confidant of the powerful and well-connected. Greer contended that "Mr. Woolsey et al have a very selective memory of this nearly 3 hour briefing of a sitting CIA Director. If anything ... my description of the meeting is incredibly understated." He went on to explain that John Petersen, who "was working very closely with" Greer at the time, had characterized the dinner as a briefing. In response to the accusation that Greer's claims "contravened" simple manners, Greer pointed out that he had kept quiet about the dinner with Woolsey for several years despite many opportunities to publicize this vital information during his appearances on television and radio programs. Instead, Greer waited until Woolsey was no longer the CIA Director. He ended his statement with a flurry of self-righteous indignation:

> Good "manners" as it pertains to this subject means speaking the truth—and being willing to stand up for it. Good manners would be public servants such as.... Woolsey ... and others doing the right thing and working ardently for the truth to be told regarding UFOs and ETI. Good manners should mean being more concerned for the health of our democracy and the Constitution than covering-up the import and purpose of such a briefing. And good manners would be joining in the effort to disclose a matter which, once made public, would allow earth-saving technologies to be revealed which would halt the wholesale destruction of our eco-system....
>
> The current attempt to minimize, obfuscate or cover-up the purpose and details of this briefing with the CIA Director is quite disconcerting—and strange.... But now, perhaps the time has come for "we the people" to demand that current and former officials such as CIA Director Woolsey and the President be held responsible for the lack of action on resolving this most pressing problem. After all, we pay their salaries, provide their perks—and they represent us. It is not I who needs defense. My actions over these long years have spoken my commitment. But we still await action from our elected and appointed officials. As the earth groans under the weight of the errosive [sic] and corrupting influences of big money and special interests, I wonder just how much longer we shall have to wait....
>
> I think it is time that the American people demand that the waiting time be over.[53]

Greer positioned Woolsey's denial of the briefing as part of the broader UFO cover-up he was trying to end and changed the subject, turning the statement away from the briefing. Greer transitioned his argument into something of a referendum on the fundamental concept of his Disclosure efforts. He reiterated his key argument about the "public" elements of the government being unable or unwilling to take action. Disclosure must come via the work of the American people.

3. The UFO Disclosure Movement

Following the 1993 meeting with Woolsey (whatever may have actually occurred at that December dinner party) Greer continued his attempts to "brief" government officials and work for the public disclosure of the alien presence on Earth. To bolster his case and generate a cadre of witnesses and whistleblowers, Greer developed a legal theory that could possibly help. Greer argued that any national security oaths which might prevent people from disclosing what they know about the Extraterrestrial cover-up were, in fact, unlawful and non-binding due to the illegitimacy of the secret government that demanded such secrecy from members of the military and intelligence communities.[54] While Greer was by no means part of the sovereign citizen movement, the notion of selectively recognizing laws based on the perceived legitimacy of the government is a familiar sovereign citizen concept. Greer also sent a letter to President Bill Clinton, dated November 15, 1996. Copying Vice President Al Gore and a number of national security figures with a subject line of "Planned Disclosure on the UFO/Extraterrestrial Subject and National Security Oaths," Greer informed the president that Project Starlight had "identified several dozen former and current military, intelligence and defense contractor related witnesses to UFO/ETI events and projects." Their statements and testimony were appended to the letter and Greer warned Clinton that these witnesses would "provide open, public testimony on this matter in the very near future." While Greer was not asking Clinton for permission, he was requesting "a clear determination regarding their freedom to speak openly on this subject" and gave Clinton a deadline. On January 1, 1997, CSETI and Project Starlight would move forward with their public revelations, unless Clinton informs Greer "specifically that such witnesses to UFO/ETI related matters are still bound to silence will our plans for a disclosure by them be altered." They would also move forward if Clinton did not reply, interpreting this as tacit approval for the testimony to be made public.[55] Clinton, perhaps unsurprisingly, did not intervene and so Project Starlight evolved. Greer and his group of witnesses met with members of Congress in 1997, presenting their information. Nothing came of this, so between 1997 and 2001, Greer filmed the witness and whistleblower testimony and compiled it for sale.[56] This work culminated in the Disclosure Project. The Disclosure Project was a May 9, 2001, event at the National Press Club in Washington, D.C. This was the public revelation of testimony from Greer's witnesses and whistleblowers.

In addition to the live event in Washington, Greer and the Disclosure Project prepared a written brief and an *Executive Summary* of the Project and the evidence their witnesses presented, in April 2001. In the summary, Greer laid out the "implications" of the disclosure of the extraterrestrial presence. He framed it in terms of implications for "the environment, world peace, world poverty and the human future." He began by asserting that those who believe the question of "whether or not we are alone in the universe" is merely conjectural or academic are "wrong—catastrophically wrong." Before discussing those implications, however, Greer described exactly what his witnesses and whistleblowers would disclose. They would reveal that humanity was "indeed being visited by advanced extraterrestrial civilizations and have been for some time" and that "advanced spacecraft of extraterrestrial origin ... have been downed, retrieved and studied since at least the 1940s and possibly as early as the 1930s." These retrievals have led to "significant technological breakthroughs in energy generation and propulsion ... utiliz[ing] a new physics not requiring the boring of fossil fuels." These advances, if released to the public, had the potential to empower a new human civilization without want, poverty or environmental damage.[57] Before getting to the actual witness testimony, Greer summarizes the benefits for humanity in more detail. With regard to the environment, the Disclosure Project's "insiders and scientists" know the means and methods to replace "all forms of currently used energy generation and transportation systems." Anti-gravity and free energy would have benefits beyond the physical damage caused by the extraction of natural resources. There would be benefits to agriculture, reduced pressure on water supplies, a reduction in noise pollution, and the elimination of "resource depletion and geo-political tensions arising form competition for fossil fuel resources."[58] With regard to the environment, Greer explained, these benefits cannot come soon enough:

> Current human civilization has reached the point of being able to commit planeticide: the killing of an entire world. We can and we must do better. These technologies exist and every single person who is concerned about the environment and the human future should call for urgent hearings to allow these technologies to be disclosed, declassified and safely applied.[59]

Greer realized that the issue of revealing the truth of the extraterrestrial presence may not be compelling enough to rouse public action. By linking environmental issues with the issue of UFO Disclosure, Greer attempted to broaden the appeal of the Disclosure Movement to anyone concerned about the environment.

He took a similar approach in discussing Disclosure's impact on "society and world poverty." The technology that the secret government has scrounged from extraterrestrial sources would have a beneficial effect on world societies, leveling the playing ground between nations:

These technologies, because they will decentralize power—literally and figuratively—will enable the billions living in misery and poverty to enter a world of new abundance. And with economic and technological development, education will rise and birth rates will fall. It is well known that as societies become more educated, prosperous and technologically advanced—and women take an increasingly equal role in society—the birth rate falls and population stabilizes. This is a good thing for world civilization and the future of humanity.[60]

Greer argued that poverty is merely the result of access to resources; that poverty is chiefly, if not entirely, the result of scarcity and poor or flawed resource allocation. His view of poverty's causes and solutions was not a nuanced one. There was no discussion of the structural causes of poverty and the differences in causes of poverty in different parts of the world. Greer presented alien technology, adapted for human use, as a cure all, with little recognition of political issues. He did, however, recognize the potential for conflict:

The international community will need to put in place safeguards to prevent such potential geo-political rapprochement between the first and third world from devolving into bellicose and disruptive behavior on the part of the newly empowered.[61]

It will be the role of the United States, Greer explained, to "lead through strength," but without becoming domineering. In general, Greer argued that issues of peace and security may also be solved by the governments of the world openly embracing these wondrous technologies:

The real threat of war over a shrinking supply of fossil fuels in the next 10–20 years further underscores the need for this disclosure. What happens when the 4 billion people living in poverty want cars, electricity and other modern conveniences—all of which depend on fossil fuels? To any thinking person, it is obvious that we must transition quickly to the use of these now classified technologies—they are powerful solutions already sitting on a shelf.[62]

Like his discussion of poverty, Greer presented the perfectibility of the human condition through alien technology as a fait accompli, revealing that through this technology, problems can be solved almost immediately. A golden age is waiting. What has kept this golden age from materializing, of course, is a deeply embedded program of secrecy and suppression that kept this information hidden not only from the general public but also the elected and appointed leaders of the United States and other nations.

After he presented the promise that these technologies held, Greer delved into a précis of the history of UFO secrecy. It largely mirrors the standard narratives of UFO cover-up conspiracy theories, both those embraced by the Disclosure Movement and accepted within wider UFOlogical circles. During the 1930s and 1940s, governments (including that of the United States) came into possession of craft that had crashed. As the Cold War began in the late 1940s, "a concerted effort was made to figure out the basic science and technologies behind these spacecraft, primarily through the direct study and reverse-engineering of the retrieved extraterrestrial objects from New Mexico and elsewhere." The New Mexico retrieval was a reference to Roswell, but Greer kept this history broad and avoided getting bogged down in individual cases—particularly where his group of witnesses and whistleblowers might have been able to provide alleged first-hand knowledge. Greer presented his history of the cover-up as a higher-level overview which concentrated on the policies and trends that made up the suppression of extraterrestrial knowledge rather than a detailed account of the entire UFO phenomenon. During the 1950s, as governments realized the potential power of these alien devices, officials were concerned that possession of such technology "could tilt the balance of power in the nuclear arms race." Greer explained that "the theme of human geo-political dysfunction appears as a recurring feature of the secrecy related to UFOs." Thus the world peace that full Disclosure could achieve would not only be the result of the technological advances extraterrestrial knowledge could provide. Disclosure would also undo the damage wrought by decades of secrecy.

In Greer's account, the rot set in during the 1950s, as "substantial progress was made on some of the basic physics behind the ET craft energy and propulsion systems" and the projects were "increasingly 'black' or unacknowledged." As a result of the reverse engineering research being moved off the official books, there was less legal oversight of these projects. As Greer described it, the projects were removed from "legal, constitutional chain-of-command oversight and control." This did not only happen in the United States but in all nations where such reverse engineering was taking place, including the United Kingdom and the Soviet Union. This was the origin of a secret government—a cabal of insiders who were dedicated to retaining the secrets of the stars for themselves. "It does not matter how high your rank or office," Greer explained, "if you are not deemed necessary to the project, you are not going to know about it. Period." As well as disabusing readers and listeners of the notion that the president could simply declassify UFO information, Greer also explained that common conceptions of the UFO cover-up as either the result of worries that the public would panic at the knowledge or to hide the presence of an enemy alien force were both incorrect. In fact, Greer and the leaders of the Disclosure Project "know of no knowledgeable insiders who regard the ETs as a hostile threat." This positive characterization of extraterrestrial beings was part and parcel of the Disclosure/Exopolitical narrative and, going back further, has been a constant in Contactee and channeler circles since the 1950s. While Greer did not pioneer it, presenting an antagonist that is wholly human—the forces hiding the truth of extraterrestrial life—allowed him to keep the focus on terrestrial political and social issues.[63]

Greer went on to explain that starting down the path of secrecy in the 1950s led to the cabal greatly fearing the social, political, economic, and cultural changes that would occur were Disclosure to happen. Greer argued that the longer the delay, the more unpredictable the consequences of Disclosure may be. Despite this uncertainty, he urged those hiding the truth to bite the bullet for the good of humanity:

> To continue the secrecy and the suppression of these new energy and propulsion technologies means something far more destabilizing: the collapse of the Earth's ecosystem and the certain depletion of the fossil fuels on which we depend. And the growing anger of the have-nots, who are needlessly being deprived of a full and dignified life. There are no more generations to which we can pass this cosmic hot potato: we must deal with it and do what should have been done in 1950.[64]

The problem, as Greer presented it in 2001, went beyond the secrecy and extended to the "extraordinary things that have been done to maintain this secrecy" and the development of the secret government that maintained the secrecy. Greer did not mince words when he described the severity of the political situation and claimed that "the entity which controls the UFO matter and its related technologies has more power than any single government in the world or any single identified world leader." This secret government, in Greer's words, was semi-privatized and the embodiment of the threat suggested by President Dwight Eisenhower in his 1961 address on the growing power of the military-industrial complex. The phenomenal power of this cabal and the illegalities involved in perpetuating it provide another justification for the secrecy:

> The complexity of the compartmentalized projects, the degree of unconstitutional and unauthorized activity, the "privatization" (or theft) by corporate partners (the "industrial" part of the military—industrial complex) of advanced technologies, the continued lying to legally elected and appointed leaders and to the public—all of these and more have contributed to a psychology of continued secrecy—because disclosure would expose the greatest scandal in recorded history.

Thus there were several compelling reasons for the continued secrecy and cover-up, summarized by Greer as "global power, economic and technological control, geo-political status quo, the fear of scandal surrounding the exposure of such projects and their behavior."[65]

To illustrate the vast array of sensitive information the secret government continued to hide from the public, The Disclosure Project presented dozens of witnesses, with their testimony offered in the Executive Summary as well as at the 2001 National Press Club event. Many of the witnesses presented were not named but "described by their positions or occupations." Witnesses held jobs such as "Senior Air Traffic Controller," "Former Head of the British Ministry of Defense," and "NRO [National Reconnaissance Office] operative." In some cases, witnesses were identified only by the organizations for which they worked: "US Air Force," "US Strategic Command," or "New York Air National Guard." Witness credibility was based as much on the national security institutions with which they were affiliated as with the actual content of their testimony.

Greer designed the Disclosure Project's May 9, 2001, public National Press Club event to highlight the credibility of the Project's witnesses. The witnesses included retired military officers, government scientists, and NASA employees. Despite their credentials, some of the witness statements were far from detailed, such as this one from a "Dr. B":

> I know that some people I worked with did disappear on certain programs and were never heard from again. They just disappeared. There has been evidence of that all through my work. You know, that people go out on projects [and disappear]. But [to protect myself from this] I wouldn't go any further on a project because I could see something strange coming. So, a lot of people have disappeared you know, that are higher up.[66]

Dr. B revealed nothing of the kind of work he did, or what these programs were—in fact, he made a point to deny being in a position to know details about the project.

More specific was this statement from John Callahan, Head of Accidents and Investigations for the Federal Aviation Administration:

> This was one of the guys from the CIA. Okay? That they were never there and this never happened. At the time I said, "well I don't know why you are saying this. I mean, there was something there and if it's not the stealth bomber, then you know, it's a UFO. And if it's a UFO, why wouldn't you want the people to know? Oh, they got all excited over that. You don't even want to say those words. He said this is the first time they ever had 30 minutes of radar data on a UFO. And they are all itching to get their hands onto the data and to find out what it is and what really goes on. He says if they come out and told the American public that they ran into a UFO out there, it would cause panic across the country. So therefore, you can't talk about it. And they

are going to take all this data...." When the CIA told us that this never happened and we never had this meeting, I believe it was because they didn't want the public to know that this was going on. Normally we would put out some type of a news release that such and such happened....[67]

Much of the testimony at the briefing event centered on similar stories—government intimidation of UFO witnesses and those who had experienced alleged contact with alien intelligences or craft, or even just reported sightings during the course of their official duties. Some witness testimony addressed the culture of institutional secrecy within government organizations. The testimony of Donna Hare, described only as a "NASA employee" fell into this category:

> There was a point in time when I had some people come out and tell me I shouldn't talk about this. They didn't threaten to kill me but I got the message I shouldn't talk about it. But I'd already talked about it so much it didn't really matter anymore. And like I said at the [1997] congressional briefings, I really started feeling like this topic was like sex. You know, everybody knew about it but nobody talked about in mixed company.

Hare was one of the witnesses who, in addition to talking about the culture of secrecy in official circles, went out of her way to praise Greer and the Disclosure Project.

> I'm waiting to tell more whenever there's a congressional hearing where I could be protected. I trust Dr. Greer. I feel he's done everything he said he would do as far as protection, secrecy of what I give him, for now. I want it to come out when it's necessary and proper and can do some good. I don't want people going around that are trying to get rid of these people or hurting them or challenging them or making them so frightened they move away-like this one particular man I know of who has just disappeared off the face of the Earth. This one man, he has disappeared. I just don't want that.[68]

These allegations were significant because, if true, they logically led to the accomplishment of the Disclosure Project's goals. The allegations and statements not only testified to the existence of secret extraterrestrial-based technology but also to a long-standing cover-up and parallel governmental structure determined to preserve these secrets.

The 2001 Disclosure Project presentation, DVD, and briefing reports did not lead to the new age for humanity that Greer anticipated. He would persist, however, throughout the 2000s, compiling hundreds of pieces of witness testimony and alleged government documents about the reality of alien visitation, the existence of advance technology, and the secret government that kept these things hidden from humanity. He also wrote commentary on current events, weaving them into his argument for Disclosure. Within weeks of the September 11, 2001, terrorist attacks on New York City and Washington, D.C., Greer issued a statement in which he asserted that the Disclosure Project was more important than ever. The secret government's hoarding of information and technology meant that

> the valid, true, legal government of We The People is deprived of both technologies and funding that could have prevented the massive national security and intelligence failure that led to the events of 9/11.... Largely privatized, these operations have both the means and the technologies to have prevented 9/11. And yet they did nothing.

Greer positioned the Disclosure Project as a savior, saying that the organization "stands ready to provide Congressional and other government investigators with the insider witnesses" that can provide the means to end the cover up, putting advanced, alien-derived technology programs "back under the control of the legitimate government—where they can do the people some good." This would, he argued, be "the means to prevent another 9/11." Greer closed by proclaiming that disclosing the existence of extraterrestrial life and sharing the secrets of their technology would be "the most fitting memorial to those innocents who left this world on 9/11."[69] After 2010, Greer's efforts would shift to using elaborate documentary films to promote his Disclosure narrative, which remained largely focused on hidden technologies and their promise for humanity.

Richard Boylan

While having a lower public profile than Steven Greer, Richard Boylan's history within the UFO field spans three decades. His time in the extraterrestrial Disclosure realm has been a steady march from ideas well within the bounds of "mainstream" UFO research and belief to a prophetic, triumphal vision of UFO Disclosure and the inevitability of humanity's coming relationship with its "Star Visitor" neighbors. As with other exponents of extraterrestrial Disclosure, Boylan's claims involve accounts of "diplomacy" between the peoples of Earth and those of other planets. Boylan has, over time, increasingly placed himself at the center of these tales, weaving fantastic tales of alien interaction with humanity, with Boylan himself as the mediator between Earth and the Star Visitors.

On the "Biography" page of his website, Richard J. Boylan described himself as a "behavioral scientist, anthropologist, university associate professor (emeritus), retired clinical hypnotherapist, consultant, and researcher."[70] Holding a Ph.D. in Anthropological Psychology from the University of California at Davis, Boylan worked as a social worker, psychologist, and family therapist throughout the 1970s and 1980s.[71] Although he had been interested in the UFO phenomenon from a young age, his professional connection to the subject began in 1989, when four of his counseling patients claimed to have had extraterrestrial encounters. "I realized," Boylan later explained, "that I would have to look into this if I wanted to be a well-informed counselor." He established a "research project" in 1991. "I started my own research and found that there was almost nothing of scientific value published in this area," said Boylan,[72] who—on his CV—describes this as "research in cross-cultural psychological conditions, and clinical hypnotherapy,"[73] downplaying the extraterrestrial aspects of the "cultures" involved.

Boylan's findings from his hypnosis sessions with patients were different from the stereotypical tales of medical examinations and sexually tinged body horror. His patients experienced positive growth from their encounters and had pleasant experiences with the visitors. Boylan claimed that his patients "are aware of the motives, emotions, and communications of the ETs they're dealing with," and see their encounters "as a pioneering experience in interspecies contact rather than an unremitting horror show."[74] His first book on the subject, 1994's *Close Extraterrestrial Encounters* consisted of a number of alien contact accounts from his patients, and Boylan's own extraterrestrial contact experiences formed part of the evidence as well. Boylan focused heavily on the culture and characteristics of the various extraterrestrial species he and his patients met. He described them as placing "a very high priority on mental development of higher consciousness." They placed a much lower value on "the fervent acquisition of material goods and a high value on reverencing life in the man forms in which life manifests itself." Because of this viewpoint, "they are distressed by what we are doing by degrading the planet, and thus our own habitat, health and future." The alien races were also concerned about the condition and development of humanity's children, "particularly in those children in whom they have engineered a subtle genetic advancement."[75]

Boylan also offered a summary of what the extraterrestrials want humanity to know. He had gained this knowledge from his patients. Many of the lessons concerned conflict and Earth's future. Boylan shared some of the impressions his patients have received. These included:

"The ETs don't understand our constant quarreling and conflict."
"The ETs are here to help us."
"There will be profound changes in the next 10 years.... I get the feeling it will evolve into peace and harmony."

"There are coming cataclysms for California, and for the earth, but these are birth pains, transformation."

"They told me, 'we won't leave you in this state.'"

"I feel that I am helping usher in the Golden Age. They tell me, 'it'll be all right.'"

"The coming out will occur very soon. Those who are mentally prepared will fare well in the changes coming up soon—a real transformation."[76]

There was a prophetic quality to Boylan's presentation of these extraterrestrial encounters that came through in these impressions from his patients. Humanity must abandon its wasteful, warlike habits to make way for a better future.

This was not dissimilar to the messages of many of the Contactees of the 1950s and 1960s. Like the beings encountered by George Adamski and others, the beings encountered by Boylan's patients were flesh and blood (or the alien equivalent). While they were not always human or humanoid, Boylan emphasized that neither were these beings "spirits, etherial [sic] shades, mental evocations, interdimensional projections, or holograms."[77] Boylan updated the trappings to reflect the UFO culture of the 1990s and swapped the jumpsuited blond men of the 50s for the more exotic creatures. Another significant difference between traditional Contactee tales and the narrative Boylan presents was the sense of triumphal inevitability. The extraterrestrials were organized into a galactic alliance or government that Earth could one day join. While the aliens had "concerns" about humanity's violent ways and possession of nuclear weapons, inability to care for its children, and destructive behavior toward the environment, they would not *force* humanity to change. However, Boylan seemed certain that a golden age is coming. The aliens would help Earth get there. Indeed, they were working to "accelerate our development by genetic engineering."[78] True believers, "those who are mentally prepared," would be the winners in this new world. The Contactees presented humanity as having a choice: peace or war? This was the same choice other planets' inhabitants had to make and those space-faring people who visited Earth could not directly help, could not interfere. The future, back in the depths of the Cold War, was still in flux. For Boylan, the future was a fait accompli, and he was certain to be on the winning side.

Boylan, like most researchers in the UFO field, contended that there was a government cover-up. Boylan became convinced that he, personally, was being targeted for persecution in 1995 when he was accused of inappropriate behavior by a number of patients. The patients, women whose diagnoses included substance abuse and post-traumatic stress disorder resulting from childhood sexual trauma, accused Boylan of leading them into claims of extraterrestrial contact during hypnosis sessions as well as taking them to supposed UFO landing sites and UFO conventions. The accusation that gained the most traction in the UFO field was that Boylan (labeled "Respondent") held therapy sessions in a hot tub:

> Respondent said that part of the meeting would be in the hot tub and that no suits were allowed. Respondent did not allow bathing suits in his hot tub because he believed residual detergent in the suits left "soap scum" in the tub.[79]

State authorities stripped Boylan of his counseling credentials, which pushed him further into the UFO field. In a December 1995 open letter to the UFO community, Boylan insisted that he had been railroaded by the California psychology licensing board and was the victim of a vicious campaign of character assassination. This was no mere professional dispute, however, for the board, he asserted, had been influenced by number of military officials, such as expert witness Jeffrey Younggren, "a psychologist who had never treated extraterrestrial encounters, but is a current Army Colonel in a unit with its headquarters at the Pentagon." Boylan denied the accusations and lamented that "the Board chose to accept the false, coached allegations from persons, whom court records established had histories as (frankly) homely, grossly obese, lesbian, poor or welfare-dependent substance-abusers, who had been suing for money."[80] In March 1997, Boylan penned another open letter, addressed to "the UFO Cover-up." This letter represented a turning point, as Boylan moved from being primarily an abduction researcher to becoming a prophet of imminent UFO Disclosure.

In the letter, he differentiated between various levels of the UFO cover-up. At the lower level was "the relatively mild official U.S. Government cover-up." This was comprised of "a basic policy of Official Denial: denial of UFO knowledge, and denial of access to physical UFO evidence and to sensitive UFO documentation." This was the conception of the UFO cover-up that dated back to the 1950s, to Donald Keyhoe and NICAP's efforts to breech the "paper curtain" of official denial of the flying saucers. The higher-level cover-up, Boylan claimed, was carried out by "an outlaw, privatized, pseudo-governmental organization's aggressive and criminal Cover-Up." Boylan labeled this the "Treasonous Paragovernmental Organization's Cover-Up" or TPOC. Boylan accused the TPOC of numerous crimes, including "UFO shoot-downs, kidnapping, forcible interrogation, mind-control experimentation and torture of civilian experiencers and captured extraterestrials [sic], nationwide disinformation campaigns." He, personally, had been on the receiving end of the "vicious intimidation, assaults upon, or character assassinations" visited upon those who, like Boylan, have gotten "too close to the truth."

Both of these models of cover-up would soon, Boylan assured his audience, come to an end at the hands of the Star Visitors themselves:

> This Spring will occur the first of a series of formal Landings and Meetings between Extraterrestrial Emissaries and Earth representation teams. These Meetings are for the purpose of beginning open and official communication between the visiting Star Nations and the general people of Earth. Since the official governments of the technologically developed countries have declined to be honest with their people about extraterrestrial contact, the Star Nations are going directly to the people. The era of open extraterrestrial contact has arrived.

Boylan did not yet fully explain his own role in this, but would presumably be one of those UFO experts brought in to help manage the transition to this new age:

> a coalition of top civilian UFO researchers, astronauts, and former Special Projects military and intelligence officers will be meeting with Congressional staff to establish open, public, televised Congressional Hearings on the evidence these experts have seen and handled of UFO reality and extraterrestrial visitation. This effort will also extend to a United Nations presentation, and will not exclude a worldwide televised public press conference.[81]

Boylan then began to go down the road of intergalactic diplomacy. He moved beyond the speculation about humanity being able to join the Extraterrestrial alliance that he mused on in *Close Extraterrestrial Encounters* and was now at the point of predicting specific timeframes for these changes to occur. Boylan dealt with these changes—his vision for the future—in a fictional context in his novel *Project Epiphany*. The book concerned Boylan stand-in Roger Maguire and his discovery of a plan for an alien landing which would establish a diplomatic relationship between extraterrestrials and humans. This plan was in danger of being thwarted by JANUS, a rogue element of the U.S. intelligence community that "took itself private without Presidential authorization" and possessed "unsupervised control of the tens of billions of dollars which it had accumulated in 'black' accounts for use in conducting the UFO cover-up."[82] The novel ends with the revelation of this entire scheme and the United Nations Secretary General declaring that efforts to prevent contact between the aliens and humanity are bad. "But their bad example only underscores the necessity for all of us, individuals and nations of the Earth, to abandon the old ways of seeking advantage over one another. We need now to come together and acknowledge our oneness as one people of Earth. And we need to prepare ourselves now to meet our cosmic future."[83]

For the remainder of the 1990s and into the early years of the 21st century, Boylan used his platform to promote the stories of those whose claims bolstered his own as well as attempting to raise the issue of the potential for the raising of human consciousness through contact with the Star Visitors and humanity's need to become "cosmic citizens" in order to fully take part in the new order. Boylan saw an important role for children in this new cosmic order. In October 2000, he gave a talk at the annual convention of the Academy of Clinical Close Encounter Therapists on "Becoming a Cosmic Human." Taking the question of the existence of extraterrestrial civilization as a settled matter, Boylan discussed the future of humanity's place in the universe.

> As we move into Fifth World cosmic society—something a number of us have been giving some thinking to, and perhaps some of our thinking has been inspired by our star friends—it occurs to me that we need some new institutions to help nurture and build Fifth World society. We're not going to be able to do it with some of the existing institutions, because frankly most of them were created to perpetuate current society, Fourth World materialistic, industrial, earthbound-perspective society.

As for the institution that would be best suited to preparing a new generation to build a new world, Boylan believed that humanity needs systemic change. Schools, as they are, are not "built particularly to prepare citizens—our kids—for cosmic society." School curriculum, he argued, needed to change "to match that new agenda." This, however, would be a long-term project. In the meantime, Boylan suggested a stopgap measure. He looked back to the 1960s—"our revolutionary little warm-up dry run getting us ready for cosmic society"—and suggested setting up supplementary schools modeled on the freedom schools of the era which he described as places where the children of "oppressed black communities, and in urban centers of the oppressed black community" could "get a quick orientation to black history, culture, everything that was left out of the curriculum of the time." This will enable humanity's children to know "who they are, what they are, and what they know" and will give them "a sense of their role in this transition to building cosmic society."[84] Boylan had a long history of awkwardly attempting to draw parallels between racial inequalities on Earth and human fear of aliens. He has argued, for example, that "it would be a terrible thing if we were to begin a new and dark chapter in our history and, in place of the 'Yellow Peril' or the 'Red Menace,' define a new ET 'Grey Menace.'"[85] More offensively, Boylan has denounced accounts of alien encounters that portray the aliens in a negative light as an attempt to turn "visiting extraterrestrials into cosmic 'niggers' by attributing all manner of evil to them as a race." Boylan complained that such an attitude "is false, unjust, blatantly racist, and does not belong in civilized discussion about the different races of extraterrestrials."[86] As awkward and offensive as his comments were, however, it was a telling feature of his perspective on the extraterrestrial connection with humanity. Boylan's persistent use of race and ethnicity as descriptors placed the extraterrestrials on a similar biological and anthropological spectrum as humanity, rather than the extraterrestrials being utterly unlike earth people. This made human ascension to their level of consciousness seem more plausible; human development became a question of political and spiritual evolution rather than biological evolution. This evolution had, as Boylan explained, been helped by the genetic manipulation of humanity and was visible through the emergence of what Boylan calls "Star Kids."

These young people who were going to usher in the "fifth world cosmic society" were the subject of Boylan's 2004 book, *Star Kids: The Emerging Cosmic Generation*. Here, Boylan described the Star Kids in comic book terms, suggesting that the then-recent Marvel *X-Men* films were an example of "art imitating life." The mutant X-Men worked to protect the humanity that hates and fears them. This was—despite the "Hollywood hyperbole and over-dramatization"— a "roughly-accurate depiction" of the Star Kids.[87] Boylan defined a Star Kid as "a child with both human and extraterrestrial contributions to their origin" who had two human parents, are born on Earth, but whose makeup was partially alien. This is a variation on the phenomenon of "Indigo Children" sometimes connected to some NESARA adherents as discussed in Chapter 2. The "extraterrestrial contribution" to the Star Kids' genetic make-up came in a variety of forms:

> "Star Visitor genes spliced into human reproductive material" during an encounter between the parents and the extraterrestrials
>
> "During an encounter with the Star Visitors when the Visitors worked on an already-born child using their advanced biomedical technology," which would result in the subject becoming "more robust, psychic, super-intelligent, etc."
>
> A "walk-in," during which a sick or dying child's "departing human spirit/soul/personality" is "simultaneously replaced by a Star Visitor spirit/soul/personality."
>
> There could be situations where the "Star Visitor personality/consciousness comes in and shares space within the human with his own consciousness/personality as a dual, or alternating, consciousness."
>
> A Star Kid could be born by way of "the deliberately-chosen 'missionary' incarnation of a Star Visitor into a human body to accomplish important

work on Earth at this point in our history, bringing useful awareness, competencies, and advanced abilities, and lofty principles, values, and ideals to share and spread here." This, Boylan asserts, is "the most prevalent" origin of Star Kids.[88]

The Star Kids, Boylan explained, had a number of talents and characteristics, including psychic powers, heads that are so large they require Cesarean section births, "cross-species communication," and the ability to affect electrical devices. The Star Kids may or may not be aware of their true nature, so their education must begin by ensuring they are "awakened" by accepting that they are a Star Kid, learning about what this means, activating their special skills and embarking on their mission on Earth, including "collaborating with other ... Star Kids to build the natural network of Fifth World builders."[89] In 2004, as part of his research, Boylan undertook a study to determine the number of Star Kids in the general population. His methodology was remarkably subjective. The earliest phase of his research utilized

> random informal sampling on several continents, utilizing detection methods such as the size of children's auras, the degree of precocious development and abilities in children, high intelligence, novel thinking styles, pronounced psychic abilities, and the large dimensions of their bodily energy fields, etc.

Boylan conducted "surveys," of young people, attempting to obtain a diverse sample by going to Disney World, "a Wal-Mart in a poverty area of South Sacramento, where there is a substantial mix of ethnicities," and "an area of Sacramento notorious for violent crime, hard-drugs trafficking, and gang drive-by shootings." Observing children in the area, Boylan used dowsing rods to detect Star Kids.

> These dowsing rods are used to compare the relative sizes of the bio-electromagnetic-photic fields around an individual if they are a Star Kid or Star Seed adult versus the size of their field if they are an ordinary human. As you might expect, the bio-electromagnetic-photic field, (what I also call their "energy signature,") around a Star Kid is so considerably larger than the one around an ordinary human than there is no chance of confusing the two.

For quality control purposes, he "intermittently cross-checked with a visual survey of the person's aura, to determine whether comparative radius of the person's aura was consistent with comparative radius of bio-electromagnetic-photic energy around a given person." Using these methods, Boylan concluded that, as of 2004, 96 percent of children 12 and under in the United States were Star Kids.[90] With this massive number of Star Kids—which does not include Star Kids (and adult "Star Seeds" over the age of 12)—surely the new cosmic age is coming soon.

Boylan also informed the Star Kids and their families about the "Geopolitical Context" they will have to navigate. In this chapter, he explained the Cabal. They are, he described, "a claque of global-scale plutocratic manipulators who use their immense wealth, prestige and power to control governments and economies to perpetuate their stranglehold on global society." The Cabal was made up of "the most selfish, megalomaniacal, and sociopathic individuals, some of whom are big-shots in the Bilderberg Council, the Council on Foreign Relations, and the Trilateral Commission global policy-making groups." Boylan's Cabal was comprised of the same shadowy groups that have haunted conspiracy realms since the earliest days of the Cold War. This group was responsible for the global UFO cover-up, which it managed through "its proxies on some of the seats in the Special Studies Group of the U.S. National Security Council, the group which controls official U.S. government UFO and Star Visitor information and access, and conducts the *government-authorized* UFO Cover-Up."[91] Boylan did not spend much time on the Cabal in *Star Kids*, mostly providing context and background to the forces that might be opposing the Star Kids in their mission.

Boylan's Star Kids were also more advanced than normal humans in terms of their understanding of sexuality. Here, Boylan turned over the narrative to a Star Kid (the pseudonymous "Aether Thetan Dragonwolf") for an explanation of Star Kid sexuality:

> This new sexuality is called spiritsexuality. It is not limited to Star Kids and not all Star Kids are spiritsexuals. In this sexuality, people choose a mate on spiritual, emotion, mental, psychic, and magickal [sic] vibrations. Physical sex will probably occur between such couples, but to them it is only an artistic expression of their love for one another and not the reason that they are together. It is a luxury to have sex, but not a major need.
>
> Some confusion may occur because spiritsexuals are not concerned with gender and neither are bisexuals. This may lead some to believe that these two sexualities are the same. In fact, they are not, because in spiritsexuality, physical attraction is least important, and bisexuals find physical characteristics important. [92]

This "spiritsexuality," Boylan argued, "leapfrogs over the current interminable debate over heterosexuality versus homosexuality" and "even outlines a new level of relationship formation and relationship conduct which transcends concerns over gender and physical sexual expression." Boylan explained that he is acquainted with several "transgender Star Seeds" and believed that "the trans-gender issues come up because of reincarnation life path trajectories which do not always mesh effortless from one lifetime to the next." As with concerns about the environment and issues of human conflict and war, Boylan framed issues of gender and sexuality in terms of humanity's increasing connection to and interaction with these extraterrestrial beings. Another example of the way in which Boylan imparted extraterrestrial meaning to disparate topics was his assertion that an adherence to "naturism" is indicative of being fully attuned with the coming Fifth World Society. Writing, he says, from a "traditional naturist beach," Boylan reported that he is "stark naked" and spending time with "30 other stark naked people." What is the deeper meaning of this? Boylan explains that near him, "a lively coed game of frisbee being played by seven high-energy people at the edge of the water." One of the people, "a shy teenage boy," is the only young person who is not nude. "Perhaps not coincidentally," Boylan reported, "he is the only one whom the dowsing rods I carry indicate is not a Star Kid." He admitted this was not a scientific study, and that not all Star Kids were naturists, and not all naturists were Star Kids, however he believed that Star Kids and Star Seeds "find the nature-affirmation and the underlying personal and social values of naturism very appealing," and that these aspects of naturism are "congruent with the consciousness and other values which Star Kids possess."[93]

Unlike many adherents of conspiratorial narratives, Boylan took active steps to bring about his vision of the future by working directly young people thought to be (or thought by their parents to be) Star Kids. Boylan conducted summer camps. These included activities largely modeled on various New Age beliefs, such as this session:

> Psychic exercises teaching, practice demonstration, sharing: e.g.,—Chakras Cleansing. —Aura Viewing. —Psychometry Exercise. —Remote Viewing Exercise. —Experiencing our Spirit Self. —Silent Communication—Telepathy Exercise.

Other sessions were devoted to activities appropriated from Native American culture:

> Native American Pipe Ceremony, Star Kids (and Star seeds) prayer circle.... Native American spiritual Star Elders ceremony, with smudging with sage, sacred pipe prayer ceremony, meditation, drumming and invocation. Invoking of the Blue Star Kachina (Star Visitor remembered in Hopi tradition) to hasten her return.[94]

Boylan has also run weekend workshops with similar activities, as well as Star Kid education on these young people's role in the coming changes. He summarized these changes—what he calls "the time of transition"— in terms of how Star Kids are going to need to respond to them. Boylan described this as "a time of regional major geophysical upheavals, (such as volcanic eruptions, major earthquakes, huge tsunamis, dramatic weather changes, etc.)" There would also be political and geopolitical aspects to the time of turmoil with "regional wars, nuclear detonation(s), biological warfare epidemics, massive famines, crop failures, economic crashes" all taking place.

Writing in 2004, Boylan predicted that the time of transition would occur before 2012. The events and the timeframe had been revealed "by the Star Visitors to experiencers" and through "indigenous people's [sic] prophecies." People around the world who lived under democratic political systems will "realize that the government no longer represents *legitimate* authority." Since, as his dowsing rod studies had demonstrated, "Star Seeds and Star Kids may quickly be forming a majority of the population," they will come to realize that the governments of the world do not have their best interests at heart. They will "chose to disempower the governmental machine, and set up alternative communities based on common values." Boylan asserted that he is not advocating for or predicting a violent uprising or sedition. The Star Kids and Star Seeds, he argued, possessed "morally superior ways to change things that need changing."[95] Boylan gave the Star Kids and Star Seeds—humans who have extraterrestrial attributes in one form or another—a central role in remaking the world into a better place. Unlike the legal and political predictions or forecasts of NESARA adherents, Boylan's narrative of the future was prophetic. It was based on received wisdom from an unearthly source. Some of this was traditionally prophetic—the vision of things to come has been handed down in "indigenous" prophecies. The extraterrestrial aspects were significant because unlike many UFO Disclosure narratives, it was handed down expressly to Boylan from the Star Visitors. In *Star Kids*, he shared what he learned from the extraterrestrials in 2003.

Boylan reported that blue-skinned Zeta Reticulan aliens had, in centuries past, assisted in building the pyramids using anti-gravity technology. These beings, and their fellow extraterrestrials with whom they are in contact, were displeased by the "developed countries" and the UFO cover-up they perpetuated "despite Star Visitor repeated requests to inform the populace of contact and their presence." The aliens, however, were also concerned by "the wars and bombings which our supposedly-civilized population persist in" and felt the need to address the problem. The Star Visitors were going to cease their calls for Earth's governments to abandon the UFO cover-up. Likewise, their individual contacts with humans, in an attempt to spread the word of their presence, "[were] proceeding too slowly." What was their hurry? The year 2012. For it would be in this year that "a time-loop for Earth will reach the end of its cycle." Here, Boylan connected his UFO Disclosure

3. The UFO Disclosure Movement

narrative to then-current predictions that the year 2012, the supposed "end of the Mayan calendar" would herald the beginning of a new phase of human consciousness. This new phase would also involve calamity, from which the Star Visitors would save humans, but their success hinged on humans being prepared to accept their help:

> The populace of Earth needs to be informed about the Star Visitors, so that they will be psychologically and socially prepared, when it is time for the Visitors to appear openly in a large-scale public way, and when they come to accomplish limited temporary retrievals of certain groups of people from zones at risk.[96]

Since time was short, the Star Visitors were attempting to engage in "public close encounters," appearing to groups of people rather than to individuals. This, Boylan predicted, "will cause the implosion of the UFO Cover-Up" and that the project would begin no later than 2006. The eventual wide-scale public revelation of the Star Visitors would have an effect on the religious beliefs of the public:

> When the Star Visitors return, many of the population will interpret the luminous humanoid (Pleiadean, Altairean, etc.). Visitors as angels or saints. Further, at a certain point in the foreseeable future, the individuals that have been historically know as Jesus and Mother Mary will return also, along with others also known on Earth as Great Teacher avatars. The churches will have a lot of explaining to do, when supposedly divine or saint figures descend from the sky and step out of starcraft. At that point, the churches' distortion of original messages will become obvious. The Visitors are working with religious leaders to educate and prepare their peoples for this return. But, like the leaders of the civic governments, church leaders generally are too timid to make public declarations to their congregants in the current government-sanctioned climate of cover-up and ridicule.[97]

Here, Boylan's prediction harkened back to Contactees, such as those who channeled various extraterrestrials that were, in reality, "Ascended Masters." Boylan linked human spiritual traditions to his teachings on the extraterrestrials but at the same time passed judgment on "the churches." The coming of the Space Visitors would shake up human religion and spirituality as well as its political affairs.

In addition to their political organization, Boylan's Star Visitors possessed a moral and ethical system far in advance of those human cultures possessed. The "11 Universal and 11 Spiritual Laws of the Cosmos" were a set of principles divulged to humanity by the Star Nations, "the governing organization of our Milky Way galaxy" which "conducts Star Trek–like outreach expeditions to potentially inhabited star systems." The laws, or principles, consisted of eleven paired concepts. These ranged from the very broad ("Universal Principle of Change/Spiritual

Principle of Growth") to those that were explicitly linked to New Age spiritual concepts ("Universal Principle of Light-Sound Vibration/Spiritual Principle of Intuition") or paranormal phenomenon ("Universal Principle of Perception/Spiritual Principle Future Sight"). When they encountered these inhabited planets, Boylan explained, they imparted the wisdom of the "11:11 Principles," which were "the highest spiritual information they can share." Boylan argued that these principles "are not couched in the Thou Shalt/Not language of Human civil and religious laws" but are "universally-valid, self-evident Principles grounded in the natural law. In the fundamentals of consciousness, and in the connection of each intelligent lifeform [sic] to Source/God." These laws were revealed to humanity via "interstellar Symbolic Language glyphs" inscribed into a piece of wreckage from the craft that crashed at Roswell in 1947. Boylan discovered this when he sought a translation of the glyphs:

> Ihanktowan Dakota (Yankton Sioux) Chief Standing Elk/Golden Eagle took Dr. Boylan s photocopy of the Roswell craft symbols into an inipi (sacred lodge), asked guidance from the Tunkasilas (Dakota word for the Grandfather spirits), spiritual persons from the stars, and learned that the symbols stood for the 11 Universal Principles ... and 11 Spiritual Principles which all Star Nations cultures accept as their common philosophical and spiritual foundation.[98]

Boylan's use of a supposed Native American connection to provide some manner of legitimacy for his claims about alien spiritual laws is not unique in the UFO field. Boylan's use of this trope—which blends the "Ancient Aliens" approach of reinterpreting myth with a tinge of cultural appropriation—was part of his broader cosmos-building and added layers of detail to this tales of the Star Visitors. He invited readers to "inform" themselves "on the ancient information given to the Hopi and Zuni tribes by the thin-framed, articulated-limbs star race, the Gansplicoids, whom the Hopi Indians call 'the Ant People.'"[99]

In 2005, Boylan revealed on his website that the Star Nations had held a hearing on the Cabal's behavior. In his "Report on Sept. 29, 2005 Formal Hearing and Indictment of the Cabal on Violations of Universal Laws," Boylan reported that a variety of figures, including Star Visitors and Star Seeds (including Boylan in his role of Councilor of/for Earth) presented a variety of evidence about the Cabal's activities. Boylan himself testified about the ways the Cabal had violated Universal Law:

> The Councillor of Earth presented Cabal violations of the following Universal Laws: Law of Free Will (citing the hundreds of victims of intimidation and coercion he has interviewed), Law of Change (citing Cabal obstruction of Earth's progress), Law of Movement and Balance (citing the emotional,

mental and spiritual imbalances caused by Cabal torture and information suppression), Law of Innocence, Truth and Family (citing especially the wholesale Cabal sexual and psychological abuse of children to turn them into mind-control sex and psychic slaves and intelligence couriers, and the wholesale Cabal disinformation campaigns), Law of Life (citing Cabal murders and harvesting the life energies of ritual victims), and the Law of Love (citing wholesale perversions and MILABS gang-rapes of kidnapped civilian victims during faked alien abductions).

The Cabal was found guilty—what did this mean for the Earth? Boylan explains that the Star Visitors will be able to work against the Cabal more actively, speeding up Earth's cosmic development. And after the Cabal is gone?

> There will be no more obstacle to our task of ushering in the long-prophecied [sic] Fifth World, a cosmic, just, non-materialistic, peaceable, extended-family society. Such a Fifth World will incorporate the soon-to-be-liberated benefits of such elements as clean non-petroleum energy, psychotronic healing machines, ZPE-powered hydroponic food-growing machines, gravity-shielded superfast airliners and sea freighters, and the immense store of spiritual, metaphysical and scientific knowledge that the Star Visitors wish to have publicly shared with the people of Earth.[100]

There is still a struggle to come, though. The Cabal will not go quietly. Boylan continued his ongoing account of human-Star Visitor relations in his 2012 book, *The Human-Star Nations Connection: Key to History, Current Secrets, and our Near Future*. In this account, Boylan went into greater detail about the relationship between the Star Visitors and humanity and what this relationship means for the future of the planet. The book was largely comprised of reprinted material that originally appeared on Boylan's website and in emailed announcements to his followers. Boylan also shared details about his own connection to the Star Visitors and his place in the coming age, describing his role as a liaison between Earth and the Star Nations. The Star Nations, he explains, are "the federation of intelligent civilizations of space."[101] This conception of an outer space coalition of alien planets was, again, not dissimilar to ideas presented in the Contactee literature of the 1950s and 1960s. As Boylan gave himself a role which included active communication with the extraterrestrials, he stepped into the shoes of some of the Contactees that came before him. In doing so, he established an alternate narrative not only of human history but of then-current events. Like promoters of the NESARA narrative and of the QAnon theories to come, Boylan predicted the future and explicated a hidden present based on a suppressed past. His predictions and forecasts would come to pass, but because of the machinations of the Cabal orchestrating the conspiracy against UFO-truth, the great mass of humanity was unaware of what was truly happening. Boylan presented an alternate reality and attempted to persuade readers that an extraterrestrial golden age was at hand.

Boylan's career as an interstellar diplomat began in early 2005. He explained that he was chosen as "the Councillor of/for Earth." When the Star Nations, he explained, believed that a planet's population "has developed to a point of readiness for cosmic contact" they will choose a person from the planet to represent their people on the Star Nations' High Council—their governing body. As a Councilor, Boylan described his duties as including "both representation and communication." This meant that he is "the official communication pathway to bring overall Earth issues to the High Council" and represented "humankind and Earth official to Star Nations for matters of policy development by its High Council as concerns Earth. And I represent Star Nations in official matters to the people of Earth." Boylan's description of the job seemed to suggest that the Councilor position worked for both parties, which was an odd sort of diplomatic position. In any case, Boylan's positions on issues usually favored the wishes of the Star Nations' Council. His job of communicating with the people of Earth was complicated by "the Cabal's choke-hold on the media" which "prevents the kind of ready and truly comprehensive sharing" of messages from the Star Nations. He asserted that "things are changing" but, until the Cabal's iron grip on power was broken, Boylan would primarily be communicating with visitors to his website and subscribers to his e-mail announcements.[102]

Boylan's career as the Councilor of/for Earth was foreordained. Speaking in the third person (and then switching back to first-person at the end), Boylan explained the process:

> A member of High Council volunteered to incarnate as a Human and to grow up to full maturity about the time that Human society was reaching this critical threshold for Earth.... Because that Councillor who incarnated as a Human was not immediately evident in his Human form, Star Nations sent down another Councillor, Asheoma to find him.... Asheoma spent many years searching and in late February, 2005 found him. Asheoma approached the Human-Incarnate and asked him if he was willing to accept appointment as Councillor of/for Earth. I consented.[103]

Thus, Boylan granted himself a dual nature: human, but with the soul or consciousness of one of the extraterrestrials. Asheoma was able to identify Boylan through his "longtime activities to educate people about Star Visitors" including his work with Star Kids and the online platforms through which he communicated with his followers. Boylan went on to explain how the Star Visitors have used the "almost-1500-member

3. The UFO Disclosure Movement

global community" of his email list to assess human attitudes to questions such as "whether typical Humans would welcome Star Visitor environmental scientists to help remedy Earth's environmental crisis. (They would.)" While there were several "Star Nations Help Humanity" storylines that Boylan recounted in *The Human-Star Nations Connection*, this tale of alien scientists who came to Earth to help with humanity's environmental concerns is a useful summary of Boylan's overall narrative.

In June 2007, Boylan contacted his followers via his email list. He announced that a group of Star Visitors needed to make a new home on Earth "because their current world will not be suitable for habitation much longer." Boylan requested that his followers vote on the issue, asking "whether the general people (as distinct from Cabal-controlled governments) would welcome them." The results, unsurprisingly, were overwhelming in support of the Star Visitors' arrival, with only 0.04 percent saying "no." Armed with this "overwhelming mandate," Boylan and his Star Nations contacts agreed to a small group of 12 beings from the planet Altimar visiting Earth. Fortunately, they possessed "hybrid lungs and musculoskeletal structure that enable them to come to Earth without needing devices to adapt to Earth atmosphere and gravity." The dozen Altimarians are scientists going to work with human scientists "and others we specify who were not operating from egotistical orientation" to "clean up Earth." Boylan provided brief biographies of the visiting scientists, along with their chosen human names, in a manner reminiscent of a film treatment.

> **Amanda** is a *Communication Specialist*, and will work with translations and language problems such as helping clear up misunderstandings, and reporting issues between Human Specialists and Teams and the Star Nations Team. She works with communications of every sort by way of telepathy, whether it be with the Earth elementals, with various species or whatever.[104]

The results of work the Altimarians were doing "will be open soon enough to public view, and this will help to dissolve the UFO Cover Up." In response to concerns about the human response to these changes, Boylan explained that he told the Altimarians that humanity was "ready and welcoming," as the poll of his email newsletter list subscribers had shown. The Altimarians had a simple message for humanity, as proclaimed by Communications Specialist Amanda: "We come in peace, to help."[105] In January 2008, the Altimarians arrived. They worked with anti–Cabal human allies to provide alternatives to fossil fuel and nuclear energy production as well as dismantling harmful devices being used by the Cabal to destroy the Earth. In addition to those efforts, Boylan engaged in several "joint psychic exercises" using the telepathic assistance of his Star Kid and Star Seed allies—set to accomplish great victories against the work and thwarting the Cabal's plans for humanity. This included destroying conspiracy-theory favorite technologies like the HAARP array[106] and "chemtrails."[107] Boylan and his allies also engaged in exercises to "stop an impending Cabal Global-Plague biowar operation,"[108] "deflect an inbound potentially-devastating asteroid by telekinesis,"[109] and other similar adventures. Boylan's summaries of these noble offensives against the Cabal relied upon readers accepting Boylan's word that the threat as well as the psychic elimination of the threat actually happened. Rarely did these threats to humanity had a basis in events in the news. When they did, such as the case of the 2009 H1N1 virus, Boylan presented a psychic mission that is similarly unverifiable, asking for psychic help to "neutralize the lethal-precursor genetics bioengineered into the Cabal's H1N1 Variant-2 virus to trigger a fatal reaction in persons immunized with Swine Flu Vaccine."[110]

Boylan has continued to publish post–2012 updates to his website, always following a consistent pattern of "revealing" what the Star Visitors/Star Nations were doing and how the Cabal was futilely attempting to stymie them. One example of the persistent, if repetitive, optimism of Boylan's vision for the future of humanity is a brief article on his website that first appeared in April 2016. It was titled "2017: The Cabal's Last Stand: Star Seeds' Coming Victory in a Peaceful 'Velvet Revolution.'" Boylan asserted that "aware Star Seeds and Star Kids" are actively at work improving society. Their work will lead to a "revolution" that will "eventually sweep through global society like the Hippie [sic] Revolution of the 60's did, and even more so." Boylan explained that although the "Cabal," which he described as "dark-energy global plutocratic oligarchy," was fearful of the change and would resist it, he remained confident that "their end is coming." The conflict between these "light" and "dark" sides, Boylan claimed, would "escalate to a peak in 2017" and that this "lightworkers-versus-Cabal End-Game struggle" would become visible, playing out across the globe, in ways that might not be readily apparent. This struggle is the result of the Cabal's "escalating resistance to Star Seeds' and other lightworkers' efforts to improve global society." The bad guys' "backs are to the wall" and they are desperately going to use "their Cabal-nurtured terrorist assets to create disruption through fake–'Islam' jihadist/terrorist violence." This claim echoed a conspiratorial trope that had become almost routine in the 21st century: the narrative of the false-flag attack. From the September 11, 2001, attack to the right-wing assault on the Capitol building on January 6, 2021, allegations that terror attacks are used by those in power to misdirect and disinform the public with the goal of implementing otherwise illegal or unpopular policies, have been predictable whenever politically charged violence has taken place. Here, Boylan used the same technique, painting terrorism as being sponsored by the Cabal and "their financed stooges: Al Qaeda, ISIL, Boko Haram, Chechen extremists, Al-Shabaab, etc." The Cabal is also controlling humanity by means of "trans-national financial manipulations, their international drug trade cartels, sex trafficking, and rigging elections to foist their politician proxies onto the public." These concerns reflected those of other conspiratorial communities, including NESARA and QAnon, as does Boylan's position that through the triumph of the light-workers—their "revolution" is all but inevitable.

In addition to conventional terror and violence, the Cabal will also "sneakily manipulate" those in power, causing them to create "conditions of chaos, deprivation, marginalization, and intimidation"—all of which serve to keep the Cabal in power. These efforts, along with use of the military will serve to "prolong the status-quo where they are on top." The turning point, he claimed, will come in "early 2017." At that time, Star Seeds and Star Kids will "join together into bands of light-warriors using psychic tools, internet wizardry, social media, music messaging, and political organizing." They will form into "lightworker action groups" in order to train and defeat the Cabal. The lightworkers' psychic skills are the most important tool they have to "confuse and subdue" members of the Cabal, who will be neutralized by "non-corrupt law enforcement and national/transnational security forces." The lightworkers' "battle cry," according to Boylan, "could well be: 'Use the Force, Luke." Boylan's reference to "non-corrupt" law enforcement personnel is a standard trope of positive, or triumphalist conspiracy narratives—like the NESARA "white hats" or government "insiders" like Q. The fulfillment of these conspiratorial prophecies rely upon a cavalry at the ready, just over the horizon, prepared to sweep down and assist the true believers in making their visions come to fruition. Boylan connected the work of these Star Seeds to "the 'new' paradigm demonstrated by Mahatma Gandhi, Martin Luther King and Cesar Chavez." The Star Seeds' work is fundamentally non-violent and the actions they take against the Cabal "will be done in accordance with the 11 Universal Laws and the 11 Spiritual Laws of the cosmos." Fortunately, because of their special powers—"precognition, intuition, reading others' energy fields, remote viewing, future-seeing, telepathic remote-influencing, and telekinetic defensive maneuvers"—casualties among the Star Seeds and Star Kids will be low. One danger, however, would be the "Cabal infiltrators" posing as Lightworkers, but overall, Boylan was upbeat. "Before 2017 is over, the Cabal will basically be losing the struggle. Their global power empire will be well into the process of being dismantled." Boylan closes the article with a final call to action for the enlightened human readers:

> Prepare now, get active, and connect with others of the light side. Seek out what you can do to help release Earth from Cabal control. Help build a transformed, family-like global society, and thus create the conditions for Humankind to fully flourish as a remade society ready for its cosmic destiny.[111]

The "Velvet Revolution" did not happen in 2017, but Boylan was undeterred. Changing nothing else about the page, he replaced all instances of "2017" in the article with "2018," without changing the name of the actual file on the website, which remained "2017caballaststand.html."[112] When 2018 came and went without a revolution, he updated the document to read "2019."[113] In 2020, heading into 2021, Boylan did not bother updating the year within the article (it remained 2019) but did update the link on the homepage to read "2020–21: the Cabal's Last Stand: a Revolution by Star Seeds Will Sweep Away the Cabal Oligarchs, their Minions and their Empires."[114] Boylan offered no explanation for why the revolution had not yet occurred, instead he pushed on with multiple claims, increasingly brief and combined with glosses on how current news stories illustrated the truth of the Star Visitors' presence and links to other people's online videos, when they bolstered his claims. In the autumn of 2020, this item appeared on his website:

> Soon peaceful Visitors from the stars will arrive in a 20-mile-long mothership, which will hover over United Nations Headquarters in New York City for two hours. The purpose of the visit is to make clear that there are other people in our galaxy, and that "UFOs" are real. The peaceful hover will provide an opportunity for many to see an actual extraterrestrial spaceship clearly and take pictures of it. Then the ship will depart.
>
> Later some Star Visitors will return to talk with UN leaders and Delegates about being of assistance, including help with fighting the COVID-19 pandemic. Star Nations, the organization of peaceful civilizations in our Milky Way Galaxy, hopes very soon to sign a Treaty of Peace and Friendship with United Nations (Earth).[115]

This announcement seemed to contradict Boylan's long-standing claims that the contact between various alien nations and Earth-based government was decades old and, as of this writing, Boylan has not confirmed nor expanded upon this amazing public display of extraterrestrial support.

Steven Greer and Richard Boylan were not the only exponents of Disclosure. In Chapter 4, we will examine some of the work of Dr.

3. The UFO Disclosure Movement

Michael Salla, whose strand of Disclosure activism, dubbed "exopolitics" took a great deal of inspiration and "corroboration" from QAnon beginning in 2018. While Greer and Boylan have positions on Disclosure that vary greatly, they have both promoted the need to end government secrecy (whether from the visible government or a secret government) on the subject of Earth's alleged interplanetary visitors. They have both touted the benefits to humanity from revealing this information, from new technologies and health benefits to solutions for myriad political, social, and environmental issues. They have both remained relentlessly positive that the necessary revelations will occur, that the righteous who have kept the faith will be justified in their perseverance in the face of ridicule and professional or career setbacks. Building from long-standing conspiratorial narratives about UFO secrecy, Disclosure advocates like Greer and Boylan flipped a story that was relentlessly downbeat, with humanity being enslaved by alien overlords, into a prophetic tale of redemption for humanity and our new partners among the stars.

Chapter 4

QAnon

> We looked for an alternative to the fake news. We found Q. Q was also fake ... but ... it brought us together and brought us hope.
> —Twitter user "DewsSox79," January 8, 2021

UFO Disclosure and NESARA represented conspiratorial narratives that promised a glorious, abundant future to those willing to keep the faith through the turbulent present and based their claims on a misrepresented past. The QAnon conspiracy theory that emerged in October 2017, was in very much the same mold but with a timeline that unfolded rapidly in comparison to the years- or decades-long slow burn of UFO truth or the fulfillment of NESARA. QAnon, like NESARA, arose in an online space, but one of social media and fringe image-board forums like 4chan rather than email newsletter lists and static websites. Thus, the QAnon message spread far more rapidly to a larger number of people. The nature of the social Internet—and the cryptic nature of the source material—also ensured that QAnon was more participatory than these earlier narratives. Because it so closely identified its triumphal goals with the Donald Trump presidency, the QAnon narrative had something of a built-in timeline and its prophetic goalposts could not be moved as nonchalantly as the predictions of UFO Disclosure advocates or NESARA promoters.

A brief note on sources: QAnon was largely an Internet-based phenomenon. Q drops first appeared on 4chan's /pol/ board, moved to 8chan and, later 8kun. Several websites have come and gone which archived Q drops. The citations presented for Q drops were operational at time of writing but the Internet is ephemeral. With regard to QAnon, perhaps no aspect of the Internet was more ephemeral than social media. During the lifecycle of QAnon from 2017 to 2021, numerous social media platforms deleted or banned QAnon content. Reddit was the first major site to restrict QAnon related posting and others eventually followed, particularly after the January 6, 2021, insurrection at the U.S. Capitol. Twitter, YouTube, and other major platforms moved to remove QAnon related material. Primary sources, whether based on social media posts from deleted accounts or entire social media ecosystems that have vanished, are sometimes limited to citations of the material in other sources which, while not ideal, has often been the only option available.

Precursors and Origins

At its core, the QAnon narrative was a relatively simple one, in comparison to other widely promulgated conspiracy narratives. "Q," a military intelligence official (or a team of such officials) released cryptic information to the public via the /pol/ board on the 4chan discussion board beginning in October 2017. This information predicted an impending takedown of entrenched, evil conspirators through the work of President Donald Trump and his allies in the military. Much of the conspiratorial content surrounding the QAnon narrative, however, was already well established. The QAnon Origins Project, which tracked the development of QAnon in painstaking detail, observed that "Q's origins can't be divorced from the culture of /pol/, which was a rich slurry of racism, anti–Semitism, and … right-wing conspiracy theories" and that "Q—far from leaking top-secret information to the anons—simply repackaged what right-wing media (and therefore the anons [participants in 4chan discussion boards]) were already discussing."[1] In examining Q's posts on 4chan and, later, other venues, it was clear that the author owed a debt to conspiracists of years and, in some cases, decades before. As with NESARA and UFO Disclosure, it presented long-standing conspiratorial narratives in a new, triumphal light. In 2019, Muirhead and Rosenblum described QAnon as "an ephemeral element at the fringe of popular political culture." Despite its position on the fringe, they saw elements of the new conspiracism such as a "claim to own reality" as well as "verification" of conspiratorial claims being "a matter of repetition and assent" rather than based on evidence. They recognized within QAnon an "assault on common sense."[2]

As the QAnon Origins Project argued, many of the themes that were central to the QAnon narrative emerged earlier in the same online venues. One of the most significant was the claim that the evil, elite cabal controlling the Deep State and, thus, the nation, had long been engaged in the trafficking and abuse of children. The accusations ranged from child sexual exploitation to outright child sacrifice. Such conspiratorial claims were not unique to QAnon. The "Satanic Panic" of the

1980s was driven by unfounded suspicions of child sacrifice. Within the broader, more secular, conspiracy community during the 1990s, several dubious memoirs of self-proclaimed CIA mind control subjects alleged politicians' violent sexual proclivities in lurid detail. Books like Cathy O'Brien's *Trance-Formation of America* and Brice Taylor's *Thanks for the Memories* popularized the notion that wealthy, powerful elites in politics, business, and entertainment not only routinely engaged in sexual violence but that their activities were part of a systematic program. The conspiracy narratives that began to build during the election of 2016 built on these themes.

4chan QAnon precursor "High Level Insider," during an August 9, 2016, question and answer session, responded to the seemingly facetious question "How many babies do the Rockefellers eat on a daily basis?" by revealing that "they don't eat children, but often have sex with them." In September 2016, the High Level Insider was asked, "Why is the trafficking and abuse of children by the us and other governments condoned? Is that where all the missing kids go?" They responded:

> Establishment people want blackmail on each other because they wouldn't be able to trust each other otherwise. To this end, they encourage each other to engage in a wide range of degenerate things that the public would find unacceptable.[3]

Similarly, "FBI Anon," who claimed to be a well-placed informant in the Bureau claimed that "the people under the magnifying glass do have an affinity for children" and specifically referred to Hillary Clinton and Bill Clinton, claiming that Hillary Clinton had "sex with kidnapped girls" and explaining:

> Sex rings are popular in all governments, but pedophilia is primarily in British parliament & Saudi Arabia, and that's why HRC and BC love foreign donors so much. They get paid in children as well as money. Dig deep and you can find it. It will sicken you.[4]

These suggestions of elite misbehavior circulated widely on Internet forums like 4chan but would soon emerge into more widely trafficked areas of the Internet. Earlier, in 2013 and 2014, another online conspiracy emerged which alleged that the elite were extracting adrenochrome from the blood of children and other victims. This, too, would be folded into later conspiracies.[5] During October 2016, in the closing days of the electoral contest between Donald Trump and Hillary Clinton, FBI Director James Comey announced that the FBI would be reopening the investigation into Clinton's use of a private email server during her time as Secretary of State. Some information from the server was identified by authorities on devices owned by Anthony Weiner, who was married to Huma Abedin, a Clinton advisor. On October 29, 2016, a Facebook post appeared from a user calling themselves "Carmen Katz":

> My NYPD source said its [sic] much more vile and serious than classified material on Weiner's device. The email DETAIL the trips made by Weiner, Bill and Hillary on their pedophile billionaire friend's plane, the Lolita Express. Yup, Hillary has a well documented predilection for underage girls.... We're talking an international child enslavement and sex ring.[6]

A number of twitter accounts amplified claims that high level Democratic party officials were involved in pedophilia, child trafficking, and Satanic ritual abuse and the story spread to various websites, eventually becoming known as "Pizzagate." Scouring leaked emails for clues to the conspiracy, Internet posters believed they discovered a connection between the Clinton campaign and a Washington, D.C., pizza restaurant, Comet Ping Pong. On the discussion site Reddit, users established a forum (or sub-reddit) to discuss Pizzagate and provided a summary which alleged that Comet Ping Pong was a hub for the violent sexual exploitation of minors. The summary revealed that "John Podesta has had campaign fundraisers there for both Barack Obama and Hillary Clinton" and proclaimed that the restaurant was a "disturbing hub of coincidences":

> Everyone associated with the business is making semi-overt, semi-tongue-in-cheek, and semi-sarcastic inferences towards sex with minors. The artists that work for and with the business also generate nothing but cultish imagery of disembodiment, blood, beheadings, sex, and of course pizza.

Reddit would ban the Pizzagate subreddit for posting private information but, while it was active, its stated purpose was to "document the evidence, raise awareness, seek justice for all of the lives that have been ruined by theses [sic] disgusting people." The goals of the discussion group went further, however, and expressed a need "to try and save these children who are being subjected to this and to prevent any future children from being subjected to this great evil of humanity that needs to be removed from our society once and for all."[7] This call to action on behalf of the supposedly exploited children subjected the owners and employees of the restaurant to harassment by believers in the conspiracy theory,[8] the most severe of which was in December 2016 when Edgar Welch travelled from North Carolina to Washington to "investigate" the restaurant and rumors that a Hillary Clinton-linked child sex ring operated there,[9] threatening patrons and employees with a rifle. Despite the outrageous nature of the Pizzagate claims, in a December 2016 poll, 46 percent of Donald Trump voters (and 17 percent of Hillary Clinton voters) agreed with the statement, "leaked email from some of Hillary Clinton's campaign staffers contained code words for pedophilia, human trafficking and satanic ritual abuse—what some people refer to as 'Pizzagate.'"[10] The child trafficking/child sexual exploitation narrative was a persistent theme in QAnon related conspiracy narratives but it pre-dated QAnon, as did many of the other themes present within the QAnon universe. But these heinous acts were only part of the broader Deep State conspiracy described by Q beginning in October 2017.

The mysterious Q missives revealed that former president Donald Trump was involved in a herculean effort to rid the United States government of "Deep State" operatives who were working to obstruct his work in "making America great again," in the words of the campaign slogan. This was not simply an act of political opposition, for the Deep State was connected to a wider conspiracy involving Satan worship, pedophilia, child trafficking, and human sacrifice. Despite this formidable enemy, which had been entrenched for decades, victory was at hand. The military (which was loyal to Trump) was preparing to arrest those responsible for numerous crimes against the people of the United States—indeed, against all humanity—in an operation referred to as "The Storm." This moniker stemmed from events surrounding an October 5, 2017, meeting between Trump and military officials. At a press call following the meeting, Trump remarked to reporters "You guys know what this represents? Maybe it's the calm before the storm." When asked for the meaning of this statement, Trump simply replied, "You'll find out."[11]

The first Q drop, on October 28, 2017, discussed in the Prologue, tied directly into the conspiracy theories that had surrounded Hillary Clinton, the most recent of which was Pizzagate, promising that she would face justice. This was a recurring theme: that Clinton and other supposed Deep State operators would be arrested and imprisoned or executed as Trump took control of the country and his people were placed in positions of authority. The second Q drop, also on October 28, introduced more concepts that would be lasting ones for the QAnon narrative including "Mockingbird,"[12] a reference to alleged CIA attempts to influence public opinion through manipulation of the mass media. The history of Mockingbird is clouded by controversy with a great deal of credible testimony but no real definitive proof of the extent of CIA meddling in mass media. In 1977, Carl Bernstein published an article, "The CIA and the Media," in *Rolling Stone* in which he asserted that throughout the 1950s and 1960s the CIA had "a series of embarrassing relationships ... with some of the most powerful organizations and individuals in American journalism" and that "the CIA's use of the American news media has been much more extensive than Agency officials have acknowledged publicly or in closed sessions with members of Congress." However, Bernstein also acknowledged that while "the general outlines of what happened are indisputable; the specifics are harder to come by."[13] This lack of specific detail led David P. Hadley, in his 2019 book *The Rising Clamor: The American Press, the Central Intelligence Agency, and the Cold War*, to assert that the "continued lack of specific details proved a breeding ground for some outlandish claims regarding CIA and the press." Hadley explained that the "Mockingbird" cryptonym was promoted by Deborah Davis in her biography of *Washington Post* publisher Katherine Graham despite the Church Committee oversight hearings on the CIA's activities revealing no such operation. There was, however, a "Mockingbird" project in the early 1960s that saw the CIA illegally wiretap two journalists.[14] Over time, this conflation of one CIA operation with another—both involving journalists and the media—became ingrained in conspiratorial narrative. Q's mention of Mockingbird fed into the mistrust of the news media that Trump's supporters already felt.

In this second drop, Q clarified that Hillary Clinton had been "detained, not arrested (yet)" and asked, rhetorically, "Why does Potus surround himself w/ generals?" and "why go around the 3 letter agencies?"[15] The Q drop repository at qanon.pub includes correlating "answers" to these rhetorical questions, summarized from the work of "bakers" who interpreted the "crumbs" supplied by Q. For these questions in the second drop, anons interpreted news of Clinton's "detention as Q 'implying HRC was detained and released on own recognizance within strict limits, passport would be flagged unable to leave the continental US (CONUS).'" This interpretation very carefully threaded a needle of accepting Q's claim that Clinton has been detained while providing an explanation for why Clinton was clearly visible going about her life. Why does the president surround himself with generals? "To prevent a coup and ensure the safety of executive." Why "go around 3 letter agencies?" This is because "the 3-letters agencies have been infiltrated by bad actors who are not acting in the interest of the US." In other words, they are part of The Deep State or "the swamp," as opposed to the military, which is loyal. Q also provided additional detail on Trump's efforts:

> POTUS will not go on tv to address nation.
> POTUS must isolate himself to prevent negative optics.
> POTUS knew removing criminal rogue elements as a first step was essential to free and pass legislation.
> Who has access to everything classified?

> Do you believe HRC, Soros, Obama etc. have more power than Trump?
> Fantasy.
> Whoever controls the office of the Presidecy [sic] controls this great land.
> They never believed for a moment they (Democrats and Republicans) would lose control.

As the "answers" section interpreted this, "POTUS will not discuss ongoing investigations into the Swamp" because the media would distort what was happening, "which would be inappropriate and damaging to the POTUS and the office." The person who has "access to everything classified" is Attorney General Jeff Sessions, who "'knows things the President doesn't know for the sake of OPSec.' His work is essential because Trump is interested in the pursuit of justice instead of obstructing it to cover their masters [sic] asses." The pieces were in place for Trump and his people to keep their promise of draining the swamp—a swamp that was much deeper and more deadly than the American public knew. The public would not hear about it, Trump would not talk about it, but it would happen.[16]

As the Q drops continued for over three years, the membership in the evil cabal grew. The first Q drop focused on the impending arrest of Trump's 2016 opponent, and perennial right-wing conspiracy villain, Hillary Clinton.[17] Within a day, the list of enemies expanded as Q claimed:

> Many in our govt worship Satan.
> Not about Republicans v Democrats at this stage.[18]

By November, Q widened the Cabal to include some cultural figures and celebrities:

> Which performers/celebs supported HRC during the election?
> Who performed during her rallies?
> What jewelry and/or tattoos present?
> What other events do they attend together?
> What does HRC represent to them?[19]

Over time, the number of people who would be arrested and locked away at Guantanamo Bay was beyond counting, and Q claimed that cells at the base in Cuba would be at "Max. cap."[20] and that "(3) detention centers [were] being prepped."[21] Eventually, the members of this evil cabal, the Deep State and their cohorts in business, entertainment, and other fields would be permanently imprisoned or, in extreme cases, executed. The public would learn the truth, and the United States would triumphantly enter a new era of freedom.

This was the basic framework of the QAnon narrative but out of that narrative would grow numerous offshoots, interpretations, and mind-bending cul-de-sacs. The thousands of Q drops themselves would delve into the minutia of nearly every aspect of Trump's words, actions, and social media posts and hundreds of followers would interpret the messages (or "bake" the "crumbs," in QAnon parlance) into full-blown theories and storylines. It is outside the scope of this study to conduct a full, in-depth examination of every aspect of the QAnon phenomenon. Rather, the focus will be on the prophetic, triumphal aspects of the Q communications and the various interpretations they spawned, followers' efforts to integrate failed (or delayed) prophecies into their worldview, and ways in which the QAnon phenomenon intersected with both the ongoing narratives of NESARA and UFO Disclosure.

One area of overlap or intersection between the QAnon narrative, NESARA, and UFO Disclosure was a reliance—almost a fetishization—of the figure of the whistleblower or government insider who deigns to share information with the people of the world not through popular mass media but through intermediaries (like Dove of Oneness, Steven Greer, or Richard Boylan) or, in the case of QAnon, though relatively obscure Internet forum sites. The importance of the information the source shared gave the recipients information, but also provided a sense of validation and importance. The role of QAnon adherents in interpreting the often cryptic Q statements and promoting them across social media by posting links, cataloging Q drops, and creating meme images raised them from the level of being merely informed citizens to members of a crusade, "digital soldiers" in the war against the Deep State. Q was not the first to appear on 4chan and other venues claiming to be an anonymous, highly placed source, as we have seen and figures such as "FBI Anon" and "High Level Insider" provided alleged secret information, some of which—such as suggestion of child sexual exploitation and human trafficking—tied directly into the themes and narratives that would later be identified with QAnon.

Throughout the remainder of 2017 and into 2018, Q continued to build several of the narratives that would persist through December 2020, when the last Q drop (to date) appeared. Q mentioned the impending declassification (often referred to simply as "DECLAS") of secret documents that would inform the public about the evil of the cabal. Q also made reference, beginning in a November 5, 2017, drop, to "ten days of darkness." This is a recurring motif that would inspire a great deal of speculation. As QAnon began to grow in prominence, notably on message boards like 4chan and 8chan (where the missives would eventually move), what might be termed "spin-off" works emerged. While Q drops tended to be fairly repetitive and cryptic, the interpretations that

QAnon followers and adherents developed had more coherent narratives from the building blocks Q supplied.

Joe M: The Plan to Save the World

"The Plan to Save the World," a YouTube video by popular QAnon personality Joe M, attempted to provide a broader historical and political context for the messages that Q conveyed. "The Plan to Save the World" blended well-worn conspiracy-theory tropes with the hopeful prediction of justice and vindication that typifies QAnon interpretations; the white hats *will* save the world. Joe M began with a series of rhetorical, leading questions:

> Have you ever wondered why we go to war? Or why you never seem to be able to get out of debt?
> Why there is poverty, division and crime?
> What if I told you there was a reason for it all?
> What if I told you it was done on purpose?
> What if I told you that those who were corrupting the world, poisoning our food and igniting conflict were—themselves—about to be permanently eradicated from the earth?

Joe M combined geopolitical events with personal ones, claimed the evils of the world were intentional, and revealed that a reckoning was imminent. Those who have done these evil things are "criminals" who "choose personal gain over the rights of others, and have no regard for the law." The wars, poverty, and tragedies that have plagued humanity are not, he explained, the result of "human nature" or "simply the way the world works." The problem was not capitalism, nor was it communism. Rather, "it was the CRIMINALS all along!" These criminals infiltrated the media, the banking system, the U.S. Presidency, the European Union, the Roman Catholic Church, and the British royal family. They seized leadership of "agricultural companies who have control over food supply" and "big pharmaceutical companies, the ones we trust to help us when we're sick." In order to keep the people subjugated, these criminals exploited economic, racial, and religious divisions and "using their influence over culture, they popularize lifestyle choices that lead to a surge in broken homes, lost youth and substance abuse." While the "bad guys" have been in control, good guys existed as well. In keeping with well-established conspiratorial lore, Joe M. presented John F. Kennedy as a martyr to the ongoing criminal conspiracy:

> Well there were good guys. Many.
> One became the president of the United States in January of 1961.

He knew about these criminals and wanted them gone.
He knew their intentions for us all and he wanted to fight them.
Sadly, he had no idea how powerful they'd become.

Joe M also placed Ronald Reagan in this category, since he had "good intentions for the American people" and "his economic policies were promising" but alleges that the March 30, 1981, attempt on Reagan's life warned him away from this righteous path. In fact, every president since Reagan has been "one of these Deep State criminals." As the Internet emerged and grew, the United States became a surveillance state, but this was not necessarily negative. While the populace was "connected, trackable, and surveilled," the Deep State malefactors were as well. "In this new age of information," Joe M explained, "it was thought that the military should also have its own intelligence agency to focus on cyber crime and espionage. They called this the NSA, the National Security Agency." Joe M suggested that the establishment of the NSA was a reaction to the growth of the Internet when, in fact, the agency was created in 1952. The NSA is crucial to the QAnon narrative and the "PLAN to reclaim the world from the cabal and return it to the people." The "good guys" realized that there were two options to save America:

> Launch a military coup to seize the government from whichever Cabal puppet was in the White House.
> Or win legitimately, take control of the NSA, expose the criminals for what they are and arrest them all.

To accomplish this, the good guys "needed a candidate who could win and who could win big" in order to overcome the "voting machines" the criminals had "electronically set up to swing votes any which way." Donald Trump was the candidate of choice for the good guys and in 2016 "he overcame the voter fraud and won." During the first two years of the Trump administration, Joe M asserted, the world began "experiencing a dramatic covert war of Biblical proportions, literally the fight for death, between the forces of good and evil," which included "false flag terror attacks, downed planes, missile alerts, assassination attempts." Despite these trials and tribulations, the good guys were winning. Joe M cited the destruction of ISIS "in the year after Trump's win" as well as North Korean dictator Kim Jong-Un's "embracing peace" as evidence. In fact, there had only been tense relations with North Korea because of the Deep State criminals:

> The Cabal had complete control over North Korea.
> They hijacked the Kim Dynasty, took them hostage and worked to build up a nuclear arsenal to threaten the world.

King Jong-Un suddenly embracing peace was simply because the Deep State were beaten and driven out.

The story was not over, however, for "most of the known criminals are still free." Joe M identified Hillary Clinton, the Bushes, and Barack Obama as the highest profile enemies still at large. The "Q intelligence dissemination program" is part of the endgame that will lead to "high-profile arrests." This will all be accomplished by way of "an online grassroots movement called 'The Great Awakening.'" For Joe M, and QAnon more generally, those who believe the narrative are an integral part of the process of "saving" humanity and defeating "the greatest force of evil the world has ever known." The "anons" who read, dissect, analyze, and share Q's messages would play a vital role in "keeping the public informed when the Deep State war breaks out onto the surface." QAnon followers, then, would have a personal stake in the disclosure of information about the Deep State and in the fight that was taking place. Failure would not only mean that they had placed their trust and hopes in someone who had failed, but that they had failed as well.[22] While "The Plan to Save the World" referred to events and narratives to which Q discussed in various posts, Joe M does not directly quote Q's missives. The visuals that accompanied his narration in the original video merely featured a brief segment displaying Q posts scrolling rapidly across a screen. "The Plan to Save the World" re-contextualizes pre-existing conspiracy narratives—including familiar villains like central banking and the British royal family—within the QAnon universe.

While overwhelmingly an online phenomenon, some QAnon material also appeared in print. These books were generally published via print-on-demand services rather than released through traditional publishers, another example of QAnon—and conspiracy culture more broadly—taking advantage of new technologies and platforms to spread their message. Ironically, several of these books proved as fleeting as online QAnon information when Amazon purged its platform of QAnon material following the January 6, 2021, attack on the U.S. Capitol.[23] Two books, in particular, provide a sample of QAnon and related conspiracy narratives crossing the boundary from the online world to the physical realm. *QAnon: An Invitation to The Great Awakening* is a collection of essays published under the author name "WWG1WGA" but edited by "Captain Roy D" and "Dustin Nemos." The book consisted of reprintings of blog posts, transcripts of YouTube videos, and some material written specifically for the collection.

The book, and others like it, provided something of an anchor point—a window into the Q community's beliefs, ambitions, and concerns during the period before the election of 2020 (or the Democratic

Party's gains in the 2018 midterm elections). A key theme running throughout *An Invitation to The Great Awakening* was the degree to which people felt transformed by their exposure to and embrace of the QAnon narrative. The editor's introduction described one of the goals of the book as sharing "what has happened in the recent past that has changed so many things for us, both together and as individuals." The greatest thing that occurred was discovering QAnon, "an online poster (or a group that speaks as one) with a different voice and an insider's perspective." The editors and contributors to the book did not question Q. They may have debated Q's identity, whether it represented an individual or a collective, but Q was real, Q was correct. Despite the messages being "cryptic" they were always "insightful and full of foresight." Q's contributions gave his followers "insights and flashes of the future, taught [them] history, shown [them] fresh possibilities." Just as significant as the information Q shared was the way that following the QAnon phenomenon has, the editors explain, "inspired us to work together." It was this collective effort and unity that had, they believe, been "the primary reason" the QAnon narrative "has been vilified by the mainstream media." The editors described the relationship between Q and adherents of the QAnon narrative in a way that emphasized the relational of the community:

> At last, it seems, we've been befriended by someone who has our best interests at heart. As decades of deceit and lies are revealed, so is the plan for dealing with them. As thinking, caring people, we know that there is a great deal at stake. We trust that the plan is well underway and that the plan is working. The intensity of the medias [*sic*] ridicule and social media censorship tells us that we are "over the target."[24]

Q was not just a source of inside information; they were a friend. Those who believed Q's messages were not just people with similar beliefs or interests, they were a community, working together to correctly interpret Q's messages and support each other in the face of criticism and abuse from the media and others who refused to see the truth. The essays in *An Invitation to the Great Awakening* provided a healthy cross-section of QAnon-related topics from the height of the phenomenon's popularity, if not the height of its public visibility. It includes the text of Joe M's "The Plan to Save the World" video, portions of speeches by Michael Flynn about "digital soldiers,"[25] a lengthy examination of the "delta" phenomenon of determining the truth of Q posts, and essays that were more personal in nature.

"Schumer's Shutdown," by "ZackoDaFracko" was an essay that appeared in *An Invitation to the Great Awakening*. In it, ZackoDaFracko informs readers that it was "time to continue expanding our thinking."

The subject at hand was the then-impending December 21, 2018, government shutdown due to Congress's inability to pass spending legislation. This was a situation that had become relatively common by that point in the 21st century. ZackoDaFracko, however, saw it as a sign that at least part of the QAnon narrative was coming to pass or, at least, that Donald Trump's control over the federal government was as total as QAnon adherents believed. ZackoDaFracko alleged that Senate Majority Leader Chuck Schumer and House Speaker Nancy Pelosi, both Democrats, were "part of the plan and … they're working with Q Team…. Trump owns these two traitors and he has for at least a year." ZackoDaFracko credited this control Trump has over the two Congressional leaders for defense budget increases and other policies Trump supported. "If they both play their roles exactly as suggested," ZackoDaFracko asked, "can they avoid the death penalty?" He also points out that "they are being threatened by quote [sic] 'them' too. Sophie's Choice."[26]

Prompted by Q posts that promised benefits from a government shutdown, ZackoDaFracko posited five things that the shutdown would provide the president. First, a shutdown would, ZackoDaFracko believed, have allowed Trump to get the "military to build the border wall." Also, Trump would be able to carry out "recess appointments" of officials who might not be able to get Senate confirmation, and he could have ordered "DC cleared out for office raids," presumably to gather evidence of Deep State crimes without interference and there would have been a "window for Congress arrests" for such crimes. Lastly, Trump would have had a "pretext for temporary martial law."[27] Trump imposing some manner of martial law often arose in QAnon narratives and was presented as a positive thing. While martial law has long been a component of right-wing conspiracy narratives, those on the right rarely—if ever—anticipated their "side" using it. Martial law was a tool of the enemy—the left, the globalists, the New World Order. QAnon narratives seemed to welcome authoritarianism—as long as "their" authoritarian was in charge.

The QAnon narrative was so broad that it accommodated numerous pre-existing conspiracy theories. Indeed, without prior storylines vilifying international bankers, the intelligence community, Hillary Clinton, and alleged Satanic cabals, QAnon would have very few villains. Linda Paris's contribution to *An Invitation to the Great Awakening*, "The Election of a Lifetime," illustrated the capaciousness of QAnon adherents' conspiratorial worldviews. The editorial introduction to Paris's essay acknowledged that the process of learning the truth is difficult: "At first there is disbelieve [sic], then disorientation, then outrage over the betrayal, combined perhaps with fear and then sadness, etc."

As one became "awakened" to the truth, however, they found "a stable foundation where we will rapidly rebuild a new, safer, more prosperous and more peaceful reality for ourselves, our children and yes, even the greater world." As they have throughout, the editors personalized the QAnon conspiracy narrative by connecting individual believers to the greater events that will take place. As individual Americans have gone through the painful awakening process, so will the process be painful for the national as a whole, but the benefits, they promised, would be worth it.

Linda Paris identified herself as someone who worked for CNN for 17 years, ending in 2000. She did not specify her precise role at the network, nor what she did afterword for "every major network ... as a freelance, or as an employee." However, she was certain that she had never seen an election resembling that of 2016. "It was," she said, "a great awakening." Like many Americans, she "had been red-pilled by Obama's anti–American language and his free and easy use of executive orders, not to mention his penchant for shredding the Constitution."[28] There were other issues as well, including Obama's "habit of consistently announcing his plans to turn the United States of American into the 'largest Muslim nation in the world'" and "the infiltration of the Muslim brotherhood into government positions." There was, however, "still ... no public outcry." During the 2016 election, Paris, explained, the media was relentless in their campaign to unfairly paint Donald Trump as a "racist and Nazi." As the year wore on, Paris educated herself on the issues at hand, particularly the refugee crisis in Europe. Thanks to "videos and photographs [that] were popping up on the Internet," she became aware of "swarms of, mostly young, men with cell phones, storming across the countryside in endless streams, hundreds upon hundreds of them, with no final destination." Paris gathered information on the Internet, watching as "the refugees burst into farmhouses, and took what they wanted," soon "the European countryside, once picturesque and pristine was left littered with corpses." Whose corpses? Those "who had invited these refugees into their towns." This was, she said, "everyone's worst nightmare, and it was headed directly toward the United States."[29] As Paris tried to cope with the threat of refugees over-running the United States, as the Internet led her to believe was happening in Europe, she learned of an even darker future awaiting the nation:

> The revelation of Fema [sic] Camps (complete with guillotines) was the point of no return for me. Sleep was non-existent and I had frequent nightmares: Women, chained together, shrouded in black from head to toe, faces covered, all of them being led through the streets of my town, the black-clad men controlling them, waved giant knives in the air, while other men ran

into homes and grabbed women and children, dragging them out of their homes.[30]

The conspiratorial fever dream of the Federal Emergency Management Agency (FEMA) herding loyal Christian Americans into death camps for mass execution has been prominent since the 1990s when right-wing lawyer Linda Thompson produced *America Under Siege*, a documentary which purported to show that the Amtrak repair facility in suburban Indianapolis, Indiana, had been converted into a FEMA detention center.[31] Conspiracy promoter Pamela Schuffert amplified these claims on various websites from the early 2000s onward.

> *In order to use this AMTRAK facility as a DEATHCAMP for future NWO resisters,* ALL THEY HAVE TO DO is simply back in *FOUR PRISONER BOXCARS WITH SHACKLES* into one former repair building, SEAL IT UP, and release the deadly gas into the building. *And within 20 seconds, PRISONERS WILL BEGIN TO DIE,* according to former CIA microbiologist Larry Wayne Harris.
>
> *When I interviewed my friend, former CIA assassin Elaine* (later becoming a Christian exposing satanism and the NWO agenda), about this facility, *she confirmed that this will be used as a FUTURE DEATHCAMP* to get RID of anticipated NWO resistance. *Elaine should KNOW.* She WAS the previous satanic high priestess over Indiana for 17 ruthless years, when hired for the CIA as an assassin.[32]

Schuffert also helped popularize the narrative that the government had purchased large numbers of guillotines to execute Christian patriots:

> *Staff Sergeant/ARMY RANGER/Spec Ops* man from Fort Lewis Washington that I just met WHILE TRAVELING FROM MONTANA TO NORTH CAROLINA REVEALS: *"THE GUILLOTINES ARE REAL* AND I WAS GOING TO TRAIN MY MEN IN MY PLATOON TO USE THEM NEXT WEEK IN HIGHLY CLASSIFIED OPERATIONS AT FORT LEWIS...UNTIL YOU TOLD ME*" THEY WILL BE USED ON YOUR FELLOW AMERICANS UNDER COMING MARTIAL LAW!" *NOW he and the men who he told about my reporting, on HOW the guillotines will be used against their fellow Americans, ARE BEING ROUNDED UP AND HUNTED DOWN LIKE DOGS.[33]

These stories spread from early promoters like Pam Schuffert to forums, message boards, email lists and, eventually, YouTube and other social media and networking platforms. By the time Linda Paris encountered Q, she was already deep into the rabbit-hole of conspiracy theories that were decades old. Neither was she alone. She recalled that "by staying connected online, and exploring chat rooms and discussion boards, I discovered a large cross-segment of the population, who were feeling the same way that I was." Like her, these other seekers "were all coming to the realization that there was no place to go. We were not going to be able to avoid this insanity, because all the major news networks were suppressing this story."[34]

After she discovered Q and the QAnon community, Paris learned about the "massive corruption" that enveloped the United States, perpetrated by "a small group of 'elites'" and their "'New World Order,' consisting of both government and big business." She continued to build her community of fellow truth-seekers, who "had been thrown together politically because we were not brainwashed by the Fake news, and we could clearly see that something terrible was coming." She learned about the Freemasons and the Illuminati and discovered that there were "13 Illuminati bloodlines" that "control their offspring from the grave." She even learned that after the Second World War, Nazis maintained a secret base in Antarctica from which they operated fleets of flying saucers. She learned that, even now, "there is something important being hidden from us in Antarctica, and it is only one aspect of our life that they have manipulated."[35] Paris closes her essay by explaining that "QAnon has told us that the world is not how we think it is.... Everything we thought was real, is fake, and everything we thought was fake, is real." The media is a "CIA operation," she said, and "the moon landing is looking sketchy." Despite all of this, Linda Paris was excited to be alive:

> When the 2016 election began, I thought we were all going to die, but after QAnon arrived on the scene, it became the movement of a lifetime, and now, there is only one thing left to do:
> Enjoy the show.[36]

Linda Paris's description of her experience exemplified both what differentiated QAnon from other conspiracy trends in recent American history and what had not changed at all. Tales of FEMA death camps, Illuminati bloodlines, and Nazi UFOs at the South Pole were nothing new and, indeed, were almost conspiratorial clichés to all but the thoroughly uninitiated. What we might term the "QAnon factor" was the intensive sense of community that grew up around these retold tales as well as the unrelenting belief that the tide had turned, that the death camps would be shut down, and that those responsible for centuries of horror would face justice.

Another of the personal awakening, or "redpilling," essays was by Lori Colley. In her contribution to the *An Invitation to the Great Awakening* collection, she described "The Day I Knew Q wasn't a Hoax." This brief essay provided insight into the level of proof QAnon adherents required to accept the narrative Q presented and illustrated the connections that formed between the QAnon narrative and Evangelical

Christianity, particularly prophetic and end-times narratives. Colley described her entry into the QAnon sphere as stemming from her work on a newsletter and blogging site, *Praying Citizen*. As she "was on YouTube doing research" she learned about a number of conspiracy theories—some new, some decades old. Colley asserts that "the Fake News media doubled down on their attacks after Trump's victory" leading her to seek information from alternative sources. She learned much:

> The first casualty was trust in the government. From the JFK assassination to 9/11 to government mind control programs like Project MK-Ultra, I have become a bona-fide conspiracy believer. If you haven't taken the time to look into these and other crisis events, like the Pulse Night Club, Las Vegas, Parkland High School, and Sutherland Springs Baptist Church shootings, you really should. Nothing about the official stories about them adds up.
> Like Q says, we have been lied to by the people we trust the most.

Like Linda Paris, Colley traveled a path through well-worn and oft-told conspiracy stories. When she first encountered Q, Colley was struck by the fact that "right from the beginning Q said we can trust Trump and the US military." This resonated with her since, she says, "those were the only two entities I was prepared to trust!" She was comforted by Q telling her who was trustworthy and that there was "an effort by Trump and the good guys to take control away from the evil globalist elite and return power to We, the People."[37] She acknowledges that some "struggle to believe Q" when authorities failed to arrest Hillary Clinton as promised, admitting that "it wasn't always easy to keep the faith" and that "it has been a long road, and the hype and lack of visible action took its toll." Although "some Q followers fell by the wayside" many have "kept the faith" and through their "praying, and spreading the word" have been rewarded. This reward was not, as many hoped, mass arrests of Deep State officials. Colley stated her "patience has paid off with 'hints from Q'" that have "led [her] down more rabbit holes than [she] can keep up with." As a result, she and others who have kept the Q faith "are probably the most informed people around."[38] In addition to the informational benefits, QAnon is a "patriot movement" that will "unite us as one people." She was also comforted by the fact that "Q is a Bible-believer." While the immediate reward of Q-faith has been an increased awareness of the conspiracy, Colley was confident that "the elitist cabal of evildoers will be removed from power." She closes on an eschatological note:

> One day, the light will be so bright, the darkness will not be able to hide from it. Believers in the Lord Jesus Christ know that day is coming when Jesus returns. But I hope to see a small measure of that kind of righteousness in America one day very soon.[39]

The future Q promised to QAnon adherents was, in this interpretation, an iteration of the Second Coming. Colley did not place Q at the same level as Christ, but she presented Q as a prophetic figure, who led the wayward masses toward righteousness. Despite posting on her *Praying Citizen* blog as recently as early 2021, Colley stopped publishing posts tagged "QAnon" in March 2019. The content of her website continued to be strongly pro–Trump and echoed the QAnon-oriented storylines of the "stolen" 2020 election, COVID-19 denialism, trans- and homophobia, and other "culture war" themed topics.[40]

While Lori Colley drew some thematic parallels between The Great Awakening promised by Q and the Second Coming of Christ, these themes were more explicit in *QAnon and the Battle of Armageddon: Destroying the New World Order and Taking the Millennial Kingdom by Force*, a book produced by "RedpillTheWorld." It was published through Amazon in 2019 and contained no publishing or copyright information. Amazon took down the book in its deletion of QAnon related materials, but the author (also known as "Melissa") republished it, purged of QAnon content, under the title *End Times and 1000 Years of Peace*, in 2021. The differences between the two editions are slight. In the acknowledgments, the author substituted "Thank you to all the patriots everywhere" for "Thank you to the entire Q Army ... the Anons everywhere." In one portion where she specifically referred to Q, the original read:

> No matter what the enemy tries, there's nothing he can do to stop this! As Q said from the beginning,
> Big.
> Bigger!
> BIGGEST!!
> This is truly the BIGGEST! That sounds in Impossible! Outrageous! Too good to be true![41]

The 2021 edition replaced "As Q said from the beginning" with "We were told from the beginning." The passive voice obscured the Q-related source from Amazon's publishing software but was clear enough to readers. RedPillTheWorld asserted that "The Great Awakening" predicted by Q was, in fact, what the Bible called "the GREAT DAY of the LORD!" The author's association of the QAnon narrative with the Second Coming emphasized the triumphal, positive aspects of it. She told readers, "Now, don't be scared! It's not what we have been told. We are not going to see worldwide catastrophe No more devastation. no need to fear. No need to panic. (At least not for us)."[42] The end of the world was a good thing for those on the correct side, those who kept the faith. RedPillTheWorld then launched into her interpretation of the Christian

End Times narrative, which she based on the prophecies of Daniel in the Hebrew Bible. Daniel interpreted a dream had by the Babylonian King Nebuchadnezzar which featured a statue comprised of different materials, each corresponding to a future empire. The final one was the weakest:

> And whereas thou sawest the feet and toes, part of potters' clay, and part of iron, the kingdom shall be divided; but there shall be in it of the strength of the iron, forasmuch as thou sawest the iron mixed with miry clay. And as the toes of the feet were part of iron, and part of clay, so the kingdom shall be partly strong, and partly broken. And whereas thou sawest iron mixed with miry clay, they shall mingle themselves with the seed of men: but they shall not cleave one to another, even as iron is not mixed with clay.[43]

RedPillTheWorld identified this final kingdom that will exist just before the Day of the Lord arrives as the New World Order, headed by a "triangle of evil" made up of the Rothschilds, George Soros, and the House of Saud. The New World Order infiltrated governments, media, religious organizations, schools, the medical field, and every other institution imaginable. All of it could be traced back through history via a number of "ultra-wealthy international bankers/bloodline families" such as the DuPonts, Kennedys, Rockefellers, and Astors.[44]

Similarly, she reinterpreted other Old Testament prophecies as commentaries on current events. This is not unique to the world of RedPillTheWorld, of course. Biblical prophecy has long been connected to contemporary political and social events, with Hal Lindsey's immensely popular book *The Late, Great, Planet Earth* (1970) spawning dozens of imitators over the decades. RedPillTheWorld, however, dispensed with many stock interpretations. There would be no Rapture, there would be no Tribulation. The Mark of the Beast, as described in the Revelation of St. John, would not be a physical mark. Rather, "the Mark of the Beast is the Mark of PURE EVIL. This is the 'mark' that the New World Order minions have taken on in order to gain wealth and privilege."[45] While the relevant Bible verse specified that "no man might buy or sell, save he that had the mark, or the name of the beast, or the number of his name,"[46] RedPillTheWorld explained that the reference to buying and selling has been taken too broadly:

> Think about it. have most people been **truly free** to buy and sell? To gain true wealth? NOOOOO! The stock market is rigged. The education system is rigged. the jobs are rigged. The prices make it almost impossible to survive without going into debt slavery![47]

Who has the Mark of the Beast? In an appeal to a vague populism, RedPillTheWorld seemed to be saying it is anyone who has experienced gains in their investments, an education, or a job. In another QAnon-oriented interpretation, RedPillTheWorld declared that Ezekiel's vision of the valley of dry bones coming to life represented the awakening of humanity to the evils of the New World Order "and the pedophiles. And the human traffickers. And the money-making wars and disease. And the chemtrails (geoengineering). And the puppet leaders. And the fake news from every direction!"[48] The trumpet sounds in Revelation, signaling the beginning of apocalyptic events, similarly, were "intended to wake up the masses, so they can fight the Beast/New World Order." RedPillTheWorld then described her own awakening:

> For me it was just before the 2016 election, when I heard something about the Wikileaks and the Weiner laptop, that had reduced hardened investigators to tears. And then I dug, I discovered that the Bushes and the Clintons were not political rivals, but were in cahoots on the drug trafficking into Mena, AK [sic]. After that, I was WIDE AWAKE.

Much like Lori Colley described in "The Day I Knew Q wasn't a Hoax," RedPillTheWorld's "awakening" was the result of encounters with a grab-bag of long-standing conspiratorial narratives combined with the populist rhetoric of the Trump campaign. She connects Trump to the awakening and trumpet sounds, saying "I LOVE that our President is named TRUMP. There is no doubt that President Donald J. Trump is the anointed of the LORD to bring judgement."[49] RedPillTheWorld connected nearly every Biblical prophecy to the QAnon-based narrative. This included conflating the Second Coming with QAnon's predictions of punishment for those complicit with the machinations of the Deep State:

> It's ALL getting shut down. Completely. Not even a candle will be left burning in their Evil Empire. Bye!
> The ones who were made right because of the New World Order can cry all they want....
> God will avenge us for all the damage they have done to our families, our unity, our health, our finances. And the LORD will restore everything, in time.

She called on readers to "relish in the vengeance of our God on our enemies," and blamed these enemies for a vast number of misfortunes including cancer, "stealing our hard-earned money and making our money practically worthless," causing the destruction of families, invading privacy through surveillance, human trafficking, abortion, child abuse, and "creating AIDS, Autism, and Clinical Depression" along with "countless other diseases." For these crimes, "the LORD will make them pay for what they have done. He is angry about what they have done to us, and **they will pay and pay and pay some more**."⁵⁰ RedPill-TheWorld reduced the end of time to a vehicle for political retribution and a redressing of grievances. While Q and QAnon are not overwhelmingly present in *QAnon and the Battle of Armageddon*—to the degree that a Q-free edition of the book was nearly the same—the same themes are present. The book made explicit the similarities between the QAnon narrative and millenarian prophetic narratives, literally identifying the fulfillment of Biblical prophecy as being the fulfillment of a political, social, and cultural agenda.

The "imageboard" nature of 4chan, 8chan, and 8kun—where Q drops appeared and where a great deal of QAnon discussion and interpretation took place—perhaps made it inevitable that graphics, particularly "memes," were a prominent feature of QAnon discourse. The editors of *An Invitation to the Great Awakening* wrote that memes, which "can spread ideas like wildfire across the Internet," are the creation of "citizen journalists" and "have become the people's media by default."⁵¹ "Liberty Lioness," who described herself as "a 70-year old Boomer lady" with a "love" for the Internet,⁵² wrote an entry for the collection on "The Power of Memes" in which she explained that Q asked anons to create memes for several reasons, including the fact that with text embedded into a graphic it was more difficult for "the spying social media giants" to use text-analysis algorithms to "censor" QAnon related posts. She urged readers to choose images that are of high resolution and provided examples of memes she believed were particularly effective. One is a billboard she claimed was "found on I-40 near Little Rock" that read:

> WAKE UP AMERICA
> SWAMP MEDIA = FAKE NEWS
> DEMOCRATS = SOCIALISM
> THE DEMOCRATS DON'T HATE TRUMP THEY HATE AMERICA

Also effective, she wrote, was "using a cartoon or other famous character" if there was no other image that fit your message. As an example, she presented a picture of Kermit the Frog sipping tea with text that read, "MSM JUST SHOWED US HOW TALENTED THEY ARE AT MAKING FAKE VIDEOS... IT'S ALMOST LIKE THEY'VE DONE IT ONCE OR TWICE BEFORE."⁵³ Meme images were often repetitive and focused on core QAnon concepts such as the untrustworthiness of news media and the supposedly treasonous intentions of anyone who did not support Donald Trump.

In addition to the nearly ubiquitous memes, there were other graphic materials supporting and promoting QAnon, such as a series of 120 graphics designed to look like a collectible card game. These "QCards" consisted of two categories, "MAGA" and "Swamp," and contained a headline with a graphic beneath, followed by a description of the text of a Q drop. Card #1 was headlined "POTUS" with a picture of Donald Trump giving two thumbs up in front of four U.S. flags. The text of the card read,

> Donald J. Trump: The President believes the United States has incredible potential and will go on to exceed even its remarkable achievements of the past. Trumps [sic] campaign slogan for President was and still is, "Make America Great Again," and this is exactly what he is doing.

Card #7 depicted "QANON" as a 1980s-style "portable" computer, complete with dual 5.25" floppy disk drives and a phosphorescent green screen with a giant "Q." The text of the "QANON" card related the legend of "Q Anonymous":

> On October 28, 2018, Q began posting a series of cryptic messages in a /pol/ thread titled "Calm Before the Storm." Q, a high-level government insider with Q clearance tasked with posting intel drops to 4chan in order to inform Patriots about POTUS's genious [sic] master counter-strike plan to defeat the deep state.

Trump and Q were, obviously, in the "MAGA" category of cards. The "Swamp" category included card #19, "Renegade: Barrack [sic] Hussein Obama":

> U.S. President for two terms, protected by the MSM and The Swamp, America has not yet seen the real Obama. BHO is a Deep State Puppet, he was president for the first 8yrs in the [16yr plan to destroy America] paving the way for the NWO plan for world domination.

Card #20, perhaps inevitably, was "Crooked Hillary":

> Was the 2016 Democrat Presidential Candidate who rigged the election and still lost to Trump. Decades of crime, scandals, cover-ups, blackmail, and murder are going to catch up with her. HRC is the Deep State Swamp, she was the 2nd part of the [16yr plan to destroy America].

In addition to significant individuals, there were QCards representing core QAnon concepts, such as card #28, "13K Indictments":

> Most years there are only about one thousand federal indictments in the system, this year an unprecedented number, higher than ever before in history. Thirteen thousand Federal indictments are soon to be unsealed, it also just so happens that GITMO is now ready for 13k new residents.

The QCards not only demonstrated the use of graphics and imagery in spreading the QAnon message but also the prevalence of QAnon merchandising. The QCards were a physical product, produced on demand through web stores, the same as books like *An Invitation to the Great Awakening* and myriad articles of clothing and household goods emblazoned with "Q" and "WWG1WGA." QAnon's hopeful, triumphal narrative was unique in conspiracy culture but so was its approach to marketing.

In 2020, the presidential campaign coincided with the global COVID-19 pandemic and QAnon adherents and influencers worked to fit the disease into their ever-evolving narrative, initially echoing rhetoric that downplayed the severity of the virus. When that was no longer possible, more complex and outlandish explanations came to the fore. David Hayes, better known as "Praying Medic," informed his hundreds of thousands of YouTube viewers that "that they may not be affected by the disease because this was 'spiritual warfare'—only those who have not been chosen by God will be affected by the disease." Q began issuing drops related to COVID-19 on March 23, 2020. Q labeled it "the CHINA virus" and implied that the crisis was an attack on the United States and, in particular, Trump's re-election bid. "What is the mathematical probability," Q asked, "this occurs at the exact point in time that allows for maximum damage prior to the P_elec? ... WHO BENEFITS THE MOST?"[54] Q consistently promoted the narrative that the COVID-19 pandemic was one aspect of an array of efforts designed by the Democratic Party and the People's Republic of China to undermine Trump's presidency and re-election chances. Q expanded on this theme in early April 2020:

> Why did WHO make several strong recommendation[s] NOT TO impose a travel ban?
> Why did select [D] govs ban the use of hydroxychloroquine [key]?
> Why does FAKE NEWS push anti-hydroxychloroquine [fear tactics re: use]?
> Why was impeachment pushed through H fast? [did they count on R's blocking new witnesses?]
> Time sensitive?
> Why?
> When did [BIDEN] become the front runner?
> Why was this critically important?
> What happened directly after?
> WHO BENEFITS THE MOST?
> EVERYTHING AT STAKE.
> When everything else FAILED....
> DO YOU ATTEMPT TO CHEAT?
> Welcome to the [D] [People's Republic of China] party.
> The Silent War continues....
> Q[55]

Already, Q raised the specter of a dishonest, rigged election in 2020—only one example of the ongoing (and, in the case of the election, anticipatory) grievances that Q presented and that QAnon adherents amplified throughout 2020. Later that same day, Q asked followers

> What is the primary benefit to keep public in mass-hysteria re: COVID-19?
> Think voting.
> Are you awake yet?
> Q[56]

Q warned that the president's enemies would use COVID as an excuse to "HOLD HOSTAGE PUBLIC AID in exchange for National 'ballot harvesting' law adopt[tion],"[57] fueling the narrative that changes to voting procedures to increase participation and to cope with the COVID-19 pandemic were part of a larger plot to steal the 2020 election. Throughout the first half of 2020, Q pushed the narrative that hydroxychloroquine was a cure for COVID-19 (a cure that was being suppressed by Democratic politicians, the Deep State, and the news media) and amplified accusations that Democratic Party governors were bolstering death figures by forcing COVID-19 patients into nursing homes. Throughout April, Q linked COVID-19 to Democratic Party attempts to thwart Trump's re-election.

> Why are they pushing back the **[D]**convention?
> COVID-19 concern or strategic for last minute change?
> Change of Batter coming?
> Why was she "saved" from officially announcing?
> Why was she "reserved" for a last minute change?
> How do you attempt to "sneak one in"?
> How do you attempt to ensure victory?
> Adopt National Vote-by-Mail?
> How do you convince American it was legitimate?
> Release fake polls indicating favorable leads in swing states?
> How do you harm opponents accomplishments re: economy, unemployment, ...?
> How do you terminate opponents highly effective rallies?
> How do you shelter [D] lead candidate from embarrassing debates and/or rallies?
> How do you shelter [D]
> corruption re:FISA-RUSSIA-FLYNN-etc. from reaching the mainstream?
> How do you extend the trade negotiation deadline w/ CHINA?
> How do you limit [test] Constitutional rights of people?
> How do you provide cover for State Govs to adopt new voter laws?
> How do you effectively control the population?
> How do you expand big tech overreach re: tracing / privacy issues?
> How do you fix [taxpayer bailout?] the long-broken economies of CA & NY?

> How do you enrich select people/co's by promoting a solution to a global crisis?
> How do you keep people living in fear and isolation in order to accept the above?
> Define "insurgency."
> How do you accomplish all of the above?
> Q[58]

While commenting on current events such as the election, the COVID-19 pandemic, and protests in the wake of police killings of African Americans (Q blamed "antifa" for any violence), Q drops also continued to suggest that ongoing investigations of anti–Trump politicians and officials would soon yield results, noting:

> THE SILENT WAR CONTINUES
> Q[59]

and

> All the walls are falling down.
> Q[60]

In the months leading up to the presidential election, many drops promoted stories that reiterated longstanding Q narratives of child sexual exploitation, focusing on supposed connections between the Clintons and Jeffrey Epstein. As the election neared, Q drops reposted numerous stories from right-wing commentary sites about Democratic candidate Joe Biden's son Hunter, accusing him of corrupt dealings in Ukraine while his father was vice president during the Obama administration. QAnon's public profile increased, however, leading to QAnon followers being increasingly in the orbit of other right-wing groups.

Kyler Ong examined the "ideological convergence" that was occurring among right-wing extremist ideologies and organizations, noting that various types of right-wing extremists generally fell into four broad categories: "racial supremacy/replacement, anti-government, policy-centered beliefs such as anti-abortion, civil liberties, and pro-gun rights, and misogyny."[61] The non-hierarchical nature of these ideologies has

> fostered a culture of culling and cherry-picking ideologies that fit a particular individual's preconceived notions of the world, allowing for multiple permutations that could be used to characterise a right-wing extremist, whose ideology is often underpinned by conspiracy theories.[62]

During the COVID-19 crisis of 2020, separate white supremacist and anti-government groups including sovereign citizens and the boogaloo movement were "coalescing over social media into a 'militia-sphere'" that found common ground in COVID-denial and opposition to lockdown orders. Ong observed that the "militia-sphere" had "latch[ed] on to QAnon conspiracy theories, [and had] grown increasingly extreme as the COVID-19 pandemic ... progressed, to the point of threatening and enacting violent attacks."[63] QAnon adherents' anti-government conspiracies contributed to the increasingly fevered rhetoric by facilitating "claims that China, in collusion with members of the US Democratic Party, were weaponizing the COVID-19 virus." At the same time, QAnon ideas—if not full-scale acceptance of the entire narrative—spread to other conspiracy-oriented right-wing groups. QAnon signage and logos were prominent at anti-lockdown protests at various state capitols, including "increasing references to a 'Q-army,' symbolized by members who wear military-style Q-army badges, all in preparation for 'The Great Awakening.'"[64]

While QAnon's reach in the world of online conspiratorial and political discourse was considerable and undeniable, some question remained about its influence—or even presence—in the broader political conversation. While QAnon *concepts* and *themes* appeared in in the wider world, many times these were often stripped of their associations with the QAnon narrative. It was not uncommon during the first two years of the Trump administration, for example, to observe conservative and Republican politicians and commentators focusing (often fixating) on a "Deep State" establishment of career bureaucrats and Obama administration appointees frustrating the Trump administration's policy ambitions. Here, however, one must remember that the Trump campaign and, later, administration's complaints about the Deep State and promises to "drain the swamp" pre-dated the emergence of the QAnon narrative. Trump's rhetoric was one source of fuel for Q and their devotees and, as we have seen, Q drops often echoed that rhetoric.

QAnon's influence outside of the Internet was often difficult to gauge. A 2018 article about QAnon on the National Public Radio website cited actress Roseanne Barr and former professional baseball player Curt Schilling as Q devotees.[65] In a February 9, 2020, *New York Times* article, Mike McIntire and Kevin Roose explored the spread of QAnon ideas in the "offline world." Using incidents where local politicians referred to Q, Trump rally attendees wearing Q t-shirts, and the fact that—at the time of the article's publication—"some 23,000 of Mr. Trump's Twitter followers had QAnon references in their profiles" to illustrate QAnon's penetration into the political sphere. Additionally, McIntire and Roose observe that the FBI had included QAnon in its list of "Fringe Political" conspiracy theories in a 2019 Intelligence Bulletin covering domestic extremism.[66] They further note that:

Beyond the mainstreaming of QAnon in certain Republican circles, a bigger concern for researchers who track conspiracy theories is the potential for violence by unstable individuals who fall under its sway, particularly in the fraught political climate of the 2020 election.[67]

Despite this attention by the mainstream media and federal law enforcement, even by early 2020, however, knowledge of the QAnon conspiracy narrative was not necessarily widespread. A Pew Research Center poll conducted in February and March of that year found that 76 percent of adults surveyed in the United States said "they have heard or read nothing at all about" QAnon. Only 3 percent answered that they had heard or read "a lot" about the narrative. Researchers also concluded that "although QAnon has gained a modest foothold among some far-right factions, liberal Democrats are the most likely of any ideological group to say they have heard or read something about it." Further, the study showed that those who were more likely to have heard about QAnon were also more likely to get their news from social media platforms such as Reddit and Twitter than mainstream news sources such as The *New York Times* or cable news networks.[68]

This seemed to indicate that—at least at the time the survey was conducted—QAnon was still a largely Internet-based phenomenon. The survey result of center-left leaning respondents being more likely to have heard of QAnon reflects the nature of the coverage journalists and commentators gave the conspiracy narrative. Many journalists who covered QAnon did so as watchdogs, tracking the influence the narrative might have had on the Trump administration and its policies. Political news website The Hill, for example, published stories such as "Florida county GOP promoted, then deleted, conspiracy theory on Twitter,"[69] "Conspiracy theory 'QAnon' jumps to prime time at Trump rally,"[70] and "South Carolina state lawmaker has promoted 'QAnon' conspiracy theory online."[71] While "Q" signs and clothing were often visible at Trump's campaign rallies, in November 2020, Marjorie Taylor Greene, who had openly expressed support for QAnon, was elected as a member of the House of Representatives from Georgia.[72] In the final days of the election campaign, QAnon became more prominent with Trump fueling adherents' devotion by refusing to denounce the belief system, notably during a town hall with NBC's Savannah Guthrie, claiming, "I don't know about QAnon" before allowing that "what I do hear about it, they are very strongly against pedophilia."[73] Two days later, Q posted this about media characterizations of QAnon:

There is 'Q.' 1
There are 'Anons.' 2
There is no 'Qanon.' 3

> Media labeling as 'Qanon' is a method [deliberate] to combine [attach] 'Q' to comments _theories _suggestions _statements **[and ACTIONS]**made by 2.
> WHAT HAPPENS WHEN YOU CANNOT ATTACK THE INFORMATION [primary source 1]?
> DO YOU ATTACK [& TYPECAST] THROUGH USE OF OTHERS?[74]

Conspiracy theorizing often involves a great deal of hair-splitting of this type. Q can state that "there is no QAnon" because Q has never used the word "QAnon" in any of their drops. By this late stage, the theories that anons had spun, driven by the rhetorical questions and vague statements that characterized many Q drops, had taken on a life of their own. The narratives promoted by Q had survived the long gaps between drops and changes of venue. In the final weeks before Election Day, Q's rhetoric became more positive and militant while, at the same time, less specific. On October 31, he asked a number of questions:

> Are you ready to finish what we started?
> "Nothing can stop what is coming" is not just a catch-phrase.
> Q[75]
> Are you ready to hold the political elite [protected] accountable?
> Q[76]
> Are you ready to take back control of this Country?
> Q[77]

During his first term, Trump had not accomplished what Q had predicted, despite the supposed thousands of secret indictments, FISA warrants, and similar claims, matters were now in the hands of the voters. When Joe Biden won, after extended counting times in some states because of the large number of early-voting ballots that could not be counted before Election Day, Q was silent until November 12, when a drop appeared with an American flag and the message:

> Nothing can stop what is coming.
> Nothing!
> Q[78]

Later the same day, in a lengthier drop, Q asked a series of questions:

> How do you "show" the public the truth?
> How do you "safeguard" US elections post–POTUS?
> How do you "remove" foreign interference and corruption and install US-owned voter ID law(s) and other safeguards?
> It had to be this way.
> Sometimes you must walk through the darkness before you see the light.
> Q[79]

Considered in light of previous 2020 drops predicting attempts to "steal" the election, Q seemed to be suggesting in this November 12 drop that a fraudulent Biden election was a necessary step to solve issues of corruption and voter fraud. As was typical with Q's messages, they suggested rather than making a specific claim of a fraudulent election. The final Q drop (as of this writing) came on December 8, 2020, and was simply a link to a YouTube video featuring the song "We're Not Gonna Take It."

Nexus Points: UFO Disclosure, NESARA, and QAnon

Disclosure is just QAnon for people who like Star-Trek [sic]
Twitter user "nuekerk," November 25, 2020

Just as QAnon built a conspiratorial backstory out of decades of paranoid narratives, adding its own triumphal twist, both the UFO Disclosure realm and advocates for NESARA made attempts to integrate aspects of QAnon into their own theories. In an October 29, 2019, article for Vice entitled, "QAnon and UFO Conspiracies Are Merging," MJ Banias reported that "many" QAnon followers had "turned to the UFO narrative for their conspiratorial fix" after the closure of 8chan and the interruption in Q posts. Banias quoted Anna Merlan, who observed that "Both Q and the broader UFO community operate fundamentally on a premise of hidden knowledge yet to be revealed, whether it's 'Disclosure' or the idea that all Q's prophecies, mass arrests, dark warnings and ominous half-messages will someday be made clear" and speculated that QAnon promoters were attempting to "build their followings by trying to graft Q onto an older, more established, more respected research community." For this purpose, "UFOs" Merlan said, "make perfect sense." The connection between QAnon and UFOlogy went both ways, with established UFO Disclosure figures incorporating QAnon into their narratives.[80]

During the Trump presidency, pioneer "exopolitics" scholar Michael Salla heavily integrated QAnon narratives into his UFO Disclosure predictions and theories. Michael Salla is a political scientist who coined the term "exopolitics" to describe "the political study of the key actors, institutions and processes associated with extraterrestrial life."[81] Beginning in 2003, Salla published dozens of "research studies" and books that sought to present the basic Disclosure narrative in terms of political science and intergalactic diplomacy. Salla's work positioned him as something of a blend of Steven Greer and Richard Boylan, with Greer's focus on relatively down-to-earth political processes and Boylan's more extreme embrace of the fringiest of alien theories. Popular topics that Salla explored included "ancient aliens"-style stories ("America's Triumph and Europe's Angst: The Secret Race to Control Iraq's Extraterrestrial Heritage"[82]) and re-visitations of classic paranoid tales of underground alien bases from the 1980s ("The Dulce Report: Investigating Alleged Human Rights Abuses at a Joint US Government-Extraterrestrial Base in New Mexico"[83])

He first discussed QAnon in an article for his exopolitics.org website in November 2017, barely a month after the first Q drops. Referring to Q credulously as an "alleged whistleblower ... who has been releasing a lot of information about what is really going on behind the scenes in Washington DC," Salla was slightly tentative in approaching the new "source." In the article "Did President Trump Endorse Q Info on Secret Indictments of Pedophile Network?" Salla argued that Donald Trump's tweeting of a link to an article on a website that also promoted Q claims represented an endorsement of the narrative in general. As with the title of his article, Salla couched this revelation as a question: "was Trump indirectly endorsing Q's information as genuine? If so, then the ramifications are enormous." In a long and winding article, Salla addressed the alleged "buzzing" of CIA headquarters by U.S. Marine Corps helicopters and claimed that "the USMC was threatening the CIA's clandestine services division to get on board with the Trump administration or else." Salla then connected this event to 2013 "whistleblower" testimony that claimed President Dwight Eisenhower threatened to "invade" Area 51 (which was controlled by the CIA) and that there was a "secret USMC intelligence group established by President Eisenhower in the early 1950's, that continues to the present day." This connection, Salla claimed, indicated that "we are on the verge of major revelations about deep systemic corruption that has plagued the US" including the truth about "systemic corruption, powerful pedophile networks, and secret space programs." While corruption and pedophile networks were certainly a well-established part of the QAnon complex of narratives, Salla inserted the UFO Disclosure theory of a secret space program based on extraterrestrial technology as a way to connect his cause to an increasingly popular trend among conspiracy minded Americans. Salla's claim of forthcoming "major revelations" was in line with his previous exopolitics career—the QAnon narrative provided a parallel story strand he presented as a form of corroboration. In subsequent writings, however, Salla moved further into the camp of those who accepted QAnon claims more broadly.[84]

On February 23, 2018, Salla continued to build the connections between QAnon and his Secret Space Program narrative. In "President Trump Validates QAnon—How Will UFO SSP Disclosure Happen?," Salla related reports that "Trump is very familiar with the cover-up of information concerning UFO's [sic] and Secret Space Programs." Salla asserted that QAnon would "be the means by which advanced technologies secretly developed in Unacknowledged Special Access Programs will be disclosed to the world." Salla, however, did not simply piggyback on to QAnon, he indicated a growing acceptance of Q's credibility and the QAnon narrative:

> The Trump Administration is locked into a no holds barred struggle against Deep State actors and forces as explained in over 800 posts to date by QAnon. These cover a multitude of issues concerning secret indictments, arrests of Deep State officials involved in pedophile networks, treasonous actions by Obama administration officials, and the January 13 false flag ballistic missile attack on Hawaii.

Salla had moved on from hedging his bets by referring to Q as "alleged whistleblower" and began to embrace the wholesale narrative. In doing so, he elevated the Secret Space Program narrative and the quest for UFO Disclosure to be part of the same narrative as the Trump assault on the Deep State. By pinning some hope on QAnon as an avenue for eventual UFO Disclosure, Salla put himself in a position of having to grant credibility to non–UFO claims. Salla argued that "it's … well worth closely monitoring QAnon's posts and President Trump's actions in supporting the release of classified information through anonymous whistleblowers, and what this is about to disclose about UFO's and secret space programs."[85] If Salla wanted his followers to take seriously a Q drop about UFO Disclosure, then he had to give credence to other claims that Q made. Salla's characterization of Q had, by April 2018, shifted from "whistleblower" to claiming that "QAnon represents several military intelligence officials who are leaking sensitive information in a cryptic and coded manner due to the pervasive influence of the Deep State over many institutions of political, financial and cultural power." In this April 7 article, Salla also demonstrated a willingness to incorporate a wider range of conspiracy tropes into his Disclosure narrative, weaving "an other-worldly Satanic influence over the Vatican, the Rothschilds, and other forces making up the Deep State" with "Reptilian extraterrestrial entities." These reptilian aliens were the "explanation" for why Q had to post such cryptic and vague messages:

> QAnon is methodically exposing the historic power behind the Deep State—a very physical Reptilian extraterrestrial force—which still has

influence through a subservient clique of leaders wishing to ingratiate themselves with their Reptilian overlords.[86]

The notion of evil reptilian creatures being the true power behind human politics did not originate with Salla, who largely based his interpretation of the reptilian agenda on the stories of another Disclosure advocate, Corey Goode, while conspiracy theorist David Icke popularized the reptilian trope more generally in the late 1990s. The Deep State, according to Salla, was under the control of the reptilian aliens—clearly too formidable an enemy for Q to openly challenge. The revelation of this reptilian cabal, and its domination of the Deep State, provides a further avenue for Salla to integrate QAnon with UFO Disclosure. throughout 2018 and 2019, the pace of Salla's QAnon-related articles quickened, and shifted toward endorsement of QAnon's political claims with only tangential connections to UFO Disclosure or Secret Space Program narratives.

Salla also saw some surprisingly specific references in the "tripcodes" used to identify QAnon posts on the 4chan and 8chan boards. Explaining that "QAnon has dropped clues about the future direction of the intelligence dumps through the specific tripcodes that have been chosen," Salla shared that some researchers have determined that the tripcodes pointed to specific books when entered into Google. Presenting a list of some of the results from Google Books searches, Salla emphasized that these books were exopolitics-related works, including *Behold a Pale Horse*, the 1991 classic by William Cooper. Salla describes Cooper as "one of the first whistleblowers to come forward to reveal what he had seen in classified U.S. Navy intelligence files" about the UFO cover-up and "most importantly for QAnon readers, he provided some pretty detailed information about the Illuminati (Deep State) and their connection to ruling bloodline families and Satanism." He also discovered that several of his own books on exopolitics were among the search results which, he believed, indicated "direction of future Q drops."[87]

In a September 19, 2018, drop, Q replied to the question, "Are we alone? Roswell?" with

No.
Highest classification.
Consider the vastness of space.
Q[88]

The following day, Salla claimed that this "makes clear that we are not alone and that the truth about the Roswell flying saucer crash has the 'highest classification'"[89] despite Q not actually addressing the Roswell portion of the question. In another September 19 post, Q responded to a reader who asked "Did NASA fake the moon landings? Have we been to the moon since then? Are there secret space programs? Is this why the Space Force was created?":

> False, moon landings are real.
> Programs exist that are outside of public domain.
> Q[90]

Salla interpreted this for his readers, explaining that by using the phrase "outside of public domain," Q revealed "the fact that much information about these secret space programs is found in the private corporate domain, and not necessarily in the hands of the US government and the military services." Like his Roswell interpretation, Salla stretched his interpretation to fit the Q drop into his existing narrative. He also moved beyond the strict boundaries of the post with his prediction that "Q will reveal much more as the general public becomes open to the possibility that the truth about secret space programs and extraterrestrial life has been hidden" and that the newly announced Space Force would be the "means of wresting control away from corporations and put back into Presidential Executive control."[91] While Salla stretched Q's words and framed them in specific ways, this was a common practice among those who "baked" Q drops to discover the deeper meaning and hidden truths contained within them. The creation of the U.S. Space Force was a signal to Salla that the American people would soon learn of the "amazing disclosures of what the USAF has secretly deployed in space for decades."[92]

Salla's turn toward QAnon should not have surprised observers of "exopolitics" and the UFO Disclosure Movement. Concerns about the entrenched military and intelligence establishments had long been a factor in Salla's work. While Salla was not the only Disclosure advocate to hitch their wagon to QAnon, he was the one of longest standing figures to do so. His embrace of the QAnon narrative was less about the domestic politics of the United States than an opportunity to connect the endless predictions and promises of UFO Disclosure to a new and popular movement. QAnon was concerned with the Deep State, obsessed with Hillary Clinton, and promised disclosures of its own. These issues overlapped with enough of Salla's longstanding theories and viewpoints that the marriage was natural, if not inevitable. While Salla was not the only UFO Disclosure advocate who latched on to QAnon-related narratives, his work up to that point showed little that would indicate political connection with QAnon ideals.

Like QAnon, NESARA had rapidly grown since its introduction. The rapid metastasis of the benefits NESARA supporters believe it would provide—whenever NESARA was eventually implemented—illustrated the incredible utility of the basic narrative as a vehicle for a wide variety of political, social, cultural, or economic agendas. Strands of the interlocking narratives that made up the NESARA "complex" began to appear in various other sectors of conspiracism in the early 21st century. From UFO belief to the story of the 2020 election cycle, the stories that Shaini "Dove of Oneness" Goodwin shared with her followers had a long reach.

There were many, many websites, blogs, social media accounts, and streaming video channels that provided updates on NESARA related events. While there have been several post–Goodwin developments, the most significant have been the globalization of the NESARA ideals and predictions. References to "GESARA"—the "Global" not "National" Economic Security and Reformation Act—began to appear in the mid-2010s. Even more than when Goodwin was alive, tracking the changes to NESARA was daunting. Fortunately, there were some summaries of these changes provided by NESARA supporters, often with links to supporting materials which, of course, are also authored by NESARA supporters. One of the most up-to-date overviews of NESARA, which illustrated the most significant developments of the 2010–2020 decade was written by blogger "Alcuin Bramerton" writing at the "Alcuin and Flutterby" blog. Based in the UK, Bramerton provided this description of himself and "Flutterby":

> a human being seeking to operate happily in the post-religious world. The New Spirituality interests him. His friend, Flutterby, is not in physical incarnation on the Earth-plane at present, but he advises Alcuin on spiritual matters.[93]

On November 1, 2020, Bramerton published a post titled "NESARA Announcements Expected in 2020" in which he presented updates on what has happened on the road to NESARA. Like Goodwin, and other NESARA advocates before him, Bramerton asserted that "the NESARA global prosperity programmes are on the cusp of being announced and activated." He held off on providing any evidence for the imminent event. First, he gave background information on NESARA—"an American legal initiative with radical and benevolent global consequences"—and informed readers of the Saint Germain World Trust, which provided one quattuordecillion U.S. dollars.[94] Bramerton explained that the money from the Saint Germain trust would "zero out (permanently cancel) all personal, corporate and national debts worldwide"—an expansion that extended NESARA's benefits beyond the United States. This money would also be used to "buy out all oil corporations, banks and pharmaceutical cartels." Like the extension of debt forgiveness to the entire world, the purchase of these "cartels" would extend beyond the traditional strictures of the NESARA legislation. The integration of the Saint Germain World Trust, and other international sources of revenue, allowed the NESARA narrative to work beyond national borders and appeal to those outside the United States whose lives would not be substantially improved by an American law.

The Saint Germain World Trust was not the only source of revenue available to these global White Knights. Bramerton explained:

> In October 2018, the Manchu family syndicate donated a $1.16 billion-worth 1934 Henry Morgenthau Bond to the White Dragon Society in Japan to seed-finance the establishment of a meritocratic future planning agency for the whole planet.[95]

In the 2010s, part of the global expansion of the NESARA concept included the involvement of various East Asian groups, particularly the White Dragon Society. This was an alleged group that originated in the online writings of financial conspiracy theorist Benjamin Fulford in 2009. The Manchu family's money did not belong to the government of the People's Republic of China but, rather, it was gold privately owned "by the successors of the last Chinese Emperor, Pu Yi." The money that these secret societies would pitch in would be "sufficient" to "begin the work of ending global poverty, stopping environmental destruction, and financing human expansion into the Solar System and beyond." The reference to the "1934 Henry Morgenthau Bond" possibly had its roots in a scam involving counterfeit U.S. Treasury Bonds that emerged in 2012.[96] Bramerton's summary also highlighted the increasing interplay between the NESARA narrative and elements of the extraterrestrial Disclosure narrative. Echoing UFO contact stories that rose to prominence in the 1950s, he explained that "most human and humanoid races live on planets and in star systems beyond Planet Earth, and always have done." Bramerton emphasized that the contributions to humanity's well-being by these trusts was distinct from NESARA.

Bremerton related the familiar story of NESARA's 2000 passage and 2001 thwarting via the Bush-engineered September 11 attacks. Things, however, were beginning to change. Several events signaled a shift toward the implementation of NESARA. One was a 2018 revelation from conspiracy theorist Benjamin Fulford. Fulford announced that "for the first time in history, Eastern and Western secret societies have agreed to work together for the benefit of the planet, secret society sources say. As one Western secret society source put it, 'Jesus Christ is going to get married to Guan Yin (the Buddhist Goddess of Mercy).'"

At the negotiations where important leaders from the Vatican and the P2 Freemasons were negotiating with their opposite numbers from Asia, "the white hats in the Pentagon and the military-industrial complex are promoting their NESARA and GESARA Global Currency Reset ideas."[97] Parallel to the effort to implement NESARA and release massive amounts of money from the Saint Germain World Trust and other sources, an important fundamental change to global finance.

This would be the quantum financial system. According to Shoshi Herscu, author of the book *Mass Awakening*, the quantum financial system was:

> an off-world monetary system which cannot be rigged, in contrast with the current financial system. As it cannot be compromised—despite the many attempts to do so by the cabal—the cabal's corrupt central banking will collapse. The cabal will have no access to this system. This system will allow the transfer of the new asset-backed currencies after the Global Currency Reset which will replace the US-controlled Swift system with all its ills of usury and manipulation. The novelty about this system is that benevolent extraterrestrial Galactics provided the Alliance with this system which does not run on a conventional computer, but a quantum computer placed on a satellite. It is protected by SSPs to prevent it from being hacked.[98]

Bremerton added that the quantum financial system would also "enable exponential global growth" in a variety of areas such as "climate repair, biodiversity support, free energy, free water, free health and healing, free housing, universal basic incomes, clean and quiet transport, new agrisystems and live ET-contact interplanetary and interstellar exploration." Thematically, nothing Bremerton (or Fulford) said was very far afield from the NESARA narrative promulgated by Shaini Goodwin. There was an announcement that was just around the corner; it will be larger than just the American NESARA law, for Saint Germain's wealth and the money contained in the prosperity programs were also waiting in the wings, ready to be unleashed. The benefits of these programs were similar as well. The difference was one of scale. Rather than being an American initiative with incidental benefits for the rest of the planet, the plan is increasingly interplanetary, if not intergalactic. Indeed, the prominence of otherworldly beings was not necessarily a break with earlier NESARA accounts but, rather, a logical expansion of them.[99]

Bremerton then brought things up to date for 2020. Under the cover of the "extended coronavirus psyop ... the QFS insiders and associated White Hats, despite the non-disclosure agreements they had signed, began to drop explicit hints about NESARA on social media channels." The only example of such a hint Bremerton cited is a YouTube video in which UK conspiracy theorist Charles Ward reported that the U.S. presidential election would go ahead despite the "virus psyop" unless President Trump finally announced NESARA before the election. If this were to happen, "the US President and Vice President and all the officials in their administration will be removed from office with immediate effect. So will all members of the US Congress and their Khazar Zionist bosses." The NESARA narrative became more explicitly entwined with traditional anti-Semitic conspiracy theories than had been the case in the past. Goodwin and others in the early days had, of course, placed the blame on "bankers," but the language that Bremerton uses is far less coded. Bremerton asserts that choices for the new "constitutionally acceptable" U.S. president could include QAnon favorites "John Fitzgerald Kennedy Jnr [sic] (if still alive)" and General Michael Flynn, one of the "retired Pentagon White Hats." Trump might be allowed to stay on temporarily in order to expose "the machinations of the Bush syndicate and the Clinton Foundation, and in releasing details about the Satanist disinformation nexus connecting the US mainstream media and PsyOps cells within the US intelligence services." Bremerton's explanation of NESARA, the Quantum Financial System, and American politics blended elements from NESARA mythology with elements of UFO Disclosure discourse as well as QAnon. While Shaini Goodwin's presentation of NESARA information was certainly broad and drew from a variety of conspiratorial tropes and story-arcs, the blossoming of the notion that occurred after her death took NESARA into areas that were far more wide ranging.

The Election of 2020 and Its Aftermath

In the morass of claims of voter fraud in the wake of the presidential election of November 3, 2020, an increasingly familiar name was L. Lin Wood, an Atlanta attorney who specialized in defamation cases. Wood had long been a strong supporter of Trump and had represented several high-profile, right wing clients. The months following Trump's loss to Biden saw Wood travel further down the road of QAnon-adjacent conspiracy narratives decrying supposed pedophilia rings involving powerful politicians while clinging to the promise that Trump would remain in office beyond January 20, 2021, and finish the job of draining the swamp and defeating the Deep State. Wood attached himself to a number of lawsuits filed in several battleground states contesting election concerns and was among those who called for Republicans to boycott the January 2021 Georgia Senate runoff election "unless officials commit to various ballot security measures, many of which are either already in place in Georgia (like voter ID rules) or rooted in evidence-free conspiracies about foreign vote-rigging."[100] Throughout November and December of 2021, Wood posted increasingly extreme claims on social media and on right wing Internet programs. He appeared to be fully aligned with the QAnon narrative in an appearance on the "Sharp Edge" program, saying "There is potentially a Great Awakening. The truth has to come out.... Every lie will be revealed. This country is going to be shocked."[101]

On December 19, Wood took to Twitter calling for martial law, expressing his hopes in religious terms, asserting that "patriots are praying tonight that @realDonaldTrump will impose martial law in disputed states, seize voting machines for forensic examination, & appoint @SidneyPowell as special counsel to investigate election fraud." On December 20, 2020, he continued this, and called for martial law in "Georgia, Michigan, Arizona, Nevada, Wisconsin, Minnesota & Pennsylvania" and for "[voting] machines/ballots seized." This, he believed, would ensure Trump's victory, explaining, "7 states under martial law. 43 states not under martial law. I like those numbers. Do it @realDonaldTrump! Nation supports you."[102] On December 31, Wood launched another conspiratorial accusation against Chief Justice John Roberts:

> A couple of more questions for Chief Justice John Roberts:
> (1) You are recorded discussing Justice Scalia's successor before date of his sudden death. How did you know Scalia was going to die?
> (2) Are you a member of any club or cabal requiring minor children as initiation fee?[103]

Wood, in days to come, would disavow any affiliation with Q or QAnon. As noted earlier, conspiratorial narratives about sinister cabals involved in child trafficking pre-dated QAnon. In the public's mind, however, they were often closely connected. When martial law failed to materialize, and Vice President Mike Pence made clear that he had no choice but to preside over the certification of electoral votes, Wood tweeted on January 1, 2021, "When arrests for treason begin, put Chief Justice John Roberts, VP Mike Pence … at top of list." On January 6, 2021, the day of the Capitol Insurrection to disrupt the certification of the presidential election, Wood tweeted a graphic of a Revolutionary War style American flag with the words "1776 Again" and "Freedom Liberty Unity Knowledge" along with the following:

> The time has come Patriots. This is our time. Time to take back our country. Time to fight for our freedom.
> Pledge your lives, your fortunes, & your sacred honor.
> There will not be another chance.

> Speak TRUTH. Be FEARLESS. Almighty God is with you.
> TODAY IS OUR DAY.

In the wake of the deadly attack in Washington, Wood's was among the several accounts Twitter suspended.[104] Like many, Wood decamped to right-wing friendly social media site Parler.

On January 7, a day after the insurrection at the Capitol, Wood posted on Parler, "get the firing squads ready. Pence goes FIRST." He followed this with a justification for the vice president's execution saying that he was "hearing rumors that Pence & leaders of coup are planning to arrest & execute President Trump & his followers." This was, he explained, a "typical move by Communist tyrants." Later that day, he called the certification of electoral votes "the greatest attempted theft in history. Now it is a completed crime." He predicted, however, that "many traitors will be arrested & jailed over the next several days" and that "President Donald J. Trump will serve 4 more years!!!" Parler removed Wood's posts calling for Pence's execution.[105] Soon Parler, itself, went dark when Amazon (which provided Parler's hosting) suspended it for "its inadequate content-moderation practices."[106]

Following the collapse of Parler, Wood moved to the Telegram messaging system to communicate with his supporters. In the weeks up to and following Joe Biden's inauguration and President Trump's exit from the White House, Wood persisted in promoting the "stolen election" conspiracy narrative. His messages also continued to reference common QAnon tropes, particularly child exploitation among the politically powerful. On January 11, Wood posted his first Telegram message, claiming that he was "being falsely attacked and accused because they cannot attack my message. They attack the messenger.... My message is simple. My message is TRUTH." Asserting that "GOD is in control," Wood reassured followers that he had not been contacted by the Secret Service and repeated his claim that his January 7 "'Get the firing squads ready...' was rhetorical hyperbole—an expression of speech intended to make a point." That point was that based on the "evidence" he had seen left him "with the belief Pence is a traitor."[107] The next day, echoing QAnon adherents across Telegram, Wood urged that followers should be "prepared to listen to President Trump or other legitimate Patriots in our government when they speak to you through the Emergency Broadcast System. They will be telling you the TRUTH. So listen carefully."[108] Wood also complained, "the truth is still being censored" and promised that "things will change soon. Patriots will never allow the theft of free speech (or our Presidential election!)."[109] As the hours wore on and no emergency broadcast arrived, Wood counseled patience: "Do not give up hope. The best is yet to come. Steady."[110] Wood also provided a more detailed promise that Trump was still on the job and would fulfill his promises:

> We are imperfect. We are impatient. We wanted this election decided on November 3. It was. 75% of the voters cast ballots on Election Day for Donald Trump. He won in a landslide.
> President Trump does not give up. He has worked hard for us and our country every day for 4 years. He has suffered the slings and arrows from many the entire 4 years.
> Do you really believe he has come this far to quit on us? He has not. He is going to drain the swamp as he promised.
> So I urge patience. Trust Trump. He will Trump them all. Most importantly, trust God who created this nation. God will never allow America to be ruled by communists. So stay strong. Be fearless. All will be well.[111]

In addition to amplifying his fellow Trump supporters' claims of election fraud, Wood also touted his experience as a lawyer to give his followers advice on navigating the world of information and disinformation. A set of rules he posted on January 18 provides some insight into the post-truth nature of 21st-century conspiracy theories:

> My suggested rules of common sense:
> If something makes perfect sense, it is perfect truth.
> If something makes sense to you, it is almost always true.
> If something does not make sense to you, it is usually a lie but is at least less than the whole story. Search for the missing parts of the story to learn whether it is truth or a lie.
> If something strikes you as nonsense, it is nonsense. It is a lie.[112]

Wood's dicta were very much in line with the notion of the "new conspiracism"—the truth is what makes sense to you, because you have the common sense to discern truth from lies. Evidence made no appearances in Wood's "rules of common sense"; truth or falsehood were in the eye of the beholder. Wood applied these rules to the outcome of the 2020 presidential election and explained that "the 'election' of Biden was a fraud" that the "propaganda media" was hiding, deceiving "almost half the country":

> Use your common sense. Do you really think Biden got more votes than Obama and Hillary??? He did not campaign. His prior runs for office were dismal failures. He had no crowds at rallies. Look at Trump. His rallies were jam packed. There was a 92 mile caravan of supporters in Arizona. Do you really think he lost Arizona??? No way![113]

Wood's assertion of "common sense" reasons why Trump won the election based on crowd size—which ignored the Biden campaign's cognizance of public health issues during the COVID-19 pandemic—provided no evidence based on the actual number of votes cast for each candidate. Rather, it encouraged readers to substitute their perception of Trump's popularity and ability to draw a crowd for electoral returns. To be sure, Wood had not abandoned his legal conspiracy theories about the election being fraudulent but this line of reasoning provided an additional avenue to shore up support for Trump. The following day, January 19, 2021, Wood transitioned to a conspiracy narrative that he would continue to promote in the early months of 2021. He called for John Roberts, Chief Justice of the Supreme Court to resign. Wood described a meeting "with a courageous whistleblower who has risked his life" to tell Wood (and the American people) that "Jeffrey Epstein arranged for the adoption of Roberts' [sic] children. Roberts used the children to gain entry into the cabal of power & influence. FBI, Rod Rosenstein & Crowdstrike knew it all."[114] He also expanded on his "treason" accusations toward Vice President Pence, calling on him to resign as well, and explained that "Pence is on videos captured by FBI. Discussions about murdering judges. Roberts was involved. So was Hillary Clinton."[115] He went on to describe Clinton's role, explaining that "Hillary Clinton thought she had rigged the 2016 election. The plan after her election was to kill federal judges so that Hillary could stack the judiciary. US Supreme Court targeted. FBI was complicit."[116] Justice Antonin Scalia learned of this plan and "reported it to the White House. As a result, Wood explained, Scalia was murdered."[117] The evidence for these crimes was the whistleblower "testimony"—which Wood provided in several brief video clips with the whistleblower's features obscured for his own protection, for he had been "brutally tortured and he and his wife have lived in fear of death." There was other "damning evidence" but this had been sealed for alleged "National Security purposes in a federal court in Maryland." Wood alleged, "False charges were brought against the whistleblower" but hoped that "in time ... he will be pardoned and honored for his courage in revealing the truth." One might believe that if the dark forces were willing to murder a Supreme Court Justice for telling the truth about this plan, that Wood's whistleblower would soon meet a similar end. Wood, however, explained that this was not the cause, for "if FBI or other nefarious actors harm him now they will only further indict themselves and prove their guilt."[118] This was a standard conspiracy theory trope: the fact that someone with a controversial and unlikely tale to tell remained alive was evidence that they were telling the truth, because if they were assassinated, it would confirm what they were saying. Ironically, such a whistleblower dying under unusual (or even banal) circumstances would *also* be sure proof that they were truthful.

4. QAnon

As of January 19, 2021, the day before Joe Biden was to be inaugurated, Wood was seemingly confident that his and his whistleblower's evidence would prevail and that Trump would remain resident. Following Trump's exit from Washington, D.C., and the opening of Biden's inauguration event, Wood expressed incredulity tinged with bewilderment:

> The events of today make no sense to me. They are close to being what I would describe as nonsense. We appear to have turned our government over to communism. I do not believe President Trump would ever do so without a fight to the finish. I also have total confidence in the in the integrity of the United States Military.[119]

His reference to the military was an example of how Wood, and other Trump supporters, were still hopeful that the military would take control. In the weeks after the inauguration, Wood continued to hold out hope that there was a plan in place but increasingly devoted his posts to the ongoing saga of his own troubles following his support for failed election challenges and outrageous social media statements, including an investigation into his actions by the Georgia State Bar Association.[120] One example of some damage control he attempted was this post from January 27, 2021:

> I believe in God, not Q. I follow Jesus Christ, not QAnon. I don't know who Q is. I don't know what QAnon stands for assuming such an organized group even exists.
> God is real. I reached that conclusion by faith, not by sight. Having made that decision by faith, I then see God everywhere....
> The enemy will not directly attack me based on my belief in God. So he attacks me by falsely claiming I am a QAnon conspiracy theorist.
> Don't be fooled by the accusations against the messenger. Most are false. Focus on the message.[121]

Wood's rhetoric often mirrored that of QAnon supporters—particularly in his references to a "plan" but Wood was always careful to identify it as "God's" plan, as he does in this message posted on February 11:

> How many of you are ready to learn "the plan" to take back our freedom and to see the return of law and order? To see the return of President Trump who was elected by a landslide to serve at least 4 more years?
> I know the response from My Followers is almost unanimously, "I am!!!"
> The truth is that we will see "the plan" when we see it. Not a second earlier nor a second later.
> "The plan" is God's plan. Until we see it, we just maintain and strengthen our faith that He has a plan and will reveal it on His schedule, not ours.[122]

He followed this post with another insisting that Trump was the true winner of the election and a wholesale assessment that the electoral system needs reform.

> I support efforts to vote for honest representatives of We The People to elected offices.
> But I do not believe that those efforts will succeed without meaningful changes to our election rules.
> And I do not believe those changes can occur until we acknowledge and correct the wrongdoing that occurred in the November 3 election and recognize the true winner—President Trump.
> If we correct November 3, we can correct the problems with future elections. Until we do so, we can have no confidence that future elections will be honest.
> I am consistent. Ask former GA Senators Loeffler and Perdue. I said then what I say now. It is a matter of principle.[123]

Wood referred here to the January 2021 runoff election in which former Republican Senators Kelly Loeffler and David Perdue lost their seats.

Lin Wood's insistence that Trump was the rightful winner of the election and would serve a second term was notable for the forthrightness with which he persisted in these claims, even in the face of severe consequences for his professional life. His increasing adherence to and use of narratives related to QAnon—if not explicit endorsement of Q or QAnon itself—illustrated the degree to which this conspiratorial framework had penetrated the sphere of Trump's supporters. Wood was not the only high-profile Trump supporter to promote the "stolen election" or Deep State child trafficking narratives, but he may have been one of the most prominent figures who was so open about these beliefs.

In 2019, Anna Merlan wrote that QAnon illustrated "how conspiracy theories reliably change form to encompass the anxieties of the day," creating an alternative explanation for concerns that Trump supporters had, such as the investigation into Russian collusion. Later, QAnon would attempt to reinterpret Trump's impeachments and trials, the loss of Republican Congressional seats in 2018, and Democratic victories in 2020. While it is foolish to make predictions, the actions of figures like Lin Wood in the months following Joe Biden's inauguration seem to be an indicator that even without new Q drops (as of March 2021), the basic narratives Q established will continue to hold sway in years to come.

The cells at Gitmo may be filled up after all.

Epilogue

Most of us expect stories to have endings.

The complex conspiracy theories that underlay, inform and permeate the NESARA, UFO Disclosure, and QAnon narratives, however, cannot have endings. An ending would change the fundamental nature of what they are, for they promise the fulfillment of prophecy. Traditional conspiracy narratives, of course, do not have endings either. But who would want those stories to come to their promised conclusion? The dark tales of subjugation by the global elite, imprisonment and execution by the denizens of the New World Order, or abduction and experimentation by malevolent gray beings from beyond the galactic rim are horrific and terrifying. For those who hold to such frightening stories, every day the conspiracy fails to reach its promised terminus may be counted as a win. Every day that goes by without NESARA being implemented, humanity's extraterrestrial friends remaining hidden from our sight, or another day in which Hillary Clinton and George Soros are not displayed on television in shackles on their way to Guantanamo Bay must be counted a loss. Positive, triumphal conspiracies, however, have a power that traditional ones do not: they provide something to fight for rather than against. For better or worse, they inspire.

It is all too easy to scoff at these belief systems or, even more arrogantly, to dismiss them as being unworthy of our attention because they are so obviously flawed. We should remember, whoever, that conspiracy theories have consequences; that sometimes people will act on their beliefs no matter how irrational they may seem to the majority.

This was apparent on January 6, 2021, at the Capitol building. Hundreds who believed they were part of the plan to save America from the Deep State, who had been drawn in by promises that the happy ending was near, engaged in acts of violence and sedition. Were they all die-hard QAnon believers? It was, and remains, difficult to trace the origins of each participant's precise beliefs and motivations. The QAnon narrative, however, even more than UFO Disclosure and NESARA, relied on its adherents to serve as operatives both online and in the real world. It was not a huge leap for some to transition from digital soldiers to actual ones. In addition to the damage such activities caused to the nation's institutions, deep adherence to QAnon often took a personal toll as well. Numerous discussion boards have appeared since 2018 to help people cope with "losing" family members to QAnon and related belief systems. In mid–2020, one user posted to the Reddit group "QAnon-Casualties" that their mother was deeply invested in the QAnon world and had fallen into a belief in the promises offered by NESARA as well:

> Most recently, she divulged her belief in a theory called NESARA, one I have never heard before. This theory, in her words, essentially claims that all of the worlds debts (loans, credit cards, car payments, mortgages, etc.) are going to be erased in the very near future. The world will become a moneyless society and everyone will live in harmony and work because "it's the right thing to do." I asked her where all this money is coming from and she said "from the trillions of dollars that has been stolen by the deep state of pedophiles and reptilians." Trump is now apparently leading a secret mission against the deep state to return this money and restore peace to the world. She told me to stop paying my student loans and credit cards. I'm becoming increasingly worried that she is digging herself into an inescapable hole of debt with the expectation that it will all soon be paid off.[1]

The two theories and the worldviews they encouraged dovetailed neatly in this woman's mind. The promised wealth—or at least freedom from want—provided by NESARA would remain unfulfilled until Trump and his fellow white hats could finally defeat the Deep State. In the wake of Donald Trump's electoral defeat, QAnon adherents had different reactions. As illustrated in Chapter 4, these reactions ranged from obstinate refusal to admit that Q might not have been entirely accurate to a heart-wrenching despair. Two posts on Parler, on the day Amazon announced it would cease hosting the platform, epitomize the two extremes. User "anonpatriotq" was unwavering:

> Anyone that says any BS about Q and the entire truth movement being a "distraction" is full of crap. We didn't sit home. We didn't get complacent. We fought the information war. We went to rallies. We woke up our friends and family. And above all, WE VOTED. The problem: the election was STOLEN. Clearly no amount [sic] of votes would have made a difference. Don't let ANYONE tell you that you were lazy or didn't do your part to get President Trump re-elected. He was re-elected. And he WILL be President another four years. Have faith.[2]

One of the most significant aspects of this post from "anonpatriotq" is that their defensive stance is not about defending Q or even defending Donald Trump and his presidency but, rather, defending themselves

4. Epilogue

and their fellow "digital soldiers" from charges of laziness. The manner in which QAnon fashioned its adherents into digital soldiers and information warriors had, in one sense, made the election a referendum on their devotion to the cause and their efforts to spread the word of Q. "Anonpatriotq" wants their fellow anons to know that they did their job to the best of their ability. The only reason they were not yet enjoying the fruits of their victory was that it had been stolen from them.

At the other extreme is "Dawnj" who posted this on Parler the same day:

> I cant [sic] stop crying. Knowing its [sic] all over ... we lost the senate and Mr trump has committed to a peaceful transfer of power ... there was never a kraken, we were tricked ... on top of it all, were [sic] being mocked all over the world for our riot.. I have been laying on my bathroom floor because I cant [sic] even stand up or I vomit.³

For "Dawnj," the story had an ending, albeit an unhappy one. As different in tone as this post was from that of "anonpatriotq," there is a similar sense of victimization. Both "anonpatriotq" and "Dawnj" were tricked but while "anonpatriotq" blamed a stolen election, "Dawnj" seemed to feel betrayed by Trump, and possibly by Q. "Dawnj" seemed to be glimpsing the reality that lay beyond the QAnon veil, but there was no promise of justice; no happy ending.

Forecasting the future is nearly always ill-advised; these narratives teach us nothing if not that. It is not unreasonable to assume, however, that the QAnon narrative will continue to evolve and persist just as NESARA has done, just as UFO Disclosure has done. The examinations here provide only snapshots of narratives that will continue to unfold.

Not all stories end.

Chapter Notes

Prologue

1. Q Drop #1, October 28, 2017. https://qanon.pub/#1.
2. Sean Robinson, "Snared by a Cybercult Queen," *The News Tribune*, July 18, 2004. Accessed March 9, 2020. https://www.thenewstribune.com/news/special-reports/article25855081.html.
3. Mike Rothschild, "Who Is Q Anon, the Internet's Most Mysterious Poster?" *The Daily Dot*, May 29, 2018. Accessed March 9, 2020. https://www.dailydot.com/debug/who-is-q-anon/.

Chapter 1

1. Aaron John Gulyas, *Conspiracy Theories: The Roots, Themes and Propagation of Paranoid Political and Cultural Narratives* (Jefferson, NC: McFarland, 2016). 5.
2. Richard Hofstadter, "The Paranoid Style in American Politics," *Harper's Magazine*, November 1964. 84.
3. *Ibid.*, 86.
4. Mark Fenster, *Conspiracy Theories: Secrecy and Power in American Culture* (Minneapolis: University of Minnesota Press, 1999), 3.
5. *Ibid.*, 108.
6. Michael Barkun, *A Culture of Conspiracy: Apocalyptic Visions in Contemporary America* (Berkeley: University of California Press, 2003), ix.
7. *Ibid.*, 4–6.
8. Russell Muirhead and Nancy L. Rosenblum, *A Lot of People Are Saying: The New Conspiracism and the Assault on Democracy* (Princeton: Princeton University Press, 2019), 3.
9. *Ibid.*, 8.
10. *Ibid.*, 52.
11. *Ibid.*, 30.
12. Monmouth University Poll, "Public Troubled by 'Deep State,'" Monmouth University Polling Institute (blog), March 19, 2018, https://www.monmouth.edu/polling-institute/reports/monmouthpoll_us_031918/.
13. Wilkinson College of Arts, Humanities, and Social Sciences, "What Aren't They Telling Us?—Chapman University Survey of American Fears," The Voice of Wilkinson (blog), October 11, 2016, https://blogs.chapman.edu/wilkinson/2016/10/11/what-arent-they-telling-us/.
14. Emma Flaherty and Laura Roselle, "Contentious Narratives and Europe: Conspiracy Theories and Strategic Narratives Surrounding RT's Brexit News Coverage," *Journal of International Affairs* 71, no. 1.5 (2018): 53–60. 54.
15. *Ibid.*, 56.
16. Q, "Q Post 4891," qposts.online/post/4891, October 18, 2020, https://qposts.online/post/4891.
17. Mark Moore, "Conway: Trump Spokesman Gave 'Alternative Facts,'" *New York Post*, January 22, 2017, https://nypost.com/2017/01/22/conway-trump-spokesman-gave-alternative-facts-on-inauguration-crowd/.
18. Kenn Thomas, *Trumpocalyspe Now!: The Triumph of the Conspiracy Spectacle* (Kempton, Ill.: Adventures Unlimited Press, 2017), 17.
19. *Ibid.*, 25.
20. Jackie Flynn Mogensen, "To Celebrate the Fourth, Michael Flynn Posts a Pledge to Conspiracy Group QAnon,"

Mother Jones (blog), July 5, 2020, https://www.motherjones.com/politics/2020/07/to-celebrate-the-fourth-michael-flynn-posts-a-pledge-to-conspiracy-group-qanon/.

21. Anna Merlan, *Republic of Lies: American Conspiracy Theorists and Their Surprising Rise to Power*, First edition (New York: Metropolitan Books/Henry Holt and Company, 2019), 5–9.

22. J.M. Berger, "Without Prejudice: What Sovereign Citizens Believe" (Washington, DC: George Washington University Program on Extremism, June 2016), https://perma.cc/9RXF-9UFX. 2.

23. *Ibid.*, 3.

24. L.B. Bork, *The Red Amendment*, 2007. https://www.scribd.com/document/32147155/Red-Amendment-Promo.

25. Daniel Rice, "The 'Uniform Rule' and Its Exceptions: A History of Congressional Naturalization Legislation," *The Ozark Historical Review* 40 (2011): 23–64. 50.

26. *The Red Amendment*.

27. University of North Carolina School of Government, "A Quick Guide to Sovereign Citizens" (Chapel Hill: University of North Carolina School of Government, November 2013), www.sog.unc.edu/publications/bulletins/quick-guide-sovereign-citizens 2.

28. David E. Robinson, "Declaration of Sovereignty," The Patriot/UCC Redemption and Redemption in Law, April 6, 2004, http://maine-patriot.com/6.htm.

29. "Chap. 6—The TRUTH About the 14th Amendment," March 4, 2012, http://usa-the-republic.com/revenue/true_history/Chap6.html.

30. "Chapter 8—United States Government Bankruptcy," USA- The Republic, March 4, 2012, http://usa-the-republic.com/revenue/true_history/Chap8.html.

31. Caesar Kalinowski IV, "A Legal Response to the Sovereign Citizen Movement," *Montana Law Review* 80, no. 2 (August 1, 2019): 153–210. 167.

32. "Meet Your Straw Man," The Redemption Service, accessed March 8, 2021, https://www.redemptionservice.com/meet-your-strawman/.

33. J.M. Berger, "Without Prejudice: What Sovereign Citizens Believe," (Washington, DC: George Washington University Program on Extremism, June 2016), https://perma.cc/9RXF-9UFX. 6.

34. "Secured Party Creditor," The Redemption Service, accessed March 8, 2021, https://www.redemptionservice.com/secured-party-creditor/.

35. "Apply for Free Membership," The Redemption Service, accessed March 8, 2021, https://www.redemptionservice.com/join-our-membership/.

36. *Ibid.*

37. *Ibid.*

38. John Stormer, *None Dare Call It Treason* (Florissant, Missouri: Liberty Bell Press, 1964), 7.

39. *Ibid.*, 226.

40. Gary Allen, *None Dare Call It Conspiracy*, electronic edition (Seal Beach, California: Concord Press, 1972). No pagination.

41. *Ibid.*

42. David Icke, *Children of the Matrix: How an Interdimensional Race Has Controlled the World for Thousands of Years and Still Does* (Isle of Wight: David Icke Books, 2001), xxiii.

Chapter 2

1. Shaini Goodwin, "NESARA, the National Economic Security and Reformation Act," NESARA.us, December 5, 2003. Accessed March 9, 2020. https://web.archive.org/web/20031205051211/http://www.nesara.us/pages/home.html.

2. Richard Hofstadter, "The Paranoid Style in American Politics," *Harper's Magazine*, November 1, 1964, https://harpers.org/archive/1964/11/the-paranoid-style-in-american-politics/.

3. "NESARA—The 'Real' NESARA," nesara.org, January 26, 2008. Accessed March 9, 2020. https://web.archive.org/web/20080126203932/http://nesara.org/articles/the_real_nesara.htm.

4. Harvey Barnard, "NESARA—The Bill, Executive Summary," nesara.org, September 11, 2001. Accessed March 9, 2020. https://web.archive.org/web/20080126203932/http://nesara.org/articles/the_real_nesara.htm.

5. Sean Robinson, "Snared by a Cybercult Queen," *The News Tribune*, July 18, 2004, https://www.thenewstribune.com/

Notes—Chapter 2

news/special-reports/article25855081.html.

6. Ibid.

7. Sharon Paul, "Press Release: Leader of Omega Trust & Trading, Ltd. Pleads Guilty to International Fraud, Money Laundering Conspiracy" (U.S. Attorney's Office- Central District of Illinois, April 10, 2001), https://web.archive.org/web/20060620003555/http://www.justice.gov/usao/ilc/press/041001hood.html.

8. Rob Stroud, "Man Convicted of Creating Omega Scam Dies," *Journal Gazette-Times Courier Online*, July 28, 2012, https://jg-tc.com/news/man-convicted-of-creating-omega-scam-dies/article_83df49c0-d831-11e1-bc18-001a4bcf887a.html.

9. Robinson, "Snared by a Cybercult Queen."

10. Ibid.

11. Ibid.

12. Bob Kerr, "Colorado Man Gives Hope to Financially Hurt Farmers in Fight Against Foreclosure," *The Lewiston Tribune*, November 7, 1993. https://lmtribune.com/nation/world/colorado-man-gives-hope-to-financially-hurt-farmers-in-fight-against-foreclosure/article_7956d913-7966-5030-8c73-00733901dbff.html.

13. "Coloradan Sows Seeds of a Farm Loan Revolt," *Los Angeles Times*, November 28, 1993. https://www.latimes.com/archives/la-xpm-1993-11-28-mn-61641-story.html.

14. Carey Goldberg, "The Freemen Sought Refuge in an Ideology That Kept the Law, and Reality, at Bay," *The New York Times*, June 16, 1996, sec. U.S. https://www.nytimes.com/1996/06/16/us/the-freemen-sought-refuge-in-an-ideology-that-kept-the-law-andreality-at-bay.html.

15. "2 Sentenced for Activist Group Fraud Scheme," *Los Angeles Times*, November 5, 1995. https://www.latimes.com/archives/la-xpm-1995-11-05-mn-65157-story.html.

16. Shaini Goodwin, "June 12, 2002—Let's Take ACTION & Get NESARA Announced!," NESARA.us, June 12, 2002, https://web.archive.org/web/20071220033017/http://www.nesara.us/june02/June_12__2002_-__Let_s_Take_ACTION___Get_NESARA_Announced_.htm.

17. Ibid.

18. Quoted in Robinson, "Snared by a Cybercult Queen."

19. Sean Robinson, "Up Against 'The Dark Agenda,'" *The News Tribune*, July 17, 2013, https://www.thenewstribune.com/news/special-reports/article25855078.html.

20. Shaini Goodwin, "NESARA -> History of NESARA (December 9, 2003)," NESARA.us, December 9, 2003, https://web.archive.org/web/20031209145956/http://www.nesara.us:80/pages/history.html.

21. Ibid.

22. Ibid.

23. Shaini Goodwin, "NESARA -> History of NESARA (May 22, 2005)," NESARA.us, May 22, 2005, https://web.archive.org/web/20050522234543/http://www.nesara.us:80/pages/history.html.

24. William G. Baskerville, Shirley A. Baskerville, J.b. Foster, Lorraine L. Foster, Also Known As Lorraine Laveda Foster; Roy E. Schwasinger; William J. Logan; Nancy L. Logan, plaintiffs-appellants, v. Federal Land Bank, a Corporation, Also Known As Farm Credit services, Also Known As Farm Credit Bank of Wichita, formerly Known As the Federal Land Bank of Wichita; First Interstate Bank of Fort Collins, N.a.; Ernest L. Wimmer, An Individual; Hill, Hill, and Manges, P.c.; William F. Dressel, an Individual; Charles E. Matheson, an Individual; Fischer, Brown, Huddleston & Gunn, P.C.; Stephen J. Jouard,an Individual; Saxton, Shively, Strommen and Holst; J.A. Simplot Company, Doing Business As Simplot Soilbuilders,defendants-appellees, 25 F.3d 1055 (10th Cir. 1994).

25. Robinson, "Snared by a Cybercult Queen."

26. NESARA -> History of NESARA (May 22, 2005).

27. Jacques Casanova de Seingalt, *The Memoires of Casanova, Complete*, (eBook, Project Gutenberg, November 2, 2006), http://www.gutenberg.org/files/2981/2981.txt.

28. J. Gordon Melton, ed., "Western Esoteric Family I: Ancient Wisdom," in *Melton's Encyclopedia of American Religions*, 9th ed., vol. 1, United States (Farmington Hills, MI: Gale, 2017), 621–35.

29. "Saint Germain, Messengers,"

Saint Germain Foundation, accessed December 1, 2020, https://www.saintgermainfoundation.org/saint-germain.

30. Melton, 621–35.

31. Robinson, "Snared by a Cybercult Queen."

32. Shaini Goodwin, "NESARA Is KEY; Avoid Anti-NESARA Info," NESARA.us, April 27, 2002, https://web.archive.org/web/20071220024337/http://www.nesara.us/apr02/April_27__2002_-_NESARA_is_KEY__Avoid_Anti-NESARA_Info.htm.

33. Shaini Goodwin, "April 28, 2002—Saint Germain Authorizes Confirmations of Ascended Masters," NESARA.us, April 28, 2002, https://web.archive.org/web/20071220015907/http://www.nesara.us/apr02/April_28__2002_-_Saint_Germain_Authorizes_Confirmations_of_Ascended_Masters.htm.

34. Shaini Goodwin, "September 26, 2002—NESARA Foretold by Ascended Master Saint Germain," NESARA.us, September 26, 2002, https://web.archive.org/web/20071220033834/http://www.nesara.us/sept2/September_26__2002_-_NESARA_Foretold_by_Ascended_Master_Saint_Germain.htm.

35. Shaini Goodwin, "April 02, 2002—NESARA Before Mid-April; Debt Forgiveness; Keep $ Onshore," NESARA.us, December 20, 2007, https://web.archive.org/web/20071220024201/http://www.nesara.us/apr02/April_02__2002_-_NESARA_Before_Mid-April__Debt_Forgiveness__Keep___Onshore.htm.

36. Shaini Goodwin, "April 04, 2002—Current Activities Bringing NESARA," NESARA.us, December 20, 2007, https://web.archive.org/web/20071220015746/http://www.nesara.us/apr02/April_04__2002_-_Current_Activities_Bringing_NESARA.htm.

37. Shaini Goodwin, "April 05, 2002—America Is Way Shower, Heralding Golden Age," NESARA.us, December 20, 2007, https://web.archive.org/web/20071220014221/http://www.nesara.us/apr02/April_05__2002_-_America_is_Way_Shower__Heralding_Golden_Age.htm.

38. Shaini Goodwin, "April 06, 2002—NESARA on Target BEFORE Mid-April," NESARA.us, December 20, 2007, https://web.archive.org/web/20071220015751/http://www.nesara.us/apr02/April_06__2002_-_NESARA_on_Target_BEFORE_Mid-April.htm.

39. Shaini Goodwin, "April 23, 2002—We The People Can Announce NESARA If Necessary!," NESARA.us, December 20, 2007, https://web.archive.org/web/20071220024321/http://www.nesara.us/apr02/April_23__2002_-_We_The_People_Can_Announce_NESARA_If_Necessary_.htm.

40. Shaini Goodwin, "August 23, 2002—NESARA, Big Money & White Knights," NESARA.us, December 20, 2007, https://web.archive.org/web/20071220024453/http://www.nesara.us/aug02/August_23__2002_-_NESARA__Big_Money___White_Knights.htm.

41. Shaini Goodwin, "April 27, 2002—NESARA Is KEY; Avoid Anti-NESARA Info," NESARA.us, December 20, 2007, https://web.archive.org/web/20071220024337/http://www.nesara.us/apr02/April_27__2002_-_NESARA_is_KEY__Avoid_Anti-NESARA_Info.htm.

42. Shaini Goodwin, "April 29, 2002—Media Prepares for NESARA Announcement," NESARA.us, December 20, 2007, https://web.archive.org/web/20071220024352/http://www.nesara.us/apr02/April_29__2002_-_Media_Prepares_for_NESARA_Announcement.htm.

43. Shaini Goodwin, "April 30, 2002—About the NESARA Announcement & Deliveries," NESARA.us, December 20, 2007, https://web.archive.org/web/20071220015912/http://www.nesara.us/apr02/April_30__2002_-_About_the_NESARA_Announcement___Deliveries.htm.

44. Shaini Goodwin, "May 1, 2002—To WKs; END Meetings; DO NESARA NOW!," NESARA.us, December 20, 2007, https://web.archive.org/web/20071220033128/http://www.nesara.us/may02/May_01__2002_-_To_WKs__END_Meetings__DO_NESARA_NOW_.htm.

45. Shaini Goodwin, "June 12, 2002—Let's Take ACTION & Get NESARA Announced!," NESARA.us, December 20, 2007, https://web.archive.org/web/20071220033017/http://www.nesara.us/june02/June_12__2002_-__Let_s_

Take_ACTION___Get_NESARA_Announced_.htm.

46. Shaini Goodwin, "NESARA -> Supporters," NESARA.us, December 17, 2007, https://web.archive.org/web/20071217042605/http://www.nesara.us/pages/supporters.html.

47. A further caveat: there is a tremendous amount of "borrowing" between different NESARA publications and websites. Sometimes a source for this borrowing is provided, but not always. I have done my best to identify original sources for these materials.

48. Department of Justice, Office of Internal Affairs, "Maine Businessman Sentenced to Prison for Tax Crimes," Department of Justice, August 27, 2015, https://www.justice.gov/opa/pr/maine-businessman-sentenced-prison-tax-crimes.

49. Nancy B. Detweiler, "History of NESARA," The Way of Love Blog, August 17, 2011, https://pathwaytoascension.wordpress.com/2011/08/17/history-of-nesara/.

50. Nancy Detweiler, "History of NESARA: The National Economic Security and Reformation Act," *Maine Republic Email Alert*, No. 115, June 7, 2012. 1–6.

51. "Hildebrand Info," n.d. https://cdn.preterhuman.net/texts/finance_and_marketing/Hildebrand_Info.txt.

52. David E. Robinson, "NESARA I: National Economic Security and Reformation Act," Brunswick, Maine: MainePatriot.com (blog), 2011, 11.

53. *Ibid.*, 11–12.
54. *Ibid.*, 13.
55. *Ibid.*, 14.
56. *Ibid.*, 16–17.
57. *Ibid.*, 17–18.
58. *Ibid.*, 18.
59. *Ibid.*, 19–20.

60. Nancy Detweiler, "History of NESARA: The National Economic Security and Reformation Act," *Maine Republic Email Alert*, June 7, 2012.

61. Peter David Beter. "Audio Letter No. 46." May 28, 1979. http://www.peterdavidbeter.com/docs/all/dbal46.html.

62. *Ibid.*, 22–24.
63. Robinson, 25.

64. "The Economic Convulsion in Agriculture," *Congressional Record* Vol. 145, No. 120 (Senate—September 15, 1999).

65. Robinson, 25.
66. Robinson, 27–28.
67. Robinson, 31–37.

68. "NESARA—the Reformation Act," February 4, 2004, https://web.archive.org/web/20040204173220/http://nesara.insights2.org/index.html.

69. "Post N.E.S.A.R.A.—What Then?—Technology," NESARA—The Reformation Act, March 1, 2004, https://web.archive.org/web/20040301074352/http://nesara.insights2.org/Tech.html.

70. Kat, "Charlie and Colleen Freak: NESARA, Tesla Towers and B. Gates Updates 8-2-20," Disclosure Chronicles Blog (blog), August 4, 2020, https://inteldinarchronicles.blogspot.com/2020/08/charlie-and-colleen-freak-nesara-tesla.html.

71. "Post N.E.S.A.R.A.—What Then?—Health," NESARA—The Reformation Act, January 5, 2004, https://web.archive.org/web/20040105202602/http://nesara.insights2.org/Health.html.

72. *Ibid.*

73. Deirdre Imus, "Is the FDA Trying to Take Away Your Vitamins?," *Fox News*, March 27, 2015, https://www.foxnews.com/health/is-the-fda-trying-to-take-away-your-vitamins.

74. "Post N.E.S.A.R.A.—What Then?—Education," NESARA—The Reformation Act, February 21, 2004, https://web.archive.org/web/20040221221950/http://nesara.insights2.org/Education.html.

75. Nancy Tappe, "Home," All About Indigos, February 6, 2009, https://web.archive.org/web/20090206083041/http://allaboutindigos.com/.

76. John Leland, "Are They Here to Save the World?," *The New York Times*, January 12, 2006, sec. Style, https://www.nytimes.com/2006/01/12/fashion/thursdaystyles/are-they-here-to-save-the-world.html.

77. Sherry Shriner, "Who Is Sherry Shriner?" The Watcher Files. Accessed July 28, 2020. http://www.thewatcherfiles.com/sherry/intro.htm.

78. Kyle Swenson, "It Looked Like a Simple Domestic Murder. Then Police Learned about the Alien Reptile Cult," *Washington Post*, July 11, 2019, https://www.washingtonpost.com/nation/2019/06/11/alien-reptile-murder-cult-barbara-rogers-sherry-shriner/.

79. Charles R. Kelley, "What Is Orgone Energy?" *The Creative Process* 2, no. 2 (September 1962). http://www.kelley-radix.org/downloads/what_is_orgone_energy.pdf.

80. Sherry Shriner, "Sherry Shriner Orgone Blasters Fight Back Against Aliens, UFOs, Chemtrails, Night Terrors, ELF," 2017. http://www.orgoneblasters.com/.

81. Sherry Shriner, "Understanding the New World Order," Sherry Shriner—New World Order—Bible Prophecy and Tribulation Last Days Prophet and Watchman. Accessed August 4, 2020. http://www.sherryshriner.com/sherry/understanding-nwo.htm.

82. Jake Flanagin, "How YouTube Became a Breeding Ground for a Diabolical Lizard Cult," *The New Republic*, June 3, 2019, https://newrepublic.com/article/154012/youtube-became-breeding-ground-diabolical-lizard-cult.

83. Robinson, *NESARA I*, 25.

84. Sherry Shriner, "Saint Germaine," Nesara Sucks, accessed December 1, 2020, http://www.nesarasucks.com/germaine.htm.

85. Sherry Shriner, "NESARA Deception NESARA Is a Lie NESARA Will Kill You," Accessed July 28, 2020. http://nesarasucks.com/.

86. *Ibid.*

87. Rev. 13:16–17, KJV.

88. "NESARA Deception NESARA Is a Lie NESARA Will Kill You."

89. Prophecy Club, "About the Prophecy Club," July 4, 2014. Accessed March 11, 2020, https://www.prophecyclub.com/about.html.

90. Stan Johnson, "THE PROPHECY CLUB May/June 1999 NEWSLETTER," Prophecy Club, September 29, 2000. https://web.archive.org/web/20000929160048/http://www.prophecyclub.com/text2/may99.htm.

91. *Ibid.* "The Prophecy Club Newsletter for March and April 2000," Prophecy Club, June 3, 2000. https://web.archive.org/web/20000603083209/http://www.prophecyclub.com/mar00/1.html.

92. "About the Prophecy Club."

93. Dumitru Duduman,"The Message For America." Hand of Help, n.d. https://www.handofhelp.com/vision_1.php.

94. "NESARA 1," The Prophecy Club, June 23, 2016.

95. "NESARA—REPUBLIC NOW—GALACTIC NEWS: 'HISTORY BEING MADE RIGHT NOW'—New Republic via GCR—'220 Points of Fact' as of May 2016," May 28, 2016, http://nesaranews.blogspot.com/2016/05/history-being-made-right-now-new.html.

96. Savvas Zannettou et al., "A Quantitative Approach to Understanding Online Antisemitism," in *Proceedings of the Fourteenth International AAAI Conference on Web and Social Media* (International AAAI Conference on Web and Social Media, Association for the Advancement of Artificial Intelligence, 2020), https://www.aaai.org/ojs/index.php/ICWSM/article/download/7343/7197.

97. "NESARA 1," The Prophecy Club.

Chapter 3

1. Brad Steiger, ed., *Project Blue Book* (New York: Ballentine, 1976), 26–36.

2. David Michael Jacobs, *The UFO Controversy in America* (New York: Signet, 1976), 38.

3. *Ibid.*

4. Meade Layne, "Fly, Lokas, Fly!," *Round Robin* 3, no. 8 (December 1948): 8–9.

5. L.H. Truettner and A.B. Deyarmond, "Unidentified Flying Objects: Project 'Sign'" (Dayton, Ohio: Air Materiel Command, United States Air Force, February 1949), http://www.nicap.org/docs/SignRptFeb1949.pdf, 23–24.

6. *Ibid.*, 25.

7. *Ibid.*

8. *Ibid.*, v.

9. Edward J. Ruppelt, *The Report on Unidentified Flying Objects* (Garden City, New York: Doubleday, 1956), 59.

10. Lt. H.W. Smith and G.W. Towles, "Unidentified Flying Objects: Project 'Grudge'" (n.p.: Technical Analysis Division, Intelligence Department, United States Air Force, August 1949), vi.

11. *Ibid.*, vii.

12. Jacobs, 47.

13. Ruppelt, 131.

14. Jacobs, 136–137.

15. Jacobs, 65–67.

16. H.P. Robertson, et al. "Report of Meetings of Scientific Advisory Panel on Unidentified Flying Objects" (n.p.: Office

of Scientific Intelligence, Central Intelligence Agency, January 1953), https://documents.theblackvault.com/documents/ufos/robertsonpanelreport.pdf. 9.
  17. *Ibid.*, 10.
  18. *Ibid.*, 15.
  19. *Ibid.*, 20.
  20. *Ibid.*
  21. *Ibid.*, 21.
  22. *Ibid.*, 24.
  23. Curtis Peebles, *Watch the Skies! A Chronicle of the Flying Saucer Myth* (Washington, DC: Smithsonian, 1994), 114.
  24. *Ibid.*, 39.
  25. Jacobs, 130.
  26. *Ibid.*, 141–143.
  27. Donald Keyhoe, *The Flying Saucer Conspiracy* (New York: Henry Holt, 1955), 7.
  28. Donald Keyhoe, *Flying Saucers: Top Secret* (New York: Putnam, 1960),154.
  29. Desmond Leslie and George Adamski, *Flying Saucers Have Landed* (London: British Book Centre, 1953), 197.
  30. *Ibid.*, 198.
  31. George Adamski, *Inside the Spaceships* (New York: Abelard-Schuman, 1955), 83, 90.
  32. *Ibid.*, 93.
  33. George Adamski, "The Kingdom of Heaven on Earth," 1937 (published online by the George Adamski Foundation: http://www.adamskifoundation.com/html/heaven.htm), 1–2.
  34. Adamski, *Pioneers of Space: A Trip to the Moon, Mars, and Venus* (Los Angeles: Leonard-Freefield Co., 1949), 1.
  35. *Ibid.*, 3.
  36. Robert S. Ellwood, "Spiritualism and UFO Religion in New Zealand: The International Transmission of Modern Spiritual Movements," in *The Gods Have Landed: New Religions from Other Worlds*, ed. James R. Lewis, SUNY Series in Religious Studies (Albany: State University of New York Press, 1995), 141.
  37. Mark O'Connell, *The Close Encounters Man: How One Man Made the World Believe in UFOs* (New York: Dey Street, 2017), 192.
  38. Jacobs, 180.
  39. "Condon Report, Section I: Conclusions & Recommendations," http://files.ncas.org/condon/text/sec-i.htm.
  40. James W. Moseley and Karl T. Pflock, *Shockingly Close to the Truth: Confessions of a Grave-Robbing Ufologist* (Amherst, N.Y: Prometheus Books, 2002). 218.
  41. "Majestic 12," FBI: The Vault, http://vault.fbi.gov/Majestic%2012.
  42. Steven Greer, "One Universe, One People," Sirius Disclosure, 1991, https://siriusdisclosure.com/cseti-papers/one-universe-one-people/.
  43. Steven Greer, "CSETI Homepage," CSETI, March 1, 2001, https://web.archive.org/web/20010301201645/http://www.cseti.org/.
  44. Steven Greer, "Close Encounters of the Fifth Kind," CSETI, 1990, https://web.archive.org/web/20010203222300/http://www.cseti.org/programs/ce_5.htm.
  45. Steven Greer, *Unacknowledged: An Expose of the World's Greatest Secret* (Afton, Virginia: Sirius Technology Advanced Research, 2017), 318.
  46. *Ibid.*, 331–332.
  47. Steven Greer, "Programs," CSETI, February 6, 2001, https://web.archive.org/web/20010206140645/http://www.cseti.org/programs/programs.htm.
  48. Greer, *Unacknowledged*, 342.
  49. *Ibid.*
  50. *Ibid.*
  51. *Ibid.*, 346–347.
  52. R. James Woolsey and John L. Petersen, "Letter to Steven Greer," Dr. Steven Greer (blog), September 16, 1999, http://siriusdisclosure.com/wp-content/uploads/2013/03/1999-Woolsey-Petersen-letter.pdf.
  53. Steven Greer, "Dr. Greer's Response to Former CIA Director Woolsey's Denial of Meeting," Dr. Steven Greer (blog), September 23, 1999, https://siriusdisclosure.com/dr-greers-response-to-former-cia-director-woolseys-denial-of-meeting/.
  54. Greer, *Unacknowledged*, 349.
  55. Steven Greer, "Letter to President Bill Clinton (1996)," Dr. Steven Greer (blog), November 15, 1996, https://siriusdisclosure.com/cseti-papers/letter-to-president-bill-clinton-1996/.
  56. Greer, *Unacknowledged*, 355.
  57. Steven M. Greer, "Executive Summary of the Disclosure Project Briefing Document" (The Disclosure Project, April 2001), https://siriusdisclosure.com/wp-content/uploads/2012/12/ExecutiveSummary-LRdocs.pdf. 2.

58. *Ibid.*, 3.
59. *Ibid.*, 4.
60. *Ibid.* 5.
61. *Ibid.*, 4.
62. *Ibid.*, 6.
63. *Ibid.*, 8.
64. *Ibid.*, 10–11.
65. *Ibid.*
66. *Ibid.*, 13.
67. *Ibid.*, 19–20.
68. *Ibid.*, 17.
69. Steven M. Greer, "Disclosure and 9/11: An Analysis," Sirius Disclosure, Dr. Steven Greer (blog), September 2001, https://siriusdisclosure.com/cseti-papers/disclosure-and-911-an-analysis/.
70. Richard Boylan, "Brief Biography of Dr. Richard J. Boylan, Ph.D.," accessed January 22, 2021, https://drboylan.com/rjbbio2.html.
71. Richard Boylan, "Dr. Richard Boylan's Curriculum Vitae," accessed January 22, 2021, https://drboylan.com/resumefullrb.html.
72. Greg Bishop, ed., "Interview: Richard Boylan, Ph.D.—Positive Experiences with Mysterious Visitors," in *Wake Up Down There! The Excluded Middle Anthology* (Kempton, Ill.: Adventures Unlimited Press, 2000), 211–22.
73. "Dr. Richard Boylan's Curriculum Vitae."
74. Bishop, 216.
75. Richard J. Boylan and Lee K. Boylan, *Close Extraterrestrial Encounters: Positive Experiences with Mysterious Visitors* (Tigard, Oregon: Wild Flower Press, 1994). 151.
76. *Ibid.*, 158–168.
77. *Ibid.*, 152.
78. *Ibid.*, 156.
79. Medical Board of California: Board of Psychology, "In the Matter of the Accusation Against: Richard J. Boylan, Ph.D," No. W-14 and LMS-57 (August 4, 1995).
80. Richard J Boylan, "An Open Letter to the Community About Government Harassment," Brother Blue, December 14, 1995, http://web.archive.org/web/19980711104056/http://www.brotherblue.org/brethren/boylanfa.htm.
81. Richard J. Boylan, "Open Letter to the UFO Cover-Up," Brother Blue, March 11, 1997, http://web.archive.org/web/19980711104117/http://www.brotherblue.org/brethren/tpoc.htm.

82. Richard J. Boylan, *Project Epiphany* (Escondido, California: The Book Tree, 1996), 19.
83. *Ibid.*, 290.
84. Richard J. Boylan, "Becoming Cosmic Citizens: Dr. Boylan's Speech to the ACCET Annual Convention, 10/15/00," October 15, 2000, https://drboylan.com/acctspech2.html.
85. Boylan, *Close Extraterrestrial Encounters*, 152.
86. Brother Blue, "Richard J. Boylan, Ph. D.—Reptoid Hugger," Brother Blue, July 11, 1998, http://web.archive.org/web/19980711104241/http://www.brotherblue.org/brethren/boylanre.htm.
87. Richard J. Boylan, *Star Kids: The Emerging Cosmic Generation*, 2004. 12.
88. *Ibid.*, 13.
89. *Ibid.*, 14–15.
90. *Ibid.*, 17–19.
91. *Ibid.*, 181–182.
92. *Ibid.*, 132.
93. *Ibid.*, 133–134.
94. *Ibid.*, 135.
95. *Ibid.*, 187.
96. *Ibid.*, 188.
97. *Ibid.*
98. Richard Boylan, "The 11:11 Universal and Spiritual Principles or Laws of the Cosmos," accessed January 20, 2021, https://drboylan.com/11.11laws.html.
99. Richard Boylan, "Dr. Richard Boylan's Official Website," accessed January 21, 2021, https://drboylan.com/.
100. Richard J. Boylan, "Report on Formal Hearing and Indictment of the Cabal on Violations of Universal Laws," October 2, 2005, https://drboylan.com/formalhearing.html.
101. Richard Boylan, *The Human-Star Nations Connections: Key to History, Current Secrets, and Our Near Future*, (Richard Boylan, 2012), 341.
102. *Ibid.*, 341–342.
103. *Ibid.*, 343.
104. *Ibid.*, 174.
105. *Ibid.*, 175.
106. *Ibid.*, 211.
107. *Ibid.*, 216.
108. *Ibid.*, 219.
109. *Ibid.*, 230.
110. *Ibid.*, 237.
111. Richard Boylan, "2017: The Cabal's Last Stand: Star Seeds' Coming Victory in a Peaceful 'Velvet Revolution,'" April 1,

2016, https://web.archive.org/web/20160401004054/http://drboylan.com/2017caballaststand.html.

112. Richard Boylan, "2018: The Cabal's Last Stand: Star Seeds' Coming Victory in a Peaceful 'Velvet Revolution,'" August 8, 2018, https://web.archive.org/web/20180827081238/https://drboylan.com/2017caballaststand.html.

113. Richard Boylan, "2019: The Cabal's Last Stand: Star Seeds' Coming Victory in a Peaceful 'Velvet Revolution,'" March 15, 2019, https://drboylan.com/2017caballaststand.html.

114. Richard Boylan, "Dr. Richard Boylan's Official Website," accessed January 21, 2021, https://drboylan.com/.

115. Richard Boylan, "Mothership Over the UN," 2020, https://drboylan.com/MothershipOverUN.html.

Chapter 4

1. The Q Origins Project, "The Making of QAnon: A Crowdsourced Conspiracy," bellingcat, January 7, 2021, https://www.bellingcat.com/news/americas/2021/01/07/the-making-of-qanon-a-crowdsourced-conspiracy/.

2. Muirhead and Rosenblum, 135.

3. "High Level Insider," March 4, 2017, http://hli.anoninfo.net/.

4. "FBI Anon AMA Transcripts," October 17, 2016, https://paulfurber.net/pdf/fbianon.pdf.

5. Brian Friedberg, "The Dark Virality of a Hollywood Blood-Harvesting Conspiracy," *Wired*, July 31, 2020, https://www.wired.com/story/opinion-the-dark-virality-of-a-hollywood-blood-harvesting-conspiracy/.

6. Amanda Robb, "Pizzagate: Anatomy of a Fake News Scandal," *Rolling Stone*, November 16, 2017, https://www.rollingstone.com/feature/anatomy-of-a-fake-news-scandal-125877/.

7. DumbScribblyUnctious, "Comet Ping Pong—Pizzagate Summary: Pizzagate," Reddit, November 17, 2016, https://web.archive.org/web/20161122231637/https://www.reddit.com/r/pizzagate/comments/5da0kp/comet_ping_pong_pizzagate_summary/.

8. Tom Kludt, "'Pizzagate': Comet Ping Pong Not the Only D.C. Business Enduring a Nightmare," *CNNMoney*, December 5, 2016, https://money.cnn.com/2016/12/05/media/pizzagate-threatening-calls-washington-dc-businesses/index.html.

9. Spencer S. Hsu, "Comet Pizza Gunman Pleads Guilty to Federal and Local Charges," *Washington Post*, March 24, 2017, https://www.washingtonpost.com/local/public-safety/comet-pizza-gunman-to-appear-at-plea-deal-hearing-friday-morning/2017/03/23/e12c91ba-0986-11e7-b77c-0047d15a24e0_story.html.

10. Catherine Rampell, "Americans—Especially but Not Exclusively Trump Voters—Believe Crazy, Wrong Things," *Washington Post*, December 28, 2016, https://www.washingtonpost.com/news/rampage/wp/2016/12/28/americans-especially-but-not-exclusively-trump-voters-believe-crazy-wrong-things/.

11. Jennifer Calfas, "President Trump Warns of 'the Calm Before the Storm' During Military Meeting," *Time*, October 5, 2017, https://time.com/4971738/donald-trump-calm-before-the-storm-military-white-house/.

12. Q Drop #2, October 28, 2017. https://qanon.pub/#2.

13. Carl Bernstein, "The CIA and the Media," Carl Bernstein, October 20, 1977, http://www.carlbernstein.com/magazine_cia_and_media.php.

14. David P. Hadley, *The Rising Clamor: The American Press, the Central Intelligence Agency, and the Cold War* (Lexington: University Press of Kentucky, 2019), 3–4.

15. Q Drop #2.

16. *Ibid*.

17. Q Drop #1, October 28, 2017. https://qanon.pub/#1.

18. Q Drop #3, October 29, 2017. https://qanon.pub/#3.

19. Q Drop #189, November 21, 2017. https://qanon.pub/#189.

20. Q Drop #740, February 11, 2018. https://qanon.pub/#740.

21. Q Drop #2623, December 12, 2018. https://qanon.pub/#2623.

22. "WWG1WGA", *QAnon: An Invitation to The Great Awakening* (Dallas: Relentlessly Creative Books, 2019), 3–9.

23. Jeffrey Dastin, "Amazon to Remove QAnon Products from Platform after U.S.

Capitol Siege," *Reuters*, January 12, 2021, https://www.reuters.com/article/us-amazon-com-qanon-idUSKBN29H03U.

24. "WWG1WGA", QAnon: An Invitation to The Great Awakening (Dallas: Relentlessly Creative Books, 2019), 1–2.

25. *Ibid.*, 11.

26. *Ibid.*, 163–164.

27. *Ibid.*

28. *Ibid.*, 171.

29. *Ibid.*, 173.

30. *Ibid.*

31. Gulyas, *Conspiracy Theories*, 50–51.

32. Pamela Rae Schuffert, "The CONFIRMED AMTRAK DEATHCAMP of Beech Grove IN," *AMERICAN HOLOCAUST and The Coming NEW WORLD ORDER* (blog), February 28, 2009, http://americanholocaustcoming.blogspot.com/2009/02/confirmed-amtrak-death camp-of-beech.html.

33. Schuffert, "Modern GUILLOTINES Confirmed at Fort Lewis, WA-Military Whistleblower Report," *AMERICAN HOLOCAUST and The Coming NEW WORLD ORDER* (blog), February 16, 2009, http://americanholocaustcoming.blogspot.com/2009/02/modern-guillotines-confirmed-at-fort.html.

34. *An Invitation to the Great Awakening*, 174.

35. *Ibid.*, 181–185.

36. *Ibid.*, 186.

37. *Ibid.*, 34.

38. *Ibid.*, 35.

39. *Ibid.*, 48.

40. Lori Colley, "Finding Fun and Joy in the Fallout," *Praying Citizen* (blog), January 28, 2021, https://prayingcitizen.wordpress.com/2021/01/28/finding-fun-and-joy-in-the-fallout/.

41. RedpillTheWorld, *QAnon and the Battle of Armageddon: Destroying the New World Order and Taking the Millennial Kingdom by Force* (n.p.: n.p., 2019), ii.

42. *Ibid.*, 1.

43. Daniel 2:41–43, KJV.

44. *Ibid.*, 6–12.

45. *Ibid.*, 26.

46. Revelation 13:17, KJV.

47. *Ibid.*, 27.

48. *Ibid.*, 14.

49. *Ibid.*, 60.

50. *Ibid.*, 162.

51. *An Invitation to the Great Awakening*, 105.

52. *Ibid.*, 119–120.

53. *Ibid.*, 114.

54. Q Drop #3896, March 23, 2020. https://qanon.pub/#3896.

55. Q Drop #3909, April 8, 2020. https://qanon.pub/#3909.

56. Q Drop #3913, April 8, 2020. https://qanon.pub/#3913.

57. Q Drop #3915, April 8, 2020. https://qanon.pub/#3915.

58. Q Drop #4014, April 30, 2020. https://qanon.pub/#4014.

59. Q Drop #3998, April 28, 2020. https://qanon.pub/#3998.

60. Q Drop #4001, April 28, 2020. https://qanon.pub/#4001.

61. Kyler Ong, "Ideological Convergence in the Extreme Right," *Counter Terrorist Trends and Analyses* 12, no. 5 (September 2020): 1–7. 7.

62. *Ibid.*, 2.

63. *Ibid.*, 2–3.

64. *Ibid.*, 5.

65. Brandon Carter, "What Is QAnon? The Conspiracy Theory Tiptoeing Into Trump World," *National Public Radio*, accessed March 31, 2020, https://www.npr.org/2018/08/02/634749387/what-is-qanon-the-conspiracy-theory-tiptoeing-into-trump-world.

66. FBI Phoenix Field Office, "FY19 Intelligence Bulletin" (Federal Bureau of Investigation, May 30, 2019), https://www.justsecurity.org/wp-content/uploads/2019/08/420379775-fbi-conspiracy-theories-domestic-extremism.pdf.

67. Mike McIntire and Kevin Roose, "What Happens When QAnon Seeps from the Web to the Offline World," *The New York Times*, February 9, 2020, sec. U.S., https://www.nytimes.com/2020/02/09/us/politics/qanon-trump-conspiracy-theory.html.

68. "QAnon's Conspiracy Theories Have Seeped into U.S. Politics, but Most Don't Know What It Is," *Pew Research Center*, March 30, 2020, https://www.pewresearch.org/fact-tank/2020/03/30/qanons-conspiracy-theories-have-seeped-into-u-s-politics-but-most-dont-know-what-it-is/.

69. Jacqueline Thomsen, "Florida County GOP Promoted, Then Deleted, Conspiracy Theory on Twitter," Text,

The Hill, July 18, 2018, https://thehill.com/blogs/blog-briefing-room/news/397615-florida-county-gop-promoted-conspiracy-theory-on-twitter.

70. *Ibid.*, "Florida County GOP Promoted, Then Deleted, Conspiracy Theory on Twitter," Text, *The Hill*, July 18, 2018, https://thehill.com/blogs/blog-briefing-room/news/397615-florida-county-gop-promoted-conspiracy-theory-on-twitter.

71. Rachel Frazin, "South Carolina State Lawmaker Has Promoted 'QAnon' Conspiracy Theory Online: Report," Text, *The Hill*, March 21, 2019, https://thehill.com/homenews/state-watch/435241-south-carolina-state-lawmaker-has-promoted-qanon-conspiracy-theory.

72. Lauren Gambino, "Who Is the Republican Extremist Marjorie Taylor Greene?," *The Guardian*, February 6, 2021, http://www.theguardian.com/us-news/2021/feb/06/who-is-marjorie-taylor-greene-republican-qanon.

73. Adam Gabbatt, "Trump Refuses to Disavow QAnon Conspiracy Theory During Town Hall," *The Guardian*, accessed March 25, 2021, https://www.theguardian.com/us-news/2020/oct/15/qanon-trump-refuses-disavow-conspiracy-theory-town-hall.

74. Q Drop #4881, October 17, 2020. https://qanon.pub/#4881.

75. Q Drop #4944, October 31, 2020. https://qanon.pub/#4944.

76. Q Drop #4945, October 31, 2020. https://qanon.pub/#4945.

77. Q Drop #4946, October 31, 2020. https://qanon.pub/#4946.

78. Q Drop #4950, November 12, 2020. https://qanon.pub/#4950.

79. Q Drop #4951, November 12, 2020. https://qanon.pub/#4951.

80. MJ Banias, "Popular UFO Conspiracy Theorists Are Cashing in on the COVID-19 Pandemic," *Vice*, October 29, 2019, https://www.vice.com/en/article/4ayyqw/david-wilcock-ufo-conspiracy-theorist-covid-19-deep-state-ascension.

81. Michael Salla, "Founder," *Exopolitics* (blog), July 10, 2012, https://exopolitics.org/about/founder/.

82. Michael Salla, "The Secret Race to Control Iraq's Extraterrestrial Heritage," *Exopolitics* (blog), March 27, 2003, https://exopolitics.net/Study-Paper3.htm.

83. Michael Salla, "Dulce Report: Investigating Alleged Human Rights Abuses at a Joint U.S. Government-Extraterrestrial Base at Dulce, New Mexico," *Exopolitics* (blog), September 25, 2003, https://exopolitics.net/Dulce-Report.htm.

84. Michael Salla, "Did President Trump Endorse Q Info on Secret Indictments of Pedophile Network?," *Exopolitics* (blog), November 27, 2017, https://exopolitics.org/did-president-trump-endorse-q-info-on-secret-indictments-of-pedophile-network/.

85. Michael Salla, "President Trump Validates QAnon—How Will UFO SSP Disclosure Happen?," *Exopolitics* (blog), February 23, 2018, https://exopolitics.org/president-trump-validates-qanon-how-will-ufo-ssp-disclosure-happen/.

86. Salla, "President Trump Validates QAnon—How Will UFO SSP Disclosure Happen?," *Exopolitics* (blog), February 23, 2018, https://exopolitics.org/president-trump-validates-qanon-how-will-ufo-ssp-disclosure-happen/.

87. Michael Salla, "QAnon Goes Mainstream at Trump Rally While Tripcodes Point to Exopolitics Books," *Exopolitics* (blog), August 3, 2018, https://exopolitics.org/qanon-goes-mainstream-at-trump-rally-while-tripcodes-point-to-exopolitics-books/.

88. Q Drop #2222, September 19, 2018, https://qanon.pub/#2222.

89. Michael Salla, "Q Confirms Secret Space Programs Real & Extraterrestrial Life Exists," *Exopolitics* (blog), September 20, 2018, https://exopolitics.org/q-confirms-secret-space-programs-real-extraterrestrial-life-exists/.

90. Q Drop #2225, September 19, 2018, https://qanon.pub/#2225.

91. Salla, "Q Confirms Secret Space Programs Real."

92. Michael Salla, "Trump Signs Space Force Act—Stage Set for Secret Space Program Disclosure," *Exopolitics* (blog), December 21, 2019, https://exopolitics.org/trump-signs-space-force-act/.

93. Alcuin Bramerton, "Blogger: User Profile: Alcuin Bramerton," accessed December 16, 2020, https://www.blogger.com/profile/14917474523744351041.

94. This is an amount that is often associated with the St. Germain trust.

Notes—Chapter 4

The definition of quattuordecillion varies, with the American usage of the term is a one followed by 45 zeros and the British usage is a 1 followed by 84 zeroes. Oddly, Bramerton defines it as "$1 with forty noughts after it."

95. Alcuin Bramerton, "Alcuin and Flutterby: NESARA Announcements Expected in 2020," *Alcuin and Flutterby* (blog), November 1, 2020, http://alcuinbramerton.blogspot.com/2007/07/nesara-announcement-expected-in-run-up.html.

96. "The Truth about $300B Worth of 'Manila' Paper," January 17, 2012, https://www.investmentnews.com/the-truth-about-300b-worth-of-manila-paper-41654.

97. Benjamin Fulford, "'Jesus Christ to Marry Asian Goddess' as East-West Secret Societies Agree to Save Planet," November 12, 2018, https://benjaminfulford.net/2018/11/12/jesus-christ-to-marry-asian-goddess-as-east-west-secret-societies-agree-to-save-planet/.

98. Shoshi Herscu, "The Global Currency Reset and Our Liberation from the Debt Slavery Financial System," *Mass Awakening* (blog), March 22, 2019, https://massawakening.org/the-global-currency-reset-and-our-liberation-from-the-debt-slavery-financial-system/.

99. Bremerton, "NESARA announcements expected in 2020."

100. Joe Walsh, "Trump's Allies Can't Decide Whether to Boycott Georgia's Runoff Elections," *Forbes*, December 2, 2020, https://www.forbes.com/sites/joewalsh/2020/12/02/trumps-allies-cant-decide-whether-to-boycott-georgias-runoff-elections/.

101. Noah, "Lin Wood: Americans Will Be Shocked at Level of Pedophilia & Satanic Worship Occupying Oval Office for Years (Before Trump)," We Love Trump, November 24, 2020, https://welovetrump.com/2020/11/23/lin-wood-americans-will-be-shocked-at-level-of-pedophilia-satanic-worship-occupying-oval-office-for-years-before-trump/.

102. Wood's Twitter account has been suspended. Unless otherwise noted, quotations from Wood's Twitter account are drawn from "Brief in Support of the City of Detroit's Motion for Sanctions, for Disciplinary Action, and for Disbarment referral and for Referral to State Bar Disciplinary Bodies in the case of *King, et al. v. Whitmer, et al.* No. 2:20-cv-13134, January 5, 2021.

103. Justin Baragona, "Trumpist Lawyer Lin Wood Casually Suggests Chief Justice John Roberts Is a Murderous Pedophile," *The Daily Beast*, December 31, 2020, https://www.thedailybeast.com/trumpist-lawyer-lin-wood-casually-suggests-chief-justice-john-roberts-is-a-murderous-pedophile.

104. Ryan Mac, "Trump-Supporting Lawyer Lin Wood Has Been Permanently Banned From Twitter," *BuzzFeed News*, January 7, 2021, https://www.buzzfeednews.com/article/ryanmac/twitter-bans-lin-wood.

105. Zachary Petrizzo, "Lin Wood Continues to Invoke Violence on Parler," *Mediaite* (blog), January 8, 2021, https://www.mediaite.com/news/pro-trump-lawyer-lin-wood-calls-for-pence-to-be-executed-posts-get-removed-from-parler/.

106. Tony Romm and Rachel Lerman, "Amazon Suspends Parler, Taking pro–Trump Site Offline Indefinitely," *Washington Post*, January 11, 2021, https://www.washingtonpost.com/technology/2021/01/09/amazon-parler-suspension/.

107. Lin Wood, Telegram post, January 11, 2021, 3:44 p.m. EST. https://t.me/linwoodspeakstruth/6.

108. Lin Wood, Telegram post, January 12, 2021, 8:36 p.m. EST. https://t.me/linwoodspeakstruth/26.

109. Lin Wood, Telegram post, January 12, 2021, 11:32 p.m. EST. https://t.me/linwoodspeakstruth/34.

110. Lin Wood, Telegram Post, January 16, 1:37 p.m. https://t.me/linwoodspeakstruth/57.

111. Lin Wood, Telegram post, January 16, 2021, 8:58 p.m. EST. https://t.me/linwoodspeakstruth/59.

112. Lin Wood, Telegram post, January 18, 2021, 1:34 p.m. EST] https://t.me/linwoodspeakstruth/68.

113. Lin Wood, Telegram post, January 18, 2021, 1:47 p.m. EST https://t.me/linwoodspeakstruth/69.

114. Lin Wood, Telegram post, January 19, 2021, 11:58 a.m. EST https://t.me/linwoodspeakstruth/100.

115. Lin Wood, Telegram post, January

19, 2021, 12:03 p.m. EST https://t.me/linwoodspeakstruth/102.
116. Lin Wood, Telegram post, January 19, 2021, 12:06 p.m. EST https://t.me/linwoodspeakstruth/104.
117. Lin Wood, Telegram post, January 19, 2021, 12:09 p.m. EST https://t.me/linwoodspeakstruth/106.
118. Lin Wood, Telegram post, January 19, 2021, 1:01 p.m. EST https://t.me/linwoodspeakstruth/109.
119. Lin Wood, Telegram post, January 20, 2021, 11:17 a.m. EST https://t.me/linwoodspeakstruth/136.
120. Kate Brumback, "State Bar Looking into Lawyer Who Pushed Voter Fraud Claims," *Washington Post*, January 29, 2021, https://www.washingtonpost.com/health/state-bar-looking-into-lawyer-who-pushed-voter-fraud-claims/2021/01/29/43e7b6f4–6275–11eb-a177–7765f29a9524_story.html.
121. Lin Wood, Telegram post, January 17, 2021, 10:40 a.m., https://t.me/linwoodspeakstruth/224.
122. Lin Wood, Telegram post, February 11, 2021, 1:27 p.m. EST. https://t.me/linwoodspeakstruth/567.
123. Lin Wood, Telegram post, February 11, 2021, 3:00 p.m. EST. https://t.me/linwoodspeakstruth/569.

Epilogue

1. imstove2, "R/QAnonCasualties—My Mom Loves Qanon & NESARA," reddit, accessed April 1, 2021, https://www.reddit.com/r/QAnonCasualties/comments/i814cc/my_mom_loves_qanon_nesara/.
2. Parler user anonpatriotq, January 11, 2021.
3. Parler user Dawnj, January 11, 2021.

Bibliography

Books

Barkun, Michael. *A Culture of Conspiracy: Apocalyptic Visions in Contemporary America*. Comparative Studies in Religion and Society 15. Berkeley: University of California Press, 2006.
Boylan, Richard. *The Human-Star Nations Connections: Key to History, Current Secrets, and Our Near Future*. Self-published, 2012.
Boylan, Richard J. *Project Epiphany*. Escondido, CA: The Book Tree, 1996.
Boylan, Richard J. *Star Kids: The Emerging Cosmic Generation*. Sun Lakes, AZ: Blue Star Productions, 2004.
Boylan, Richard J., and Lee K. Boylan. *Close Extraterrestrial Encounters: Positive Experiences with Mysterious Visitors*. Tigard, OR: Wild Flower Press, 1994.
DeHaven-Smith, Lance. *Conspiracy Theory in America*. Austin: University of Texas Press, 2014.
Fenster, Mark. *Conspiracy Theories: Secrecy and Power in American Culture*. Minneapolis: University of Minnesota Press, 1999.
Greer, Steven. *Unacknowledged: An Expose of the World's Greatest Secret*. Afton, VA: Sirius Technology Advanced Research, 2017.
Gulyas, Aaron John. *Conspiracy Theories: The Roots, Themes and Propagation of Paranoid Political and Cultural Narratives*. Jefferson, NC: McFarland, 2016.
Hadley, David P. *The Rising Clamor: The American Press, the Central Intelligence Agency, and the Cold War*. Lexington: University Press of Kentucky, 2019.
Jacobs, David Michael. *The UFO Controversy in America*. New York: Signet, 1976.
Knight, Peter, ed. *Conspiracy Nation: The Politics of Paranoia in Postwar America*. New York: New York University Press, 2002.
Krulos, Tea. *American Madness: The Story of the Phantom Patriot and How Conspiracy Theories Hijacked American Consciousness*. Port Townsend, WA: Feral House, 2020.
Merlan, Anna. *Republic of Lies: American Conspiracy Theorists and Their Surprising Rise to Power*. First edition. New York: Metropolitan Books/Henry Holt and Company, 2019.
Muirhead, Russell, and Nancy L. Rosenblum. *A Lot of People Are Saying: The New Conspiracism and the Assault on Democracy*. Princeton: Princeton University Press, 2019.
O'Connell, Mark. *The Close Encounters Man: How One Man Made the World Believe in UFOs*. New York: Dey Street, 2017.
Redpill The World. *QAnon and the Battle of Armageddon: Destroying the New World Order and Taking the Millennial Kingdom by Force*. n.p.: n.p., 2019.
Robinson, David E. *NESARA I: National Economic Security and Reformation Act*. Brunswick, Maine: Maine-Patriot.com, 2011.
_____. *NESARA II: National Economic Security and Reformation Act*. Brunswick, Maine: Maine-Patriot.com, 2011.
Ruppelt, Edward J. *The Report on Unidentified Flying Objects*. Garden City, NY: Doubleday, 1956.

Stormer, John. *None Dare Call It Treason.* Florissant, Missouri: Liberty Bell Press, 1964.
Thomas, Kenn. *Trumpocalyspe Now!: The Triumph of the Conspiracy Spectacle.* Kempton, Ill.: Adventures Unlimited Press, 2017.
Wesser, Chris J., and Dov M. Szego. *The Anti-Government Movement Guidebook.* Williamsburg, VA: The National Center for State Courts, 1999.
WWG1WGA. *QAnon: An Invitation to The Great Awakening.* Dallas: Relentlessly Creative Books, 2019.

Internet Sources

Baragona, Justin. "Trumpist Lawyer Lin Wood Casually Suggests Chief Justice John Roberts Is a Murderous Pedophile." *The Daily Beast*, December 31, 2020. https://www.thedailybeast.com/trumpist-lawyer-lin-wood-casually-suggests-chief-justice-john-roberts-is-a-murderous-pedophile.
Barnard, Harvey. "NESARA—The Bill, Executive Summary." nesara.org, September 11, 2001. https://web.archive.org/web/20080126203932/http://nesara.org/articles/the_real_nesara.htm.
———. "NESARA—The 'Real' NESARA." nesara.org, January 26, 2008. https://web.archive.org/web/20080126203932/http://nesara.org/articles/the_real_nesara.htm.
Barry, Dan, Mike McIntire, and Matthew Rosenberg. "'Our President Wants Us Here': The Mob That Stormed the Capitol." *The New York Times*, January 9, 2021, sec. U.S. https://www.nytimes.com/2021/01/09/us/capitol-rioters.html.
Bekow, Steve. "What Is NESARA?" Golden Age of Gaia, April 15, 2020. https://goldenageofgaia.com/2020/04/15/what-is-nesara-3/.
bellingcat. "The QAnon Timeline: Four Years, 5,000 Drops and Countless Failed Prophecies," January 29, 2021. https://www.bellingcat.com/news/americas/2021/01/29/the-qanon-timeline/.
Berger, J.M. "Without Prejudice: What Sovereign Citizens Believe." Washington, D.C.: George Washington University Program on Extremism, June 2016. https://perma.cc/9RXF-9UFX.
Berstein, Carl. "The CIA and the Media." Carl Bernstein, October 20, 1977. http://www.carlbernstein.com/magazine_cia_and_media.php.
Beter, Peter David. "Audio Letter No. 46.," n.d. http://www.peterdavidbeter.com/docs/all/dbal46.html.
Bethea, Charles. "A Trump Holdout in Atlanta." *The New Yorker*, January 23, 2021. https://www.newyorker.com/magazine/2021/02/01/a-trump-holdout-in-atlanta.
Blake, Aaron. "A Trio of Brutal Rulings for Trump's Voter Fraud Push." *Washington Post*, December 7, 2020. https://www.washingtonpost.com/politics/2020/12/07/another-weekend-another-batch-brutal-legal-filings-trump-backed-voter-fraud-effort/.
Bonn, Tony. "The American Chronicle: The Murder of Admiral Jeremy Boorda." *The American Chronicle* (blog), March 9, 2014. http://theamericanchronicle.blogspot.com/2014/03/the-murder-of-admiral-jeremy-boorda.html.
Boylan, Richard. "Brief Biography of Dr. Richard J. Boylan, Ph.D." Accessed January 22, 2021. https://drboylan.com/rjbbio2.html.
———. "Dr. Richard Boylan's Curriculum Vitae." Accessed January 22, 2021. https://drboylan.com/resumefullrb.html.
———. "Dr. Richard Boylan's Official Website." Accessed January 21, 2021. https://drboylan.com/.
———. "Mothership Over the UN," 2020. https://drboylan.com/MothershipOverUN.html.
———. "The 11:11 Universal and Spiritual Principles or Laws of the Cosmos." Accessed January 20, 2021. https://drboylan.com/11.11laws.html.
———. "2018: The Cabal's Last Stand: Star Seeds' Coming Victory in a Peaceful 'Velvet Revolution,'" August 8, 2018. https://web.archive.org/web/20180827081238/https://drboylan.com/2017caballaststand.html.

Bibliography

———. "2019: The Cabal's Last Stand: Star Seeds' Coming Victory in a Peaceful 'Velvet Revolution,'" March 15, 2019. https://drboylan.com/2017caballaststand.html.

———. "2017: The Cabal's Last Stand: Star Seeds' Coming Victory in a Peaceful 'Velvet Revolution,'" April 1, 2016. https://web.archive.org/web/20160401004054/http://drboylan.com/2017caballaststand.html.

Boylan, Richard J. "Becoming Cosmic Citizens: Dr. Boylan's Speech to the ACCET Annual Convention, 10/15/00," October 15, 2000. https://drboylan.com/acctspech2.html.

———. "An Open Letter to the Community About Government Harassment." Brother Blue, December 14, 1995. http://web.archive.org/web/19980711104056/http://www.brotherblue.org/brethren/boylanfa.htm.

———. "Open Letter to the UFO Cover-Up." Brother Blue, March 11, 1997. http://web.archive.org/web/19980711104117/http://www.brotherblue.org/brethren/tpoc.htm.

———. "Report on Formal Hearing and Indictment of the Cabal on Violations of Universal Laws," October 2, 2005. https://drboylan.com/formalhearing.html.

Bramerton, Alcuin. "Alcuin and Flutterby: NESARA Announcements Expected in 2020." *Alcuin and Flutterby* (blog), November 1, 2020. http://alcuinbramerton.blogspot.com/2007/07/nesara-announcement-expected-in-run-up.html.

———. "Blogger: User Profile: Alcuin Bramerton." Accessed December 16, 2020. https://www.blogger.com/profile/14917474523744351041.

Brother Blue. "Richard J. Boylan, Ph. D.—Reptoid Hugger." Brother Blue, July 11, 1998. http://web.archive.org/web/19980711104241/http://www.brotherblue.org/brethren/boylanre.htm.

Brumback, Kate. "State Bar Looking into Lawyer Who Pushed Voter Fraud Claims." *Washington Post*, January 29, 2021. https://www.washingtonpost.com/health/state-bar-looking-into-lawyer-who-pushed-voter-fraud-claims/2021/01/29/43e7b6f4-6275-11eb-a177-7765f29a9524_story.html.

Calfas, Jennifer. "President Trump Warns of 'the Calm Before the Storm' During Military Meeting." *Time*, October 5, 2017. https://time.com/4971738/donald-trump-calm-before-the-storm-military-white-house/.

Carter, Brandon. "What Is QAnon? The Conspiracy Theory Tiptoeing Into Trump World." *National Public Radio*, August 2018. Accessed March 31, 2020. https://www.npr.org/2018/08/02/634749387/what-is-qanon-the-conspiracy-theory-tiptoeing-into-trump-world.

Dastin, Jeffrey. "Amazon to Remove QAnon Products from Platform after U.S. Capitol Siege." *Reuters*, January 12, 2021. https://www.reuters.com/article/us-amazon-com-qanon-idUSKBN29H03U.

DeCanio, Samuel. "Populism, Paranoia, and the Politics of Free Silver." *Studies in American Political Development* 25, no. 1 (2011): 1–26. https://doi.org/10.1017/S0898588X11000010.

Department of Justice, Office of Internal Affairs. "Maine Businessman Sentenced to Prison for Tax Crimes." Department of Justice, August 27, 2015. https://www.justice.gov/opa/pr/maine-businessman-sentenced-prison-tax-crimes.

Detweiler, Nancy. "History of NESARA: The National Economic Security and Reformation Act." *Maine Republic Email Alert*, June 7, 2012.

Detweiler, Nancy B. "History of NESARA." *The Way of Love* (blog), August 17, 2011. https://pathwaytoascension.wordpress.com/2011/08/17/history-of-nesara/.

———. "NESARA Rights the Unthinkable Wrongs Perpetrated on the American People & the World >> Four Winds 10—Truth Winds." Accessed March 10, 2020. http://fourwinds10.com/siterun_data/nesara/history/news.php?q=1339170793.

Duduman, Dumitru. "The Message for America." Hand of Help, n.d. https://www.handofhelp.com/vision_1.php.

DumbScribblyUnctious. "Comet Ping Pong—Pizzagate Summary : Pizzagate." Reddit, November 17, 2016. https://web.archive.org/web/20161122231637/https://www.reddit.com/r/pizzagate/comments/5da0kp/comet_ping_pong_pizzagate_summary/.

Eisen, Norman, and Joanna Lydgate. "The Lawyers Who Pushed Trump's Falsehoods

May Soon Be Done Lawyering." *Washington Post,* February 3, 2021. https://www.washingtonpost.com/outlook/2021/02/03/powell-wood-accountability-lawyer/.

"FBI Anon AMA Transcripts," October 17, 2016. https://paulfurber.net/pdf/fbianon.pdf.

Finkelstein, Joel, Savvas Zannettou, Barry Bradlyn, and Jeremy Blackburn. "A Quantitative Approach to Understanding Online Antisemitism." In *Proceedings of the Fourteenth International AAAI Conference on Web and Social Media.* Association for the Advancement of Artificial Intelligence, 2020: 786–797.

Fisher, Marc, John Woodrow Cox, and Peter Hermann. "Pizzagate: From Rumor, to Hashtag, to Gunfire in D.C." *Washington Post,* December 6, 2016, sec. Local. https://www.washingtonpost.com/local/pizzagate-from-rumor-to-hashtag-to-gunfire-in-dc/2016/12/06/4c7def50-bbd4-11e6-94ac-3d324840106c_story.html.

Flaherty, Emma, and Laura Roselle. "Contentious Narratives and Europe: Conspiracy Theories and Strategic Narratives Surrounding RT's Brexit News Coverage." *Journal of International Affairs* 71, no. 1.5 (2018): 53–60.

Friedberg, Brian. "The Dark Virality of a Hollywood Blood-Harvesting Conspiracy." *Wired,* July 31, 2020. https://www.wired.com/story/opinion-the-dark-virality-of-a-hollywood-blood-harvesting-conspiracy/.

Fulford, Benjamin. "'Jesus Christ to Marry Asian Goddess' as East-West Secret Societies Agree to Save Planet," November 12, 2018. https://benjaminfulford.net/2018/11/12/jesus-christ-to-marry-asian-goddess-as-east-west-secret-societies-agree-to-save-planet/.

Gabbatt, Adam. "Trump Refuses to Disavow QAnon Conspiracy Theory during Town Hall." *The Guardian.* Accessed March 25, 2021. https://www.theguardian.com/us-news/2020/oct/15/qanon-trump-refuses-disavow-conspiracy-theory-town-hall.

Gambino, Lauren. "Who Is the Republican Extremist Marjorie Taylor Greene?" *The Guardian,* February 6, 2021. http://www.theguardian.com/us-news/2021/feb/06/who-is-marjorie-taylor-greene-republican-qanon.

Georgieva, Kristalina. "The Great Reset." *International Monetary Fund,* June 3, 2020. https://www.imf.org/en/News/Articles/2020/06/03/sp060320-remarks-to-world-economic-forum-the-great-reset.

GESARA HELP—Global Economic Security and Reformation Act. "GESARA HELP—Global Economic Security and Reformation Act." Accessed December 7, 2020. http://www.gesarahelp.org.

Goldberg, Carey. "The Freemen Sought Refuge in an Ideology That Kept the Law, and Reality, at Bay." *The New York Times,* June 16, 1996, sec. U.S. https://www.nytimes.com/1996/06/16/us/the-freemen-sought-refuge-in-an-ideology-that-kept-the-law-andreality-at-bay.html.

Goodwin, Shaini. "April 02, 2002—NESARA Before Mid-April; Debt Forgiveness; Keep $ Onshore." NESARA.us, December 20, 2007. https://web.archive.org/web/20071220024201/http://www.nesara.us/apr02/April_02__2002_-_NESARA_Before_Mid-April__Debt_Forgiveness__Keep___Onshore.htm.

_____. "April 04, 2002—Current Activities Bringing NESARA." NESARA.us, December 20, 2007. https://web.archive.org/web/20071220015746/http://www.nesara.us/apr02/April_04__2002_-_Current_Activities_Bringing_NESARA.htm.

_____. "April 05, 2002—America Is Way Shower, Heralding Golden Age." NESARA.us, December 20, 2007. https://web.archive.org/web/20071220024221/http://www.nesara.us/apr02/April_05__2002_-_America_is_Way_Shower__Heralding_Golden_Age.htm.

_____. "April 06, 2002—NESARA on Target BEFORE Mid-April." NESARA.us, December 20, 2007. https://web.archive.org/web/20071220015751/http://www.nesara.us/apr02/April_06__2002_-_NESARA_on_Target_BEFORE_Mid-April.htm.

_____. "April 10, 2002—Answering Some of Your Questions." NESARA.us, December 20, 2007. https://web.archive.org/web/20071220024226/http://www.nesara.us/apr02/April_10__2002_-_Answering_Some_of_Your_Questions.htm.

_____. "April 23, 2002—We the People Can Announce NESARA If Necessary!" NESARA.us, December 20, 2007. https://web.archive.org/web/20071220024321/http://www.

nesara.us/apr02/April_23__2002_-_We_The_People_Can_Announce_NESARA_If_ Necessary_.htm.

———. "April 27, 2002—NESARA Is KEY; Avoid Anti-NESARA Info." NESARA.us, December 20, 2007. https://web.archive.org/web/20071220024337/http://www.nesara. us/apr02/April_27__2002_-_NESARA_is_KEY__Avoid-NESARA_Info.htm.

———. "April 28, 2002—Saint Germain Authorizes Confirmations of Ascended Masters." NESARA.us, April 28, 2002. https://web.archive.org/web/20071220015907/http://www.nesara.us/apr02/April_28__2002_-_Saint_Germain_Authorizes_Confirmations_of_Ascended_Masters.htm.

———. "April 29, 2002—Media Prepares for NESARA Announcement." NESARA.us, December 20, 2007. https://web.archive.org/web/20071220024352/http://www.nesara.us/apr02/April_29__2002_-_Media_Prepares_for_NESARA_Announcement. htm.

———. "April 30, 2002—About the NESARA Announcement & Deliveries." NESARA.us, December 20, 2007. https://web.archive.org/web/20071220015912/http://www.nesara.us/apr02/April_30__2002_-_About_the_NESARA_Announcement___Deliveries.htm.

———. "August 23, 2002—NESARA, Big Money & White Knights." NESARA.us, December 20, 2007. https://web.archive.org/web/20071220024453/http://www.nesara.us/aug02/August_23__2002_-_NESARA__Big_Money___White_Knights.htm.

———. "Friday, March 15, 2002 9:33 Pm." NESARA.us, December 20, 2007. https://web.archive.org/web/20071220024201/http://www.nesara.us/apr02/April_02__2002_-_NESARA_Before_Mid-April__Debt_Forgiveness__Keep___Onshore.htm.

———. "June 12, 2002—Let's Take ACTION & Get NESARA Announced!" NESARA.us, December 20, 2007. https://web.archive.org/web/20071220033017/http://www.nesara.us/june02/June_12__2002_-__Let_s_Take_ACTION___Get_NESARA_Announced_.htm.

———. "June 12, 2002—Let's Take ACTION & Get NESARA Announced!" NESARA.us, June 12, 2002. https://web.archive.org/web/20071220033017/http://www.nesara.us/june02/June_12__2002_-__Let_s_Take_ACTION___Get_NESARA_Announced_.htm.

———. "May 1, 2002—To WKs; END Meetings; DO NESARA NOW!" NESARA.us, December 20, 2007. https://web.archive.org/web/20071220033128/http://www.nesara.us/may02/May_01__2002_-_To_WKs__END_Meetings__DO_NESARA_NOW_.htm.

———. "May 30, 2002—NESARA & Prosperity Actions in Process." NESARA.us, December 20, 2007. https://web.archive.org/web/20071220023758/http://www.nesara.us/may02/May_30__2002_-_NESARA___Prosperity_Actions_in_Process.htm.

———. "THE NATIONAL ECONOMIC SECURITY & REFORMATION ACT—A SUMMARY BY DOVE." *The Way of Love Blog* (blog), June 18, 2012. https://pathwaytoascension.wordpress.com/2012/06/18/the-national-economic-security-reformation-act-a-summary-by-dove/.

———. "NESARA -> Action Plan." NESARA.us, August 28, 2009. https://web.archive.org/web/20090828135001/http://www.nesara.us/pages/actionplan.html.

———. "NESARA -> Benefits." NESARA.us, August 28, 2009. https://web.archive.org/web/20090828142240/http://www.nesara.us/pages/benefits.html.

———. "NESARA -> Confirmations." NESARA.us, August 28, 2009. https://web.archive.org/web/20090828141433/http://nesara.us/pages/confirmations.html.

———. "NESARA -> History of NESARA (December 9, 2003)." NESARA.us, December 9, 2003. https://web.archive.org/web/20031209145956/http://www.nesara.us:80/pages/history.html.

———. "NESARA -> History of NESARA (May 22, 2005)." NESARA.us, May 22, 2005. https://web.archive.org/web/20050522234543/http://www.nesara.us:80/pages/history.html.

———. "NESARA -> History of NESARA." NESARA.us, August 23, 2009. https://web.archive.org/web/20090823064340/http://www.nesara.us/pages/history.html.

———. "NESARA -> Supporters." NESARA.us, December 17, 2007. https://web.archive.org/web/20071217042605/http://www.nesara.us/pages/supporters.html.

———. "NESARA Is KEY; Avoid Anti-NESARA Info." NESARA.us, April 27, 2002. https://web.archive.org/web/20071220024337/http://www.nesara.us/apr02/April_27__2002_-_NESARA_is_KEY__Avoid_Anti-NESARA_Info.htm.

———. "NESARA, the National Economic Security and Reformation Act." NESARA.us, December 5, 2003. https://web.archive.org/web/20031205051211/http://www.nesara.us/pages/home.html.

———. "September 26, 2002—NESARA Foretold by Ascended Master Saint Germain." NESARA.us, September 26, 2002. https://web.archive.org/web/20071220033834/http://www.nesara.us/sept2/September_26__2002_-_NESARA_Foretold_by_Ascended_Master_Saint_Germain.htm.

Greer, Steven. "CSETI Homepage." CSETI, March 1, 2001. https://web.archive.org/web/20010301201645/http://www.cseti.org/.

———. "Programs." CSETI, February 6, 2001. https://web.archive.org/web/20010206140645/http://www.cseti.org/programs/programs.htm.

Greer, Steven M. "Close Encounters of the Fifth Kind." CSETI, February 3, 2001. https://web.archive.org/web/20010203222300/http://www.cseti.org/programs/ce_5.htm.

———. "Disclosure and 9/11: An Analysis." Sirius Disclosure. *Dr. Steven Greer* (blog), September 2001. https://siriusdisclosure.com/cseti-papers/disclosure-and-911-an-analysis/.

———. "Dr. Greer's Response to Former CIA Director Woolsey's Denial of Meeting." *Dr. Steven Greer* (blog), September 23, 1999. https://siriusdisclosure.com/dr-greers-response-to-former-cia-director-woolseys-denial-of-meeting/.

———. "Executive Summary of the Disclosure Project Briefing Document." The Disclosure Project, April 2001. https://siriusdisclosure.com/wp-content/uploads/2012/12/ExecutiveSummary-LRdocs.pdf.

———. "Exopolitics or Xenopolitics?" *Sirius Disclosure* (blog), May 2, 2006. https://siriusdisclosure.com/cseti-papers/exopolitics-or-xenopolitics/.

———. "Letter to President Bill Clinton (1996)." *Dr. Steven Greer* (blog), November 15, 1996. https://siriusdisclosure.com/cseti-papers/letter-to-president-bill-clinton-1996/.

———. "One Universe, One People." Sirius Disclosure, 1991. https://siriusdisclosure.com/cseti-papers/one-universe-one-people/.

Greer, Steven M., and Thomas C. Loder III. "Disclosure Project Briefing Document." The Disclosure Project, April 2001. https://web.archive.org/web/20110526124303/http://www.disclosureproject.org/access/docs/pdf/DisclosureProjectBriefingDocument.pdf.

Harwell, Drew. "QAnon Believers Seek to Adapt Their Extremist Ideology for a New Era: 'Things Have Just Started.'" *Washington Post*, January 21, 2021. https://www.washingtonpost.com/technology/2021/01/21/qanon-faithful-biden-trump/.

Harwell, Drew, and Craig Timberg. "QAnon Believers Grapple with Doubt, Spin New Theories as Trump Era Ends: 'We All Got Played.'" *Washington Post*. Accessed January 20, 2021. https://www.washingtonpost.com/technology/2021/01/20/qanon-trump-era-ends/.

Herscu, Shoshi. "The Global Currency Reset and Our Liberation from the Debt Slavery Financial System." *Mass Awakening* (blog), March 22, 2019. https://massawakening.org/the-global-currency-reset-and-our-liberation-from-the-debt-slavery-financial-system/.

"High Level Insider," March 4, 2017. http://hli.anoninfo.net/.

Hofstadter, Richard. "The Paranoid Style in American Politics." *Harper's Magazine*, November 1, 1964. https://harpers.org/archive/1964/11/the-paranoid-style-in-american-politics/.

Hsu, Spencer S. "Comet Pizza Gunman Pleads Guilty to Federal and Local Charges." *Washington Post*, March 24, 2017. https://www.washingtonpost.com/local/public-safety/comet-pizza-gunman-to-appear-at-plea-deal-hearing-friday-morning/2017/03/23/e12c91ba-0986-11e7-b77c-0047d15a24e0_story.html.

imstove2. "R/QAnonCasualties—My Mom Loves Qanon & NESARA." reddit. Accessed

April 1, 2021. https://www.reddit.com/r/QAnonCasualties/comments/i814cc/my_mom_loves_qanon_nesara/.
Johnson, Stan. "About The Prophecy Club." Prophecy Club, July 4, 2014. https://www.prophecyclub.com/about.html.
———. "THE PROPHECY CLUB May/June 1999 NEWSLETTER." Prophecy Club, September 29, 2000. https://web.archive.org/web/20000929160048/http://www.prophecyclub.com/text2/may99.htm#Anchor3.
———. "The Prophecy Club Newsletter for March and April 2000." Prophecy Club, June 3, 2000. https://web.archive.org/web/20000603083209/http://www.prophecyclub.com/mar00/1.html.
———. "Radio Schedule." Prophecy Club. Accessed March 11, 2020. https://www.prophecyclub.com/radio-schedule.html.
Kalinowski IV, Caesar. "A Legal Response to the Sovereign Citizen Movement." *Montana Law Review* 80, no. 2 (August 1, 2019): 153–210.
Kat. "Charlie and Colleen Freak: NESARA, Tesla Towers and B. Gates Updates 8–2-20." *Disclosure Chronicles Blog* (blog), August 4, 2020. https://inteldinarchronicles.blogspot.com/2020/08/charlie-and-colleen-freak-nesara-tesla.html.
Kelley, Charles R. "What Is Orgone Energy?" *The Creative Process* 2, no. 2 (September 1962). http://www.kelley-radix.org/downloads/what_is_orgone_energy.pdf.
Kerr, Bob. "Colorado Man Gives Hope to Financially Hurt Farmers in Fight Against Foreclosure." *The Lewiston Tribune*, November 7, 1993. https://lmtribune.com/nation/world/colorado-man-gives-hope-to-financially-hurt-farmers-in-fight-against-foreclosure/article_7956d913-7966-5030-8c73-00733901dbff.html.
Kludt, Tom. "'Pizzagate': Comet Ping Pong Not the Only D.C. Business Enduring a Nightmare." *CNNMoney*, December 5, 2016. https://money.cnn.com/2016/12/05/media/pizzagate-threatening-calls-washington-dc-businesses/index.html.
Layne, Meade. "Fly, Lokas, Fly!" *Round Robin* 3, no. 8 (December 1948): 8–9.
Leland, John. "Are They Here to Save the World?" *The New York Times*, January 12, 2006, sec. Style. https://www.nytimes.com/2006/01/12/fashion/thursdaystyles/are-they-here-to-save-the-world.html.
Los Angeles Times. "Coloradan Sows Seeds of a Farm Loan Revolt," November 28, 1993. https://www.latimes.com/archives/la-xpm-1993-11-28-mn-61641-story.html.
———. "2 Sentenced for Activist Group Fraud Scheme," November 5, 1995. https://www.latimes.com/archives/la-xpm-1995-11-05-mn-65157-story.html.
Mac, Ryan. "Trump-Supporting Lawyer Lin Wood Has Been Permanently Banned From Twitter." *BuzzFeed News*, January 7, 2021. https://www.buzzfeednews.com/article/ryanmac/twitter-bans-lin-wood.
McConnell, James. "MUST READ: Saint Germain ~ The Beginning of the Next Phase." Golden Age of Gaia, October 16, 2020. https://goldenageofgaia.com/2020/10/16/must-read-saint-germain-the-beginning-of-the-next-phase/.
Medical Board of California—Board of Psychology. In the Matter of the Accusation Against: Richard J. Boylan, Ph.D, No. W-14 and LMS-57 (August 4, 1995).
Meier, Barry. "The Lien King on the Attack." *The New York Times*, June 29, 1995, sec. Business. https://www.nytimes.com/1995/06/29/business/the-lien-king-on-the-attack.html.
Meyer, Peter B. "The Change—The Final Wakeup Call—English." *The Final Wakeup Call* (blog). Accessed March 12, 2020. http://finalwakeupcall.info/en/2018/03/28/the-change/.
———. "QFS Off-World Monetary System." *The Final Wakeup Call* (blog). Accessed March 12, 2020. http://finalwakeupcall.info/en/2019/03/06/qfs-off-world-monetary-system/.
Mogensen, Jackie Flynn. "To Celebrate the Fourth, Michael Flynn Posts a Pledge to Conspiracy Group Qanon." *Mother Jones* (blog), July 5, 2020, https://www.motherjones.com/politics/2020/07/to-celebrate-the-fourth-michael-flynn-posts-a-pledge-to-conspiracy-group-qanon/.
Monmouth University Poll. "Public Troubled by 'Deep State.'" *Monmouth University Polling Institute* (blog), March 19, 2018. https://www.monmouth.edu/polling-institute/reports/monmouthpoll_us_031918/.

Moore, Mark. "Conway: Trump Spokesman Gave 'Alternative Facts.'" *New York Post*, January 22, 2017. https://nypost.com/2017/01/22/conway-trump-spokesman-gave-alternative-facts-on-inauguration-crowd/.

NESARA—The Reformation Act. "NESARA—The Reformation Act," February 4, 2004. https://web.archive.org/web/20040204173220/http://nesara.insights2.org/index.html.

———. Post N.E.S.A.R.A.—What Then?—Cost of Living: Monetary and Other Financial Matters," February 21, 2004. https://web.archive.org/web/20040221222514/http://nesara.insights2.org/Living.html.

———. "Post N.E.S.A.R.A.—What Then?—Education," February 21, 2004. https://web.archive.org/web/20040221221950/http://nesara.insights2.org/Education.html.

———. "Post N.E.S.A.R.A.—What Then?—Health," January 5, 2004. https://web.archive.org/web/20040105202602/http://nesara.insights2.org/Health.html.

———. "Post N.E.S.A.R.A.—What Then?—Meeting with ETs," February 21, 2004. https://web.archive.org/web/20040221221417/http://nesara.insights2.org/ETs.html.

———. "Post N.E.S.A.R.A.—What Then?—Sports," March 1, 2004. https://web.archive.org/web/20040301073950/http://nesara.insights2.org/Sports.html.

———. "Post N.E.S.A.R.A.—What Then?—Technology," March 1, 2004. https://web.archive.org/web/20040301074352/http://nesara.insights2.org/Tech.html.

"NESARA—REPUBLIC NOW—GALACTIC NEWS." Accessed December 22, 2020. http://nesaranews.blogspot.com/.

"NESARA—REPUBLIC NOW—GALACTIC NEWS: 'HISTORY BEING MADE RIGHT NOW'—New Republic via GCR—220 Points of Fact' as of May 2016," May 28, 2016. http://nesaranews.blogspot.com/2016/05/history-being-made-right-now-new.html.

Noah. "Lin Wood: Americans Will Be Shocked at Level of Pedophilia & Satanic Worship Occupying Oval Office for Years (Before Trump)." We Love Trump, November 24, 2020. https://welovetrump.com/2020/11/23/lin-wood-americans-will-be-shocked-at-level-of-pedophilia-satanic-worship-occupying-oval-office-for-years-before-trump/.

Ong, Kyler. "Ideological Convergence in the Extreme Right." *Counter Terrorist Trends and Analyses* 12, no. 5 (September 2020): 1–7.

Paul, Sharon. "Press Release: Leader of Omega Trust & Trading, Ltd. Pleads Guilty to International Fraud, Money Laundering Conspiracy." US Attorney's Office-Central District of Illinois, April 10, 2001. https://web.archive.org/web/20060620003555/http://www.justice.gov/usao/ilc/press/041001hood.html.

Petrizzo, Zachary. "Lin Wood Continues to Invoke Violence on Parler." *Mediaite* (blog), January 8, 2021. https://www.mediaite.com/news/pro-trump-lawyer-lin-wood-calls-for-pence-to-be-executed-posts-get-removed-from-parler/.

Pew Research Center. "QAnon's Conspiracy Theories Have Seeped into U.S. Politics, but Most Don't Know What It Is," March 30, 2020. https://www.pewresearch.org/fact-tank/2020/03/30/qanons-conspiracy-theories-have-seeped-into-u-s-politics-but-most-dont-know-what-it-is/.

Q Origins Project. "The Making of QAnon: A Crowdsourced Conspiracy." belling cat, January 7, 2021. https://www.bellingcat.com/news/americas/2021/01/07/the-making-of-qanon-a-crowdsourced-conspiracy/.

Rampell, Catherine. "Americans—Especially but Not Exclusively Trump Voters—Believe Crazy, Wrong Things." *Washington Post*, December 28, 2016. https://www.washingtonpost.com/news/rampage/wp/2016/12/28/americans-especially-but-not-exclusively-trump-voters-believe-crazy-wrong-things/.

The Redemption Service. "Apply for Free Membership." Accessed March 8, 2021. https://www.redemptionservice.com/join-our-membership/.

———. "Meet Your Straw Man." Accessed March 8, 2021. https://www.redemptionservice.com/meet-your-strawman/.

———. "Secured Party Creditor." Accessed March 8, 2021. https://www.redemptionservice.com/secured-party-creditor/.

Rice, Daniel. "The 'Uniform Rule' and Its Exceptions: A History of Congressional Naturalization Legislation." *The Ozark Historical Review* 40 (2011): 23–64.

Robb, Amanda. "Pizzagate: Anatomy of a Fake News Scandal." *Rolling Stone*, November 16, 2017. https://www.rollingstone.com/feature/anatomy-of-a-fake-news-scandal-125877/.

Robertson, H.P. "Report of Meetings of Scientific Advisory Panel on Unidentified Flying Objects." n.p.: Office of Scientific Intelligence, Central Intelligence Agency, January 1953. https://documents.theblackvault.com/documents/ufos/robertsonpanelreport.pdf.

Robinson, David E. "Declaration of Sovereignty." The Patriot/UCC Redemption and Redemption in Law, April 6, 2004. http://maine-patriot.com/6.htm.

Robinson, Sean. "Snared by a Cybercult Queen." *The News Tribune*, July 18, 2004. https://www.thenewstribune.com/news/special-reports/article25855081.html.

———. "Up Against 'The Dark Agenda.'" *The News Tribune*, July 17, 2013. https://www.thenewstribune.com/news/special-reports/article25855078.html.

Romm, Tony, and Rachel Lerman. "Amazon Suspends Parler, Taking pro–Trump Site Offline Indefinitely." *Washington Post*, January 11, 2021. https://www.washingtonpost.com/technology/2021/01/09/amazon-parler-suspension/.

Romm, Tony, Elizabeth Dwoskin, and Drew Harwell. "Twitter, Facebook Lock Trump's Accounts amid D.C. Riots." *Washington Post*, January 6, 2021. https://www.washingtonpost.com/technology/2021/01/06/trump-tweet-violence/.

Saint Germain Foundation. "Saint Germain, Messengers." Accessed December 1, 2020. https://www.saintgermainfoundation.org/saint-germain.

Salla, Michael. "Are Secret Space Program Disclosures Prelude to a False Flag Alien Invasion?" *Exopolitics* (blog), November 19, 2016. https://exopolitics.org/are-secret-space-program-disclosures-prelude-to-a-false-flag-alien-invasion/.

———. "The Big (Exopolitics) Picture behind Trump Russia Collusion Narrative & Its Collapse." *Exopolitics* (blog), March 26, 2019. https://exopolitics.org/big-exopolitics-picture-behind-trump-russia-collusion-narrative-its-collapse/.

———. "Bombshell QAnon Posts Link Clintons & CIA to JFK Jr Plane Crash." *Exopolitics* (blog), April 10, 2018. https://exopolitics.org/bombshell-qanon-posts-link-clintons-cia-to-jfk-jr-plane-crash/.

———. "Did Hillary Clinton Sell Secret Space Program Technologies to China?" *Exopolitics* (blog), March 13, 2019. https://exopolitics.org/did-hillary-clinton-sell-secret-space-program-technologies-to-china/.

———. "Did President Trump Endorse Q Info on Secret Indictments of Pedophile Network?" *Exopolitics* (blog), November 27, 2017. https://exopolitics.org/did-president-trump-endorse-q-info-on-secret-indictments-of-pedophile-network/.

———. "Did President Trump Just Acknowledge Extraterrestrials Crashed at Roswell?" *Exopolitics* (blog), June 19, 2020. https://exopolitics.org/did-president-trump-just-acknowledge-extraterrestrials-crashed-at-roswell/.

———. "Did the USSR Destroy a Secret US Moon Base in 1977?" *Exopolitics* (blog), April 19, 2019. https://exopolitics.org/did-the-ussr-destroy-a-secret-us-moon-base-in-1977/.

———. "Dulce Report: Investigating Alleged Human Rights Abuses at a Joint US Government-Extraterrestrial Base at Dulce, New Mexico." *Exopolitics*, September 25, 2003. https://exopolitics.net/Dulce-Report.htm.

———. "Epstein Arrest Supports Q Anon Claims of Global Satanic Cult Blackmailing Political Elites." *Exopolitics* (blog), July 10, 2019. https://exopolitics.org/epstein-arrest-supports-q-anon-claims-of-global-satanic-cult-blackmailing-political-elites/.

———. "Founder." *Exopolitics* (blog), July 10, 2012. https://exopolitics.org/about/founder/.

———. "Interview with Corey Goode on UFO Disclosure War, QAnon, Military Arrests & Dark Fleets." *Exopolitics* (blog), August 23, 2020. https://exopolitics.org/interview-with-corey-goode-on-ufo-disclosure-war-qanon-military-arrests-dark-fleets/.

———. "Kennedy's Last Stand & the Trump Card: Space Cooperation Used against Deep State." *Exopolitics* (blog), November 13, 2020. https://exopolitics.org/kennedys-last-stand-the-trump-card/.

———. "Man in the High Castle Is Soft Disclosure of Temporal War Revealed in Cosmic

Secret." *Exopolitics* (blog), November 25, 2019. https://exopolitics.org/man-in-the-high-castle-is-soft-disclosure-of-temporal-war-revealed-in-cosmic-secret/.

———. "President Trump Validates QAnon—How Will UFO SSP Disclosure Happen?" *Exopolitics* (blog), February 23, 2018. https://exopolitics.org/president-trump-validates-qanon-how-will-ufo-ssp-disclosure-happen/.

———. "Project Looking Glass—The Q Anon & Deep State Temporal War." *Exopolitics* (blog), November 13, 2019. https://exopolitics.org/project-looking-glass-the-q-anon-deep-state-temporal-war/.

———. "Q Confirms Secret Space Programs Real & Extraterrestrial Life Exists." *Exopolitics* (blog), September 20, 2018. https://exopolitics.org/q-confirms-secret-space-programs-real-extraterrestrial-life-exists/.

———. "QAnon Corroborates Hawaii Missile Attack & Hunt for Rogue CIA Submarine." *Exopolitics* (blog), February 18, 2018. https://exopolitics.org/qanon-corroborates-hawaii-missile-attack-hunt-for-rogue-cia-submarine/.

———. "The QAnon Deep State Temporal War & Its Galactic Implications." *Exopolitics* (blog), November 19, 2019. https://exopolitics.org/the-qanon-deep-state-temporal-war-its-galactic-implications/.

———. "QAnon Exposes Hawaii False Flag Missile Attack & Points to Secret Space Program Intervention." *Exopolitics* (blog), August 30, 2018. https://exopolitics.org/qanon-exposes-hawaii-false-flag-missile-attack-points-to-secret-space-program-intervention/.

———. "QAnon Goes Mainstream at Trump Rally While Tripcodes Point to Exopolitics Books." *Exopolitics* (blog), August 3, 2018. https://exopolitics.org/qanon-goes-mainstream-at-trump-rally-while-tripcodes-point-to-exopolitics-books/.

———. "QAnon Is US Military Intelligence That Recruited Trump for President to Prevent Coup D'etat." *Exopolitics* (blog), April 12, 2018. https://exopolitics.org/qanon-is-us-military-intelligence-that-recruited-trump-for-president-to-prevent-coup-detat/.

———. "QAnon Links US Attorney with Thousands of Sealed Indictments Decimating the Deep State." *Exopolitics* (blog), July 2, 2018. https://exopolitics.org/qanon-links-us-attorney-with-thousands-of-sealed-indictments-decimating-the-deep-state/.

———. "QAnon on How Ending Iran Peace Deal Thwarts Deep State Plans for Nuclear False Flag Attack." *Exopolitics* (blog), May 13, 2018. https://exopolitics.org/qanon-on-how-ending-iran-peace-deal-thwarts-deep-state-plans-for-nuclear-false-flag-attack/.

———. "QAnon on the Rothschild, Saudi & Soros Puppet Masters behind the Deep State." *Exopolitics* (blog), April 21, 2018. https://exopolitics.org/qanon-on-the-rothschild-saudi-soros-puppet-masters-behind-the-deep-state/.

———. "QAnon Reveals Deep State Nazi Connection & Attempt to Foment US Russia War." *Exopolitics* (blog), August 29, 2018. https://exopolitics.org/qanon-reveals-deep-state-naz-connection-fomenting-us-russia-war/.

———. "QAnon Reveals Effort to Frame Russia in False Flag Nuclear Attack on US—the Fourth Reich Connection." *Exopolitics* (blog), May 2, 2018. https://exopolitics.org/qanon-reveals-effort-to-frame-russia-in-false-flag-nuclear-attack-on-us-the-fourth-reich-connection/.

———. "QAnon Reveals Vatican Rothschild Reptilian Connection behind the Deep State." *Exopolitics* (blog), April 7, 2018. https://exopolitics.org/qanon-reveals-vatican-rothschild-reptilian-connection-behind-the-deep-state/.

———. "QAnon Unmasks Britain as State Actor That Interfered in US Presidential Election." *Exopolitics* (blog), July 28, 2018. https://exopolitics.org/qanon-unmasks-britain-as-state-actor-that-interfered-in-us-presidential-election/.

———. "Roswell UFO Crash to Be Officially Disclosed as Time-Traveling Future Humans." *Exopolitics* (blog), July 14, 2020. https://exopolitics.org/roswell-ufo-crash-to-be-officially-disclosed-as-time-traveling-future-humans/.

———. "The Secret Race to Control Iraq's Extraterrestrial Heritage," *Exopolitics* (blog), March 27, 2003. https://exopolitics.net/Study-Paper3.htm.

———. "Trump and Q on the Invisible Enemy—the Extraterrestrial Factor." *Exopolitics* (blog), July 1, 2020. https://exopolitics.org/trump-and-q-on-invisible-enemy-extraterrestrial-factor/.

———. "Trump Confirms Q Claims of UK & Deep State Panic over FISA Declassification." *Exopolitics* (blog), September 22, 2018. https://exopolitics.org/trump-confirms-q-claims-of-uk-deep-state-panic-over-fisa-declassification/.

———. "Trump Signs Space Force Act—Stage Set for Secret Space Program Disclosure." *Exopolitics* (blog), December 21, 2019. https://exopolitics.org/trump-signs-space-force-act/.

———. "Vice News Claims UFO & QAnon Connection Is Disinformation." *Exopolitics* (blog), October 31, 2019. https://exopolitics.org/vice-news-claims-ufo-qanon-connection-is-disinformation/.

———. "Von Braun's False Flag Alien Invasion—a Genuine Warning or Fourth Reich Deception?" *Exopolitics* (blog), June 12, 2020. https://exopolitics.org/von-brauns-false-flag-alien-invasion-genuine-warning-or-deception/.

———. "When Secrecy Is Better than Official Disclosure of Extraterrestrial Life." *Exopolitics* (blog), February 6, 2019. https://exopolitics.org/when-secrecy-is-better-than-official-disclosure-of-extraterrestrial-life/.

———. "Will a False Flag Asteroid Attack Be Staged to Delay the 2020 Presidential Election?" *Exopolitics* (blog), August 31, 2020. https://exopolitics.org/will-false-flag-asteroid-attack-be-staged-to-delay-2020-election/.

———. "Will Deep State Launch False Flag Alien Invasion after Exhausting Global Control Cards?" *Exopolitics* (blog), June 6, 2020. https://exopolitics.org/will-deep-state-launch-false-flag-alien-invasion-after-exhausting-global-control-cards/.

———. "Will General Flynn Exoneration Impact UFO/SSP Disclosure?" *Exopolitics* (blog), May 9, 2020. https://exopolitics.org/will-general-flynn-exoneration-impact-ufo-ssp-disclosure/.

Schuffert, Pamela Rae. "The CONFIRMED AMTRAK DEATHCAMP of Beech Grove IN." *AMERICAN HOLOCAUST and The Coming NEW WORLD ORDER* (blog), February 28, 2009. http://americanholocaustcoming.blogspot.com/2009/02/confirmed-amtrak-deathcamp-of-beech.html.

———. "Modern GUILLOTINES Confirmed at Fort Lewis, WA—Military Whistleblower Report." *AMERICAN HOLOCAUST and The Coming NEW WORLD ORDER* (blog), February 16, 2009. http://americanholocaustcoming.blogspot.com/2009/02/modern-guillotines-confirmed-at-fort.html.

Seingalt, Jacques Casanova de. *The Memoirs of Casanova, Complete*. (eBook, Project Gutenberg), November 2, 2006. http://www.gutenberg.org/files/2981/2981.txt.

Shipman, Dennis. "GESARA: No Poverty, No Hunger, No Debt, Global Prosperity and Peace." Blissful Visions, March 27, 2018. http://www.blissfulvisions.com/articles/GESARA-NESARA.html.

Shriner, Sherry. "The Antichrist and NESARA." Nesara Sucks. Accessed August 13, 2020. http://www.nesarasucks.com/nesara-sucks.htm.

———. "NESARA Deception NESARA Is a Lie NESARA Will Kill You." Nesara Sucks. Accessed July 28, 2020. http://nesarasucks.com/.

———. "Saint Germaine." Nesara Sucks. Accessed December 1, 2020. http://www.nesarasucks.com/germaine.htm.

———. "Sherry Shriner Orgone Blasters Fight Back Against Aliens, UFOs, Chemtrails, Night Terrors, ELF." Orgone Blasters, 2017. http://www.orgoneblasters.com/.

———. "Understanding the New World Order." Sherry Shriner. Accessed August 4, 2020. http://www.sherryshriner.com/sherry/understanding-nwo.htm.

———. "Who Is Sherry Shriner?" The Watcher Files. Accessed July 28, 2020. http://www.thewatcherfiles.com/sherry/intro.htm.

Smith, Lt. H.W., and G.W. Towles. "Unidentified Flying Objects: Project 'Grudge.'" Technical Analysis Division, Intelligence Department, United States Air Force, August 1949.

Strom, Ron. "Monetary Changes Promise Prosperity for All." *World News Daily*, March 9, 2005. https://www.wnd.com/2005/03/29265/#HzSc5ZwITDIxe2IP.99.

Stroud, Rob. "Man Convicted of Creating Omega Scam Dies." *Journal Gazette-Times Courier Online*, July 28, 2012. https://jg-tc.com/news/man-convicted-of-creating-omega-scam-dies/article_83df49c0-d831-11e1-bc18-001a4bcf887a.html.

Swenson, Kyle. "It Looked like a Simple Domestic Murder. Then Police Learned about the Alien Reptile Cult." *Washington Post,* July 11, 2019. https://www.washingtonpost.com/nation/2019/06/11/alien-reptile-murder-cult-barbara-rogers-sherry-shriner/.

Thomas, Pam Belluck, and Jo Thomas. "Wads of Cash, Gossip, Then Fraud Charges." *The New York Times,* September 2, 2000, sec. U.S. https://www.nytimes.com/2000/09/02/us/wads-of-cash-gossip-then-fraud-charges.html.

Truettner, L.H., and A.B. Deyarmond. "Unidentified Flying Objects: Project 'Sign.'" Dayton, Ohio: Air Material Command, United States Air Force, February 1949. http://www.nicap.org/docs/SignRptFeb1949.pdf.

"The Truth about $300B Worth of 'Manila' Paper," January 17, 2012. https://www.investmentnews.com/the-truth-about-300b-worth-of-manila-paper-41654.

USA—The Republic. "Chap. 6—The TRUTH About the 14th Amendment," March 4, 2012. http://usa-the-republic.com/revenue/true_history/Chap6.html.

———. "Chapter 8—United States Government Bankruptcy," March 4, 2012. http://usa-the-republic.com/revenue/true_history/Chap8.html.

Von Reitz, Anna. "The Truth as I Know It About NESARA." *Paul Stramer: Lincoln County Watch* (blog), August 20, 2020. http://www.paulstramer.net/2020/08/the-truth-as-i-know-it-about-nesara.html.

Walsh, Joe. "Trump's Allies Can't Decide Whether to Boycott Georgia's Runoff Elections." *Forbes,* December 2, 2020. https://www.forbes.com/sites/joewalsh/2020/12/02/trumps-allies-cant-decide-whether-to-boycott-georgias-runoff-elections/.

Wilkinson College of Arts, Humanities, and Social Sciences. "What Aren't They Telling Us?—Chapman University Survey of American Fears." *The Voice of Wilkinson* (blog), October 11, 2016. https://blogs.chapman.edu/wilkinson/2016/10/11/what-arent-they-telling-us/.

Writer, David Jackson, Tribune Staff. "The Reluctant Citizens: Bruised and Bitter." *Chicago Tribune,* chicagotribune.com. Accessed May 27, 2020. https://www.chicagotribune.com/news/ct-xpm-1995-05-17-9505170229-story.html.

Index

Abedin, Huma 131
Adamski, George 88–92, 110, 181
Aerial Phenomenon Research Organization (APRO) 81, 86, 93
Allen, Gary 30–31
anti–Semitism 9–10, 30, 77, 92, 129, 164
Arnold, Kenneth 81, 93

Ballard, Guy 47–50
Bank of International Settlements 77
Barkun, Michael 12
Barnard, Harvey 35–36, 38–39, 42, 69
Berger, J.M. 18, 31
Beter, Peter 63
Biden, Hunter 15–16, 152,
Biden, Joe 150, 152, 155–156, 164, 166–167, 169–170
Boorda, Jeremy 62
Bork, J.B. 19–22
Boylan, Richard 94, 108–127, 135, 157
Bramerton, Alcuin 161–162
Bush, George H.W. 62, 66, 138, 147
Bush, George W. 38–39, 42, 55, 57, 138, 147, 162

Central Intelligence Agency (CIA) 55–56, 62, 65, 85–86, 88, 91, 98–100, 106–107, 130, 132–133, 142–143, 157
child trafficking 79, 131–132, 165, 170
Clinton, Bill 2, 39, 41, 44–45, 56, 62–64, 98, 101, 130, 152
Clinton, Hillary Rodham 2–3, 13, 130–134, 138, 140, 144. 152, 160, 168, 171
Clinton Foundation 164
Colby, William 62
Comte St. Germain 47–50, 53–54, 56–58, 72, 161–163
Condon Committee 92–93
contactees 81, 90–92, 94–95, 105, 110, 119, 121
Conway, Kellyanne 16
Council on Foreign Relations 31, 77, 116
COVID-19 Pandemic 126, 145, 150–153, 168

"Deep State" 3–4, 6, 14–15, 31, 129, 132–135, 137–138, 140, 144, 147, 149, 151, 153, 158–160, 164, 170–172
Detweiler, Nancy 59–60, 63–66
"Dove of Oneness" *see* Goodwin, Shaini
Duduman, Dumitru 74–76, 78

8chan 3, 6, 128, 135, 148, 156, 159
Eisenhower, Dwight 96, 105, 157
eschatology 2, 4, 77, 144
exopolitics 105, 156–157, 159–160

Facebook 72, 131
"Farmers Claims" cases 44
Federal Emergency Management Agency (FEMA) 13, 141–143
Federal Reserve 18, 26, 30, 43, 61–66, 68, 77–78
Fenster, Mark 11
Flaherty, Emma 15
Flynn, Michael 139, 151, 164
4chan 2–3, 6, 128–130, 135, 148–149, 159
14th Amendment 19–26
Freemasonry 9, 32, 143, 163

Gitmo *see* Guantanamo Bay
Goode, Corey 159
Goodwin, Shaini 6, 33, 36–60, 62, 64–65, 69, 73, 78–79, 135, 161, 163–164
Gore, Al 73, 101
Greer, Steven 94–108, 126–127, 135, 157
Grudge, Project 83–84
Guantanamo Bay 134, 149, 162, 170

Herscu, Shoshi 163
Hofstadter, Richard 10–11, 35
Hood, Clyde D. 36–38, 41
Hynek, J. Allen 92

I AM Activity *see* Ballard, Guy
Icke, David 70, 159
International Monetary Fund (IMF) 42–43, 55, 77

Index

Joe M 136–139
Johnson, Stan 69, 73–78

Kelley, Charles R. 71
Kennedy, John F. 136
Kennedy, John F., Jr. 164
Keyhoe, Donald E. 87–88, 91, 111

Leoffler, Kelly 170

Mantell, Thomas 82–83
McCain, John 3
McCloud, David 62
McVeigh, Timothy 12
Merlan, Anna 17, 156, 170
MJ-12 Papers 93
Moseley, James W. 93
Muirhead, Russell 12–14, 75–76, 79, 129
Mutual UFO Network (MUFON) 81

National Economic Security and Recovery Act (NESARA) 5–6, 14, 16–17, 30–83, 75, 77–79, 114, 118, 121, 125, 128–129, 135, 156, 160–164, 171–173
National Investigations Committee on Aerial Phenomenon (NICAP) 81, 86–88, 91–94, 111
9/11 *see* September 11, 2001, terror attacks
"North Dakota Crash" 15

Obama, Barack 2, 15–16, 73, 78, 98, 131, 134, 138, 141, 149, 152–153, 158, 167
O'Connell, Mark 92
Omega Trust 35–39, 41–42, 54–55, 62

Parler 166, 172–173
pedophile rings 3, 77, 78, 157–158, 172
Pence, Mike 165–166, 168
Perdue, David 170
Petersen, John 99–100
"PizzaGate" 3, 131–132
Project Blue Book 81, 83–85, 92–93
Prophecy Club, The *see* Johnson, Stan

Q 3, 6–7, 16, 125, 128–129, 132, 135–136, 139–140, 142–145, 147–160, 165–170, 172–173
Q-Clearance Patriot *see* "Q"
Quantum Financial System (QFS) 163–164

RedPillTheWorld 145–147
Reich, Wilhelm 71
Reno, Janet 23–24, 63, 130
Rich, Seth 3
Roberts, John 165, 168
Robertson, Howard P. *see* Robertson Panel
Robertson Panel 81, 85
Robinson, David E. 19–20, 24, 59–61, 63–66

Rockefeller, David 55
Rockefeller, Laurence 99
Rockefeller family 63, 99, 130, 146
Roosevelt, Franklin D. 45, 64
Roselle, Laura 15
Rosenblum, Nancy L. 12–14, 75–76, 79, 129
Rubin, Robert 63
Ruppelt, Edward J. 83–85, 88

Saint Germain World Trust *see* Comte St. Germain
Salla, Michael 127, 156–160
Scalia, Antonin 15, 165, 168
Schuffert, Pam 142
Schwasinger, Roy 39–41, 44, 60–63
"secret government" 4, 29, 32, 94, 97, 99, 101, 105, 107–108, 127
September 11, 2001, terror attacks 16, 41, 55, 57, 66, 108, 124, 144, 162
Sessions, Jeff 134
Shriner, Sherry 69–73, 77, 78
Sign, Project 81–84
Soros, George 3, 134, 146, 171
sovereign citizen movement 4, 7, 17–19, 24–28, 45, 59, 61, 65, 76, 77, 78, 101, 152
Spicer, Sean 16
Star Kids 114–118, 122, 124–125
Star Seeds 115–118, 120, 124–126
Stormer, John 30, 32

Tappe, Nancy 69
Tesla, Nikola 67, 69
Thomas, Kenn 16
Trilateral Commission 77, 116
Trump, Donald 3, 5–6, 9, 12, 14, 15–17, 31, 58, 128–135, 137, 140–141, 144–145, 147–158, 164–170, 172–173
Trutwin, Elizabeth 59
Twitter 72, 128–129, 131, 153–154, 156, 165–166

unidentified flying objects (UFO) 4, 6, 12, 14, 17, 32, 40, 47, 65, 69–70, 79–129, 143, 156–162, 164, 171, 173
United Nations 2, 30, 112, 126
United States Supreme Court 22, 39, 22, 39, 41–46, 48, 51, 60–62, 64, 65–66, 168

Van Tassel, George 91

Weiner, Anthony 130–131, 147
Wellstone, Paul 65
"White Knights" 5, 33, 40–43, 46, 50–58, 64, 66, 162
Wood, L. Lin 164–170
Woolsey, James 99–101
World Court 41–42, 44, 51
World Trade Organization 77

www.ingramcontent.com/pod-product-compliance
Ingram Content Group UK Ltd.
Pitfield, Milton Keynes, MK11 3LW, UK
UKHW042005140426
5217IPUK00015B/993